GoodCheapEats

Also by Jessica Fisher
Not Your Mother's Make-Ahead and Freeze Cookbook
Best 100 Juices for Kids

GoodCheapEats

Everyday Dinners and Fantastic Feasts for $10 or Less

JESSICA FISHER

The Harvard Common Press
Boston, Massachusetts

The Harvard Common Press
www.harvardcommonpress.com

Printed in China
Printed on acid-free paper

Library of Congress Cataloging-in-Publication Data
Fisher, Jessica (Jessica Getskow)
   Good cheap eats : everyday dinners and fantastic feasts
for $10 or less / Jessica Fisher.
     pages cm
   Includes index.
    ISBN 978-1-55832-843-3 (paperback)
  1. Low budget cooking. I. Title.
   TX714.F5738 2014
   641.5'52--dc23

                        2014001628

Special bulk-order discounts are available on this and other Harvard
Common Press books. Companies and organizations may purchase books
for premiums or resale, or may arrange a custom edition, by contacting
the Marketing Director at the web address above.

Book design by Elizabeth Van Itallie
Photographs by Jessica Getskow Fisher
Author photograph by Sharon Leppellere

10 9 8 7 6 5 4 3 2 1

To my parents, Jack and Veronica Getskow,
for sharing their love of good food with me and
modeling frugality in the process

Contents

Introduction 9

Going Meatless 16
Stretching It 54
Something Meatier 92
Grilling and Eating Outdoors 124
Company Dinners 154
Make-Ahead Meals 200
Breakfast for Supper 234
Meals On the Run 264

Acknowledgments 303
Measurement Equivalents 304
Index 305

Introduction

I love food.

My mom says it started when I was two, at a steak house with my parents and their friends. The adults were so busy conversing that they didn't notice that the toddler had eaten the entire side order of sautéed mushrooms, a plate big enough to feed four adults.

What can I say? They were good.

And so started my foodie career. I've always liked to eat. It didn't bother me (much) that the kids at school mocked the strange toppings on my pizza or the tuna salad and sprouts that I packed in my Mork and Mindy lunch box. If it tasted good, I'd eat it.

I made a point to surround myself with food and to learn as much as I could about it. For my first job, I worked in the grocery store, bagging groceries, pushing carts, and asking customers what they were going to do with the ingredients that came down the line. One summer I got a job at an amusement park, hawking frozen bananas from a cart in the Southern California sunshine. In college I worked for the university's dining services, prepping salads, sandwiches, and other platters for the college catering company. Later I worked in a bakery and restaurant, first as a barista, then as a waitress.

While my degree may be in French literature, my heart has always belonged to food. Speaking of which, I ate my way through France during my junior year abroad. But, I bet you guessed that already.

When I married and settled down in Santa Barbara—an expensive town to live and dine in—my husband and I were surrounded not only by great restaurants but also by great friends who showed us the art of eating well at home. That was the only way any of us could enjoy top-notch food and still make ends meet in such an affluent community.

For our part, we lived in a 200-square-foot studio apartment in order to stay in town and under budget. I would cook up a storm on Sunday afternoons so that we could bring friends home with us from church that evening for supper. We'd squeeze as many people as we could into that tiny studio, with some folks lounging on the bed, others gathered around the table. We'd share a meal, a bottle of wine, and plenty of good conversation.

The joys of eating well at home have provided the sustenance we rely on, first to make our way as a newlywed couple and later to nourish our brood of six growing and seemingly always hungry children. When the first FishBaby arrived and I became a stay-at-home mom, we learned through trial and error how to feed a family on a budget. As subsequent FishKids were added to our clan, we learned more about feeding a crowd with healthy yet frugal food. Home-cooked meals have also served to comfort us through unemployment, debt, loss of family members, and cross-country moves. Good food has been there through feast and famine, comfort and celebration.

If we're together and eating well, our hearts are happy.

For us, good cheap eats is an integral part of all that. We've always lived on a tight budget, so it's been important for us to stretch each dollar as far as it could go. Even during the process of paying off excessive consumer debt in a down economy, we made it a priority to eat the tastiest and healthiest food we could afford.

Why Good Cheap Eats?

Good food is a part of every culture. It brings comfort and nourishment as well as a social connection. Gathering around the supper table is not only a time to refuel physically after a long day, but it's also a time to reconnect with friends and family.

As a college student and later a new bride, I pored over gourmet magazines and pined over fancy restaurant menus, wishing that our budget could accommodate my foodie cravings. What I learned through practice—and failure—was that I could cook just as well as—if not better than—some of the restaurants we loved, and furthermore, that I could do it for pennies on the dollar.

In life and on my blog, Good Cheap Eats, my motto has been, "Eat well, enjoy life, act your wage." That last part I learned the hard way.

Our Wrestle with Debt

In 1998, we had just taken out our first mortgage, a stepping-stone to years of debt. Up until that point, I'd never even carried a balance on my credit card. We'd paid off my student loans within two years of graduation. We built a sizeable emergency fund before the birth of our first child, which marked my "retirement" from public school teaching.

And then we bought a house, moved far from family and friends, and started to live beyond our means. It didn't happen all at once. We'd always been frugal people, cooking meals at home and searching for bargains when we were out. But our spending started to exceed our income, and before long we had nickel-and-dimed ourselves into debt.

Nine years later, we found ourselves in the hole with two homes mortgaged, sky-high credit card bills, and nonexistent savings. That was 2007. We were lucky enough to get a wake-up call before the rest of the country. It was then that we got serious about learning to manage our money better. We cut up our credit cards and created a zero-based budget where every expense was planned and agreed upon. We read up on resources for getting out of debt and followed Dave Ramsey's unique plan for getting our financial house in order. And we ate beans and rice. A lot of beans and rice. In the end, we paid off $18,000 over the course of 18 months—and we lived to tell about it.

One of the keys to our survival was learning how to eat well on a budget. We learned over time how to shop and how to eat in ways that pleased our foodie taste buds and the more "selective" preferences of the FishKids without sending us to the poorhouse.

That's what this book is about: great food, happy hearts, and balanced bank accounts.

But this doesn't mean that you have to subsist on cheap ramen noodles and macaroni skillet dishes—we sure don't. Some of the best from-scratch meals in the world are crafted from wholesome ingredients using simple preparations. In addition, you'll find shopping tricks, meal planning strategies, and tips to build a pantry that will serve you and your wallet effectively. They will enable you to stretch your dollar, eat well, and really enjoy your life.

About This Book

This book is a road map toward shopping wisely, choosing ingredients carefully, and planning meals that your family will enjoy; and of course, it's full of recipes to help you do it with taste and style, all while staying under budget.

Don't be afraid to serve simple food; it's kept civilization going for centuries. When you mix up the flavor profile and introduce various gourmet touches, simple food becomes a feast for kings. It's comforting, stick-to-your-ribs, give-you-strength-to-face-the-day kind of food. And it's good cheap eats.

Good taste doesn't have to be expensive. It doesn't need to be complicated. It just needs to be real and wholesome and honest. We often get confused into thinking that meals that come in a package or from a restaurant are better because they demand a high-ticket price. But that's just not true. The recipes in this book are better for your health—and your pocketbook—because you make them from scratch.

There's no doubt that cooking at home from whole ingredients is more healthful and generally more economical than buying commercial convenience items or eating restaurant fare. While there's a place for all of these approaches, my heart is with home-

made. Not only do you feed your body better, but you also create connections with family and friends when you can gather in the kitchen, preparing a meal together and later enjoying it *à table*. That is one of the main reasons I'm dedicated to helping the home cook gain independence from the box, the drive-thru line, and high food costs.

Throughout the book, you will find my 101 top tips for shopping for and preparing budget-friendly meals. These strategies guide the $10 price point of the meals in this book. While all of the recipes are made with generally inexpensive ingredients, you'll reduce your costs even further by following the good cheap eats standards.

About Ingredients

In my perfect world, all animals would be raised without added hormones or the need for antibiotics and then slaughtered humanely; all produce and grain would be grown the old-fashioned way (that is, without toxic chemicals or genetically modified organisms); and all convenience items would be crafted carefully from real ingredients. Unfortunately, that world is still a dream.

With grandparents and great-grandparents who farmed the lands of Minnesota, I have a heart for the farmer and for real food. While I've done my time being swayed by brightly colored packaging and catchy jingles, I've come to the conclusion that whole foods are better for us. I know that how I spend my dollar supports the farmer and serves as an investment in my family's health. I'm also a firm believer in getting the biggest bang for your buck. These are sometimes conflicting values: food quality versus cost. I know from experience the temptation of going for the rock-bottom price—which sometimes, but not always, signifies rock-bottom quality.

In my family, we're intent on buying the highest quality that our budget will allow and making baby steps toward that perfect world. Living in Southern California as we do, this means that a $40 organic produce delivery each week is very doable. We eat most of our vegetables fresh as opposed to canned or frozen because that is the best deal for where we live.

Chicken and meats, on the other hand, are a bit pricier. While I would love to buy grass-fed, free-range, and organic all the time, I just can't swing the high prices those items command in this neck of the woods. We do the best we can, watching for sales and specials and strategizing ways to have the best of both worlds.

That's my recommendation for you, too, wherever you find yourself shopping: Buy the best quality that your wallet will allow, enjoy real food, and work toward making positive changes in your family's diet.

Tools of the Trade

Since we've already established that home-cooked, whole foods are a pretty good thing to shoot for, it's important to set ourselves up for success. Making a task easier means it will happen more frequently and it will be more fun to do. (How's that for some sweet justification to buy a new bread machine?)

Kidding!

Kitchen fantasies aside, you don't need to outfit your kitchen with all new appliances and drawers full of gadgets. But there are some tools of the trade that will make cooking and eating at home easier. Here are some of the basics that I've found to be especially helpful in the kitchen:

Good knives: There are few things more frustrating to a cook than to have dull, junky knives. It will make you want to throw up your hands and fill the freezer with TV dinners. Don't do it—but don't go out and buy a deluxe set of knives, either. A good chef's knife and a bread knife will do just fine. We invested in a good set when we married, and they've lasted us more than 20 years. A few years ago we bought a sharpener so that we can keep a sharp blade going. Cooking is so much more pleasant an experience when the knives are well sharpened.

Cutting boards: Have enough cutting boards so that you can dedicate one to meats and one to fruits and vegetables. Keep them clean and sanitized and ready to help you get chopping.

Pots and pans: Again, you don't need a fancy 12-piece set; a stockpot, a large skillet, and a saucepan are a great start. As with knives, choose quality over quantity, but there's no need to buy top of the line.

Slow cooker: A slow cooker can be your best friend. Who else will spend all day cooking your supper and have it ready when you get home? These go on sale for as low as $20, making them an inexpensive addition to your kitchen that will repay you generously.

Bread machine: Store-bought or bakery bread can be expensive. Homemade not only tastes better, but it's also much more economical. Mixing and kneading bread dough by hand works just fine, but a bread machine can take a lot of the work and mess out of the experience. I've had a bread machine for more than 13 years and really rely on it to help me with my baking.

Handheld mixer: Folks rave about stand mixers, but honestly, I think they're overrated. I can do everything I want to do with an inexpensive handheld electric mixer. My stand mixer, a Mother's Day gift years ago, usually serves as a fruit bowl.

Food processor: Food processors are a whiz at completing any number of tasks in a matter of seconds. This is my workhorse for making everything from pie crust to salsa, as well as shredding cheese, chopping vegetables, and pureeing sauces.

Immersion blender: While the food processor can do everything the immersion blender can do, I turn to this gadget when I want to blend sauces and soups without dirtying another pan—or spilling piping-hot liquid all over myself. I resisted buying one for years, but I have since found it to be one of my very favorite kitchen appliances. Immersion blenders are inexpensive, too, starting at about $20, which is a lot cheaper than their countertop cousins.

Food scale: A food scale is a godsend for portioning out bulk purchases for freezing, something I do often in order to cut unit costs. When I measure things out, I find that we can get by with a lot less, and that saves us money.

Meat thermometer: One of the most perplexing issues for novice cooks is how to know when a roast or chicken is done. With an instant-read meat thermometer, you'll know exactly when a meat has been cooked long enough to be safe to eat—but not so long that it's dried out. (See page 117 for helpful tips on testing doneness.)

About the Recipes: Costs, Yields, and Accompaniments

Each meal in this book is designed to feed four adults (or four adult-size appetites, if you've got growing teens in your family!) for $10 or less when frugal shopping techniques are applied. While savvy shopping is a prerequisite to meeting the $10 price point, these recipes contain generally inexpensive ingredients anyway, so if you need to break the good cheap eats rules, yours can still be an economical meal.

There are some recipes, however, that yield a larger number of servings, as in the case of a roast, a pot of soup, or a cake. It's simply easier and more economical to make that bigger batch. Where these recipes are concerned, the cost applied to your dinner's total will include only the portion that will be consumed in that sitting. For instance, a full pan of lasagna can feed up to eight people, and a batch of four dozen cookies will keep the whole family happy for days. Therefore, in such instances, the cost of about half a pan of lasagna and eight to twelve cookies is what counts toward the hypothetical dinner total. For tips on what to do with leftovers, read about Werewolf Meals on page 263. You can easily and tastefully turn leftovers into something else the next night.

The recipes included in each menu are designed to complement one another, but please feel free to mix and match them in other ways. I've tried to create recipes with an inherent versatility that will allow you great freedom as well as hundreds of possible combinations. Many recipes can stand alone instead of being part of the menu, and the recipe notes offer lots of alternative serving suggestions.

If you're a visual person, you'll be pleased to know that there is a database of photographs of recipes in this book located at GoodCheapEats.com/gallery, in addition to the photos that appear in these pages.

Many families nowadays follow special diets due to food allergies and sensitivities. My youngest daughter is allergic to walnuts and peanuts, so we are very careful to read labels and adapt recipes so that she can enjoy them safely. Even though a food item might not contain the allergen in question, the risk of cross-contamination at the factory is often a concern. Cooking most foods at home allows us to save money as well as ensure a healthy and safe diet for her. The following designations are provided for each recipe to help you know at a glance how it fits into the bigger picture of your life and dietary preferences.

Meatless: Making meals without meat is a great way to eat more healthfully—and cut costs.

Dairy-free: Many recipes can easily be adapted for dairy-free eating, but those that are naturally dairy-free are indicated as such.

Gluten-free: The same goes for gluten-free eating. However, manufacturers hide gluten in crazy places, so be sure to read all ingredient labels to ensure, for example, that there is no gluten lurking in your bacon, soy sauce, or chili powder. Naturally gluten-free recipes are designated as such, though countless others can easily be adapted to work without gluten.

Slow cooker: The slow cooker has seen a fresh and creative new life in modern times. It's the ideal vessel for braising inexpensive cuts of meat and for prepping dinner while you're gone, making it even easier to bypass expensive alternatives on your way home from work or school.

Make-ahead: One of the enemies of home cooking is hunger, believe it or not. It drives you to the fast-food restaurant, having convinced you that it'll be quicker than cooking at home. With make-ahead meals, you can do the prep work the night before or first thing in the morning and tell hunger to take a hike, knowing that supper is just a few minutes from being served after you walk in the door that evening.

Freezer-friendly: I am a huge fan of freezer meals—after all, I wrote the book on it! If you liked my first book, *Not Your Mother's Make-Ahead and Freeze Cookbook*, then you'll appreciate the freezer-friendly options peppered throughout this book. If you're not yet familiar with that book or with freezer cooking in general, then these recipes will be a good way to get your feet wet. Having a meal in the freezer can be a godsend on busy weeknights. You can also wrap leftovers for freezing to enjoy a week or a month later if you like. Cooking in bulk and freezing the meals to use later is a fantastic way to save money.

Shopping and Cooking the Good Cheap Eats Way

Since prices vary by location and season, I haven't assigned a specific dollar amount to each meal, but I'm confident that you will keep your food costs low if you follow the 101 tips for good cheap eats.

For an example of how the 101 tips can transform your grocery receipts, let's see how the numbers crunched on one of my favorite meals: a chicken Caesar salad with mint iced tea and a cookie for dessert. For the recipes, head to page 294.

Eating at a Café

Chicken Caesar Salad = $10.95

Mint Iced Tea = $2.00

Gourmet Chocolate Chip Cookie = $1.50

Total: $14.45 per person, or $59.80 for four people, plus tip

Preparing the Meal with Store-Bought Convenience Items

1 bag washed, torn romaine lettuce = $2.49

⅓ bottle prepared dressing = $1.50

½ package prepared croutons = $1.75

½ ounce Parmigiano-Reggiano = $0.62

12 ounces grilled chicken breast = $7.98

4 bottles mint iced tea = $8.00

1 package gourmet cookies = $4.00

Total: $26.34 for four people

Preparing the Meal the Good Cheap Eats Way

1 head romaine lettuce = $0.99

Homemade dressing = $1.13

Homemade croutons = $0.33

½ ounce Romano cheese = $0.22

1 pound raw chicken breast = $1.99

Home-brewed iced tea with fresh mint and honey = $0.70

12 home-baked cookies = $1.00

Total: $6.36 for four people

Going Meatless

Meatless meals have a lot going for them. They are often healthier, more environmentally friendly, and less expensive than their beefier counterparts. At my house, we eat a meatless meal several times a week as a way to bring balance to our diets as well as to our pocketbook.

While it may take a little getting used to, there are a number of delicious options to help you eat well and still stay under budget without eating meat. Vegetarian proteins, including beans, eggs, and dairy, make dishes just as filling while cutting costs. A dose of healthy fat, as found in foods like avocados or nuts, adds substance and rounds out the flavors. Since proteins are typically the most expensive ingredients in the meal, going meatless allows you to spend a little more on other ingredients that add richness, texture, and flavor.

Poblano Chile Enchiladas 18
South of the Border Slaw 20
Zesty Mexican Rice 21

Creamy Herbed Tomato Soup 24
Garlicky Grilled Cheese Sandwiches 25
Broccoli Slaw with Pecans and Cranberries 27

Potato-Corn Chowder 28
Cloverleaf Garlic Rolls 29
Baked Apple Porcupines 30

Fire-Roasted Mushroom Marinara 31
Cheesy Polenta 32
Roasted Broccoli with Garlic 33

Simple Bean Tostadas 34
Chunky Tomato Salsa 35
Lemon Pie with Honey-Ginger Cream 36

Simplest Butternut Squash and Carrot Soup 39
Versatile Vegetable Tart 40
Michèle's *Salade* 41

Spinach and Mushroom Pizza with Roasted Tomato Sauce 42
Baby Greens with Lemon-Basil Vinaigrette 44
Salted Caramel *Affogato* 46

Hot Cheese Dip with Sun-Dried Tomatoes 48
Lemony Linguini with Broccoli and Mushrooms 49

Potato-Leek Soup 50
Honey Whole-Wheat Bread 52

MENU

Poblano Chile
Enchiladas

South of the
Border Slaw

Zesty Mexican
Rice

This meal is a throw-back to our newly-wed days and is now one of our all-time family favorites. It's classy enough to serve to company but comforting enough for every day. It makes a perfect economy meal, thanks to inexpensive pantry staples. A favorite family addition is to add a side of black beans to the menu.

Poblano Chile Enchiladas

Makes 12 enchiladas

MEATLESS **GLUTEN-FREE** **MAKE-AHEAD**

This dish will have everyone fighting over the leftovers—who *gets* to eat them, not who *has* to eat them. It's an adaptation of a recipe I found years ago in a chile cookbook. The original called for red salsa, which was tasty but turned the sour cream Pepto-Bismol pink. This salsa verde version works much better. While the chiles certainly add heat, the sour cream and cheese cool things down. And if you have time to make homemade tortillas, they'll really make the dish out of this world.

1 pound sour cream
1 (16-ounce) jar salsa verde (I prefer Herdez or Trader Joe's.)
12 corn tortillas, preferably homemade (page 222)
6 poblano chiles, roasted, halved, and seeded (see page 245)
2 cups shredded cheese, such as cheddar or Monterey Jack

1. Preheat the oven to 350°F. Grease a 9 x 13-inch pan with non-stick cooking spray.

2. In a large bowl, whisk the sour cream and salsa verde together until smooth. Spread ¼ cup of the sauce over the bottom of the prepared dish.

3. Soften the tortillas by warming them briefly in the microwave or on a hot griddle.

4. Assemble each enchilada by placing half a chile and a small handful of cheese atop a tortilla. Roll up the tortilla and place the enchilada, seam side down, in the prepared pan. Continue rolling until all the enchiladas are assembled, reserving ½ cup of the cheese for the topping.

5. Pour the remaining sauce over the top of the enchiladas. Sprinkle the reserved ½ cup cheese over the top.

6. Bake the enchiladas until heated through and starting to bubble, 20 to 30 minutes.

MAKE IT AHEAD: Prepare the dish through step 5, cover, and refrigerate up to 1 day in advance. Bake as directed, adding a few minutes of baking time since the pan will be cold.

#1

GO MEATLESS

Since proteins tend to be the highest-priced ingredients in a meal, you can cut your costs dramatically by eating meatless a few times a week. This might take some getting used to for some folks. In our serious debt-fighting days, we ate meatless three or four times a week, enjoying beans, grains, vegetables, and dairy instead.

South of the Border Slaw

Serves 4 to 6

`MEATLESS` `GLUTEN-FREE` `MAKE-AHEAD`

Cabbage is a wonderfully inexpensive ingredient, often just 15 cents a pound. Slice it into thin ribbons and toss with fresh herbs and a tangy dressing for a flavorful addition to any Latin-themed supper. Or add grilled chicken to make this a main-dish salad.

5 cups thinly sliced green cabbage (1 medium head)
1 carrot, peeled and shredded
2 tablespoons chopped red onion
2 tablespoons chopped fresh dill
2 tablespoons chopped fresh cilantro
Juice of 1 lemon
1 tablespoon plain Greek yogurt
1 tablespoon mayonnaise
1 tablespoon olive oil
¼ teaspoon ground cumin
Pinch of cayenne pepper
Kosher salt and freshly ground black pepper
Finely chopped tomato, for topping (optional)
Finely chopped avocado, for topping (optional)

1. In a large bowl, combine the cabbage, carrot, onion, dill, and cilantro.

2. In a small bowl, whisk together the lemon juice, yogurt, mayonnaise, olive oil, cumin, cayenne, and salt and pepper to taste.

3. Toss the dressing with the salad mixture. Add tomato and avocado, if desired, right before serving.

MAKE IT AHEAD: If you prefer a very crisp slaw, store the salad mixture and the dressing separately in the refrigerator, and then toss just before serving. Otherwise, the mixed salad can be stored in the refrigerator for a few hours, until ready to serve.

2

Rice bowls are an easy and cheap meal to pull together, especially if you've got different leftovers waiting to be used up. Lay out a pot of cooked rice as well as a buffet of cooked meats, beans, cheeses, and vegetables for toppings.

Zesty Mexican Rice

Serves 4

MEATLESS **DAIRY-FREE** **GLUTEN-FREE**

I grew up in Southern California, so despite my Norwegian-Polish-German heritage, I had the advantage of enjoying authentic Mexican food in my formative years. An added bonus was having Latino friends who taught me the art of making rice, beans, and home-made tortillas the proper way. This rice dish is an adaptation of one that my friend Elva taught me to make in college. The leftovers are great warmed up the next day and topped with beans, cheese, and other toppings.

2 tablespoons vegetable oil
1 cup white rice
1 cup tomato sauce
½ teaspoon ground cumin
½ teaspoon dried oregano
½ teaspoon onion powder
½ teaspoon garlic powder
¼ teaspoon kosher salt
¼ teaspoon freshly ground black pepper
2 cups vegetable broth or water

1. In a large skillet with a lid, heat the oil over medium heat. Add the rice and cook, stirring, until the rice turns opaque and then very light brown.

2. Remove the pan from the heat and stir in the tomato sauce, cumin, oregano, onion powder, garlic powder, salt, and pepper, being careful of splatters. Stir well.

3. Stir in the vegetable broth. Return the pan to the heat and turn it to medium-high. Bring the mixture to bubbling.

4. Cover and reduce the heat to low. Cook until almost all the liquid is absorbed, 15 to 20 minutes. Remove the lid and fluff with a fork. Continue to cook on low heat, uncovered, for about 5 minutes to absorb any extra liquid. Taste and adjust the seasonings.

BEAN AND RICE BOWLS

Serves 4

I credit beans and rice with getting us out of debt so many years ago. It's filling, it's affordable, and it tastes great. And it's so easy to pull together that it's been a go-to meal for years for our family, before and after debt.

We eat beans and rice about once a week for dinner. Sometimes I serve them as accompaniments to enchiladas, tamales, or tacos, but usually they make up the bulk of the meal. I like to cook beans from scratch (see page 38), but often I'll just bust open a can. We might serve plain cooked rice (see page 172) or a pilaf, like the Zesty Mexican Rice on page 21.

During very lean times, we have just beans and rice and perhaps a little shredded cheese. But when we can, we dude things up with our favorite toppings. Homemade salsa is very inexpensive, and I buy sour cream on sale. In season, we'll add chopped tomatoes and sweet bell peppers, and maybe some corn. Sliced olives, chopped scallions, shredded lettuce, and tortilla chips are nice additions if you've got them on hand.

4 cups hot cooked plain rice or rice pilaf
2 cups cooked or canned beans of your choice (rinsed and drained if canned)
1 cup shredded cheese, such as Monterey Jack or cheddar
Optional toppings (choose as many as will fit your budget):
    2 cups shredded lettuce
    1 cup salsa
    1 cup chopped tomatoes
    1 (9- to 13-ounce) bag tortilla chips
    ½ cup sour cream
    Sliced black olives
    Chopped scallions
    Chopped bell peppers
    Frozen corn kernels, thawed
    Sliced avocado
    Hot pepper sauce

Set out dishes of rice, beans, and toppings for diners to serve themselves, buffet-style.

MENU

Creamy Herbed
Tomato Soup

Garlicky
Grilled Cheese
Sandwiches

Broccoli Slaw
with Pecans and
Cranberries

It wasn't until adulthood that I discovered the delectable combination of tomato soup and grilled cheese sandwiches. I know—what cave was I living in? Well, better late than never, I say.

This meal, similar to one that you might order at a bakery café, comes together quickly. It's full of flavor, easy to prep ahead of time, and friendly on the wallet.

Creamy Herbed Tomato Soup

Makes about 4 cups

`MEATLESS` `GLUTEN-FREE` `MAKE-AHEAD`

I'm a big fan of making soup yourself rather than opening a can that is likely to be loaded with salt and preservatives. This soup comes together very quickly on the stovetop, taking only a few more minutes than if you just opened a can but delivering much more enjoyment.

If you can find them, fire-roasted tomatoes add a sweet but slightly smoky flavor to this dish. Some testers preferred this soup without the cream, which makes it a great dairy-free option as well.

¼ cup olive oil
1 cup finely chopped onion
2 teaspoons minced garlic
1 (28-ounce) can diced tomatoes, undrained
1 teaspoon dried Italian herb blend
½ cup heavy cream or half-and-half
Kosher salt and freshly ground black pepper

1. In a medium-size saucepan, heat the oil over medium-high heat until shimmering. Add the onion and garlic and cook until the onion is translucent, 7 to 10 minutes.

2. Add the tomatoes with their juices and the Italian herbs and simmer for 15 minutes, stirring occasionally.

3. Blend the mixture with an immersion blender until very smooth. Alternatively, you can puree it in a blender or food processor fitted with a metal blade. Be sure to vent the lid according to the manufacturer's directions.

4. Stir in the cream. Season to taste with salt and pepper. If the soup is too thick, you can add a little water to achieve the consistency you prefer. Reheat gently as needed.

MAKE IT AHEAD: Let the soup cool, then store it an airtight container in the refrigerator for up to three days. Warm in the microwave or on the stovetop.

STAY SHARP

Buy sharp or very flavorful cheeses and you will be able to use less, thus reducing the cost.

Garlicky Grilled Cheese Sandwiches

Serves 4

MEATLESS

When I was a kid, grilled cheese sandwiches were frequently on the menu. My mom, making a joke about her lack of griddling prowess, dubbed hers "burnt cheese sandwiches." I didn't hear her properly or understand her joke, instead calling them "bird cheese sandwiches." The name stuck for years. In my version, roasted garlic adds rich flavor to the common grilled cheese.

4 tablespoons (½ stick) butter, softened
8 slices sourdough sandwich bread
8 cloves roasted garlic (page 26)
1 cup baby spinach
4 ounces cheddar cheese, thinly sliced

1. Butter each slice of bread lightly on one side.
2. Spread the roasted garlic on the unbuttered side of 4 slices of bread.
3. Divide the spinach among the 4 slices, layering it atop the garlic. Lay the cheese over the spinach. Top each sandwich with another slice of bread, buttered side on the outside.
4. Cook the sandwiches on a hot griddle or skillet or in a panini press until the bread is golden and the cheese is melted.

Buy aluminum foil, food storage bags, and other food wraps on holiday clearance. They may have snowmen on them, but your freezer doesn't care what they look like. You'll save so much money buying them this way. Stock up for the year if you can.

roasted garlic

Makes 1 head roasted garlic

You'll laugh when you see how easy it is to roast garlic. The result is a smooth, spreadable garlic paste that has mellowed in flavor. It's tasty as a spread for toasted baguettes and sandwiches, but you can also toss the roasted cloves into salads or mashed potatoes to add zippy flavor. Slide a packet of these into the oven while you're baking something else so that you can have rich garlic nuggets on hand.

1 head garlic, cloves separated and peeled
2 tablespoons olive oil
Kosher salt and freshly ground black pepper

1. Preheat the oven to 400°F.

2. Spread out the garlic cloves on a sheet of heavy-duty aluminum foil. Drizzle them with the oil and season to taste with kosher salt and freshly ground black pepper. Fold the foil around the cloves to make a snug packet. Place the packet in a baking dish to catch any drips.

3. Roast until the cloves are soft and slightly brown, about 30 minutes. Use as desired in your recipe, or store in an airtight container in the refrigerator for up to 4 days or in the freezer for up to 1 month. Thaw completely before using in recipes.

Broccoli Slaw with Pecans and Cranberries

Serves 4 to 6

`MEATLESS` `DAIRY-FREE` `GLUTEN-FREE` `MAKE-AHEAD`

This broccoli salad is different from the overly sweet version often served at church potlucks. (My husband would be apt to say, "This one is *good*.") Whether you have an affinity for the traditional recipe or not, you'll like this one. It's not too sweet, it's got some crunch, and the flavors play well together. Thanks go out to the Small Notebook, Smitten Kitchen, and The Kitchn blogs for their original recipes, which I adapted for this version.

I like this salad best the day it's made, but my husband, Bryan, prefers it when the flavors have had a chance to mingle a bit.

2 heads broccoli, finely chopped
1 cup pecan pieces, toasted
⅓ cup dried cranberries
⅓ cup diced red onion
½ cup mayonnaise
2 tablespoons freshly squeezed lime juice
2 tablespoons red wine vinegar
1 tablespoon dark brown sugar
½ teaspoon fine sea salt

1. Combine the broccoli, pecans, cranberries, and onion in a large bowl.

2. In a small bowl, whisk together the mayonnaise, lime juice, red wine vinegar, brown sugar, and salt.

3. Pour the dressing over the broccoli mixture and toss to combine. Refrigerate until ready to serve.

MAKE IT AHEAD: Store the salad in an airtight container in the refrigerator for up to 2 days.

Potato-Corn
Chowder

Cloverleaf Garlic
Rolls

Baked Apple
Porcupines

Soup and bread is a favorite meal for cultures across the globe and throughout time. A warm hearth, a slurp of soup, and a bite of bread have satisfied many a hungry wanderer. This meal, with its creamy chowder, garlicky rolls, and baked apples for dessert, is homey and filling without the meat. Kids—and some husbands—might not naturally take to soup night, but it's a wonderfully economical meal. I've found that if I include a fun bread and a tempting dessert as part of the menu, soups go down the hatch easily.

Potato-Corn Chowder

Makes 8 cups

MEATLESS   **MAKE-AHEAD**   **FREEZER-FRIENDLY**

The black pepper gives this soup a nice warm kick. Feel free to add cooked chicken, fish, bacon, or ham if you're in the mood for something meatier. Leftover vegetables from a previous meal can also be stirred in to give it a different twist.

4 tablespoons (½ stick) butter
1 cup chopped onion
1 cup chopped peeled carrot
½ cup chopped celery
¼ cup unbleached all-purpose flour
4 cups vegetable broth or water
2 cups milk
1½ cups cubed potato (1 large)
1¼ cups frozen corn kernels, thawed
1 teaspoon fine sea salt
1 teaspoon dried rubbed sage
¼ teaspoon ground nutmeg
¼ teaspoon freshly ground black pepper, or more to taste

1. In a large stockpot, melt the butter over medium-high heat. Sauté the onion, carrot, and celery in the butter until the onions are translucent, 5 to 8 minutes.

2. Stir in the flour and cook for 2 minutes, stirring. Stir in the broth and milk, blending well.

3. Add the potato, corn, salt, sage, nutmeg, and pepper. Simmer until the potatoes are cooked and the soup is slightly thickened, 20 to 30 minutes.

MAKE IT AHEAD: Let the soup cool, then store it in an airtight container in the refrigerator for up to 3 days or in the freezer for up to 2 months. If frozen, thaw completely in the refrigerator before reheating in the microwave or on the stovetop.

FUN WITH GARLIC BREAD

Leftover rolls or hamburger or hot dog buns make great stand-ins for Italian loaves or baguettes when it comes to garlic bread. An eclectic mix of breads is just as tasty as one large loaf.

Cloverleaf Garlic Rolls

Makes 12 rolls

`MEATLESS` `DAIRY-FREE` `MAKE-AHEAD`

Even when I make a double batch of these rolls, there are never any left over. If you're new to baking bread, you'll find that these are easy to assemble and so much tastier than store-bought. It's been my experience that using a bread machine to mix the dough saves me time and hassle. That, in turn, encourages me to bake more often, which saves us money.

½ cup water
4 tablespoons olive oil
2 tablespoons honey
1½ cups unbleached all-purpose flour
½ teaspoon fine sea salt
½ teaspoon garlic powder
1 teaspoon active dry yeast
½ teaspoon dried Italian herb blend

1. Combine the water, 2 tablespoons of the oil, the honey, flour, salt, garlic powder, and yeast in the pan of your bread machine according to the manufacturer's directions. Set on the dough cycle and start the machine. (If making the dough by hand: Combine the water, 2 tablespoons of the oil, and the honey in a small saucepan and warm slightly over medium heat. Transfer the mixture to a large bowl and add the yeast. Stir and allow the yeast to proof for 5 minutes. Add the flour, salt, and garlic powder and stir to combine well. Turn the mixture out onto a lightly floured surface and knead for 5 minutes to create a smooth, elastic dough, adding more flour as necessary. Transfer to a greased bowl and turn the dough ball to coat. Allow to rise until doubled in bulk, about 1 hour.)

2. Grease a 12-cup muffin pan with nonstick cooking spray. When the machine beeps or the dough has doubled in bulk, remove the dough from the pan or bowl and divide it into 12 equal parts. Divide each part into 3 portions, shaping each portion into a ball. Place 3 dough balls in each muffin cup.

3. Preheat the oven to 400°F.

4. Brush the tops of the rolls with the remaining 2 tablespoons oil and sprinkle them with the Italian herbs. Allow to rise for 20 minutes.

5. Bake the rolls until golden brown, about 20 minutes. Cool on a rack before serving.

MAKE IT AHEAD: Store the rolls in an airtight container at room temperature for up to 2 days.

Get to know the
real people behind
your CSA, farm-
ers' market, or farm
stand. The folks who
grow and sell fresh
produce love to
share their passion
for it. Developing
a relationship with
them can also make
you privy to the
better deals and
higher-quality
foodstuffs.

Baked Apple Porcupines

Serves 4

MAKE-AHEAD

I've always found traditional baked apples to be a little unwieldy, requiring a knife and fork to eat them and the apple invariably attempting to escape across the plate. These apples are partially sliced before being sent into the oven, helping them cook a bit more quickly and also making them easier to enjoy.

4 firm apples, such as Jonathan or Braeburn, peeled, cored,
    and halved
1 tablespoon freshly squeezed lemon juice
½ cup unbleached all-purpose flour
2 tablespoons dark brown sugar
½ teaspoon ground cinnamon
2 tablespoons butter
2 tablespoons honey

1. Preheat the oven to 350°F. Grease a 9 x 13-inch pan with non-stick cooking spray.

2. Place each apple half on a cutting board, flat side down, and partially cut through the rounded side into thin slices, but do not cut all the way through.

3. Brush the cut apples with the lemon juice and place them, flat sides up, in the prepared baking dish.

4. In a small bowl, combine the flour, brown sugar, and cinnamon. Using a pastry blender or two knives, cut the butter into the flour mixture until coarse crumbs form. You can also pulse this together quickly in a food processor.

5. Sprinkle the crumb mixture over the 8 apple halves. Drizzle the honey over the tops of each.

6. Bake until the apples are tender and the crumb topping is lightly browned, about 30 minutes.

MAKE IT AHEAD: Cool, wrap, and refrigerate the baked apples for up to 2 days. Serve cold or at room temperature, or reheat in the oven or microwave.

MENU

Fire-Roasted
Mushroom
Marinara

Cheesy Polenta

Roasted Broccoli
with Garlic

This meal is one of my favorite meatless combinations. Mushroom-laden marinara soaks into cheesy polenta, while roasted broccoli adds an extra bit of texture and veg. Love this!

The sauce can be made ahead and frozen, and it reheats on the stove in about the same amount of time it takes to stir up the polenta and slide the pan of broccoli into the oven.

Fire-Roasted Mushroom Marinara

Makes 4 cups

`MEATLESS` `DAIRY-FREE` `GLUTEN-FREE` `MAKE-AHEAD` `FREEZER-FRIENDLY`

This sauce is rich in flavor thanks to the umami elements of the mushrooms. If you're in the mood for some meat, you can easily add some browned ground beef or sliced sausages.

¼ cup olive oil
1 medium onion, chopped
6 ounces mushrooms, coarsely chopped
1 teaspoon minced garlic
1 (28-ounce) can diced fire-roasted tomatoes, undrained
1½ teaspoons dried Italian herb blend
Kosher salt and freshly ground black pepper
1½ teaspoons balsamic vinegar (optional)

1. In a large stockpot, heat the olive oil over medium heat until shimmering. Add the onion, mushrooms, and garlic and cook, stirring, until the onion is translucent and the mushrooms have given up their liquid, 10 to 15 minutes.

2. Add the tomatoes with their juices, Italian herbs, and salt and pepper to taste. Simmer for 20 minutes. Taste and adjust the seasonings, adding the balsamic vinegar if you like.

3. For a smoother sauce, blend it in batches in a blender or food processor, or puree it using an immersion blender until you reach the texture you prefer.

MAKE IT AHEAD: Cool the sauce and store it in airtight container in the refrigerator for up to 3 days or in the freezer for up to 2 months. If frozen, thaw completely in the refrigerator. Reheat in a saucepan over low heat, whisking to recombine. Add a small amount of water if necessary to achieve the desired consistency.

#7

CLIP IT

I'm not sure we could have made it out of debt as quickly as we did if it hadn't been for the power of the coupon. Redeeming grocery coupons can be a great way to save money. While coupon policies vary from store to store and region to region, good deals can be had, especially when you pair a coupon with a sale. Check your newspaper, your grocery store website, and Coupons.com for a wide variety of grocery coupons. There are even digital coupons that load to your mobile device or store shopping card.

Cheesy Polenta

Serves 4

MEATLESS **GLUTEN-FREE**

Polenta is one of my favorite comfort foods. I love it even for leftovers, cut into squares and topped with pizza toppings or reheated and served with a fried egg on top. This version with mozzarella is great with the marinara ladled over it. So warm and soothing!

4 cups water
½ teaspoon kosher salt
1 cup polenta or coarse cornmeal
1 cup shredded mozzarella cheese

1. In a medium-size saucepan, combine the water and salt. Bring to a boil.

2. Stir in the polenta and reduce the heat to a simmer. Cook for 30 minutes, stirring occasionally to prevent sticking.

3. Stir in the cheese in small handfuls to melt and combine. Serve immediately.

Roasted Broccoli with Garlic

Serves 4

MEATLESS DAIRY-FREE GLUTEN-FREE

My family loves this roasted broccoli side with nuggets of spicy garlic. For less heat, reduce or omit the red pepper flakes. The broccoli and garlic can be prepped and refrigerated in advance, making for a convenient side dish that appears to be the fruit of much labor. Make extra so that you have leftovers to fold into omelets the next day.

1 large head broccoli, cut into florets
1 head garlic, cloves peeled and halved if large
2 tablespoons olive oil
⅛ teaspoon red pepper flakes
Kosher salt and freshly ground black pepper

1. Preheat the oven to 450°F. Grease a 9 x 13-inch baking dish with nonstick cooking spray.
2. Place the broccoli and garlic cloves in the prepared dish. Drizzle with the olive oil and season with the pepper flakes and salt and pepper to taste.
3. Roast until crisp-tender and lightly browned in spots, 10 to 15 minutes, stirring at least once to prevent sticking. Serve hot or at room temperature.

MENU

Simple Bean
Tostadas

Chunky Tomato
Salsa

Lemon Pie with
Honey-Ginger
Cream

This meal has been a mainstay in our family since the early years of digging out of debt. It has been known to cause some children to break out in song and dance. Bean tostadas are filling and tasty, especially when topped with homemade salsa and a drizzle of sour cream. Since you've scrimped with a bean-based dinner, you've got room to splurge on a decadent lemon tart for dessert.

Simple Bean Tostadas

Makes 12 tostadas

MEATLESS **GLUTEN-FREE**

You can buy tostada shells commercially packaged, but it's tastier to fry your own. In many cases, it's also cheaper. Consider shopping at your local Mexican market. Not only will they have the Latino ingredients you're looking for, but they also offer lower prices on those items than a regular grocery store.

Vegetable oil for frying
12 corn tortillas
2 (15-ounce) cans refried beans or 4 cups From-Scratch Refried
   Black Beans (page 183)
2 cups shredded cheddar cheese
2 large tomatoes, diced
2 cups shredded lettuce
½ cup sour cream
Chunky Tomato Salsa (recipe follows)

1. Preheat the oven to 425°F. In a small skillet, heat ½ inch of oil over medium-high heat until very hot. A small bit of tortilla will sizzle when the oil is ready. Fry the tortillas until stiff. Place the tortillas on a rimmed baking sheet and bake until brown and crunchy, 5 to 7 minutes.

2. Warm the refried beans in a saucepan until bubbly.

3. Spread the beans over the crisp tortilla shells. Top with the cheese, tomatoes, lettuce, and sour cream. Serve with salsa.

#8

GETTIN' DRIZZLY WITH IT

Condiments like sour cream or plain yogurt add great flavor as a topping for a number of dishes. Stretch your supply by drizzling instead of dolloping. (You'll get better coverage and make the dish more visually interesting, too.) Place a few tablespoons in a small zip-top plastic bag. Cut off a corner of the bag for an instant piping bag. Squeeze to drizzle on the topping.

Chunky Tomato Salsa

Makes 2 cups

`MEATLESS` `DAIRY-FREE` `GLUTEN-FREE` `MAKE-AHEAD`

The flavor of homemade salsa far surpasses any commercial preparations. Make this with fresh summer tomatoes for an extra wow factor.

2 large tomatoes, cored and chopped
1 jalapeño, seeded and chopped
¼ cup chopped red onion
¼ cup chopped fresh cilantro
Juice of 1 lemon
½ teaspoon kosher salt, or more to taste
¼ teaspoon red pepper flakes, or more to taste (optional)

Place the tomatoes, jalapeño, onion, cilantro, lemon juice, salt, and pepper flakes in a small bowl. Stir gently to combine. Adjust the seasonings to taste.

MAKE IT AHEAD: Store the salsa in an airtight container in the refrigerator for up to 2 days.

#9

PLANT A TREE

If you live in the right climate, fruit trees are a wonderful investment. My dad planted a lemon tree over 40 years ago that still yields hundreds of lemons every season. We zest and juice the lemons, package the zest and juice separately, and freeze them to use all year long for baking, cooking, and making lemonade. You can also freeze lemon slices in ice cube trays or muffin tins filled with water for refreshing lemon cubes. They take a glass of water to a whole new level.

Lemon Pie with Honey-Ginger Cream

Makes 1 (9-inch) pie

MAKE-AHEAD

Lemon meringue pie has always been a favorite of mine. My love was so deep that I taught myself to make it when I was 10 years old. This adaptation of the classic is just as tasty, but cooler and more refreshing thanks to the whipped cream topping.

    1⅓ cups sugar
    ⅓ cup cornstarch
    ¼ teaspoon fine sea salt
    1½ cups water
    3 large egg yolks, beaten
    2 tablespoons butter
    ¼ cup freshly squeezed lemon juice
    1 teaspoon grated lemon zest
    1 (9-inch) baked and cooled Versatile Buttery Pie Crust
      (recipe follows)
    1 cup heavy cream
    2 tablespoons honey
    ½ teaspoon ground ginger

1. In a medium-size saucepan, combine the sugar, cornstarch, and salt. Stir in the water, whisking until smooth. Cook the mixture over medium heat until thick and bubby, 5 to 10 minutes, stirring.

2. Remove the pot from the heat. Blend a small amount of the hot mixture into the beaten egg yolks to temper them. Return this mixture to the saucepan, mixing well. Cook just until the mixture starts to boil, stirring constantly. Add the butter, lemon juice, and zest and stir until incorporated. Let cool slightly in the saucepan.

3. Pour the filling into the pie crust and let cool to room temperature. Cover and refrigerate until fully chilled, about 2 hours.

4. When ready to serve, combine the heavy cream, honey, and ginger in a bowl. Whip with electric beaters until soft peaks form. Serve the pie with the whipped cream.

MAKE IT AHEAD: The pie can be prepared through step 3 and refrigerated for up to 2 days. When ready to serve, proceed with step 4.

versatile buttery pie crust

Makes 1 (8- or 9-inch) single-crust pie crust

I use this for nearly every pie I make. With a food processor, this crust comes together as easy as, well, pie. Even better, you don't need to roll it out if you don't want to—simply press it gently into the pie plate and up the sides.

  1 cup unbleached all-purpose flour
  8 tablespoons (1 stick) cold butter, cut into chunks
  ½ teaspoon fine sea salt
  1 to 2 tablespoons cold water

1. Preheat the oven to 350°F.

2. In the bowl of a food processor, combine the flour, butter, and salt. Run the processor until coarse crumbs form, 15 to 20 seconds. Alternatively, in a medium-size bowl, combine the flour, butter, and salt with a pastry blender or two knives. Work these ingredients together until they form pea-size crumbs.

3. Quickly pulse or stir in the cold water and combine until a dough forms. Form into a ball and chill in the refrigerator for a few minutes. (The dough can be made up to this point and frozen for later. Wrap the dough in plastic wrap, slip into a zip-top plastic bag, and store in the freezer for up to 1 month. Thaw in the refrigerator before proceeding.)

4. Roll out the dough on a flat work surface and transfer it to the pie plate, or pat it out directly in the pie plate. Bake until light golden brown, 10 to 15 minutes. Cool completely before adding the filling.

DRIED VERSUS CANNED BEANS

I t's no secret that we pay for convenience when we buy processed foods. But the suggestion, from a marketing perspective, is that we just aren't capable of doing it ourselves.

This raises the questions: Does it really take more time, effort, or knowledge to make our own? And is the cost benefit there? I say it's very often worth your while to make homemade. A great example of this is canned beans.

Consider these price points:

• A 15-ounce can of beans ranges in price from 68 cents to a buck twenty-five, though I see the price rising. What's inside? Beans and cooking liquid, and perhaps a few other things, depending on the brand and their love of additives.

• A 5-pound bag of dried beans costs between $5 and $7. Once cooked, that's the equivalent of about 15 cans of beans. Your cost per 2-cup portion is about 33 cents, making dried beans the best deal by far.

Home-cooked beans are also an excellent candidate for freezer cooking. Not only are they cheaper, but dried beans that you cook yourself are also healthier. You can add whatever seasonings you want and keep out additives and other dubious ingredients that you'd rather avoid. Cook up a big batch of beans in the slow cooker, divide it into 2-cup portions, and freeze them for later use. Then you will always have beans ready for any recipe.

Here's my preferred cooking method: Soak the beans in cool water to cover for at least 8 hours, but preferably a full 24 hours. (I've found that longer soaking results in a tenderer bean.) Drain and rinse, and drain again. Cover with 1 inch of water in the slow cooker and cook on High until tender, 3 to 4 hours. There will be extra cooking water at the end of this process. I usually drain most of it away, but leave some for added moisture and insulation when freezing. Season to taste (with salt, pepper, herbs, and spices) after the beans are fully cooked. Be sure to cool them to room temperature and then chill them in the refrigerator before freezing.

That said, if you find a great sale on canned beans that meet your family's ingredient preferences, stock up. If I find them for 50 cents or less, I know that the convenience truly is paying for itself.

MENU

Simplest
Butternut Squash
and Carrot Soup

Versatile
Vegetable Tart

Michèle's *Salade*

I lived in France for
10 months during
college. There I stud-
ied French literature,
learned how to speak
a little more flu-
ently, and ate some
of the best meals of
my life. This meal is
inspired by some of
those great meals I
enjoyed. Serve it in
courses to have the
true French experi-
ence. If you've got a
bottle of wine, a ba-
guette, and a wedge
of cheese, you'll take
it over the top.

Simplest Butternut Squash and Carrot Soup

Makes 4 cups

`MEATLESS` `DAIRY-FREE` `GLUTEN-FREE` `MAKE-AHEAD` `FREEZER-FRIENDLY`

I didn't grow up eating blended soups. Ours were always chunky and, for that matter, canned. It wasn't until I traveled to France that I discovered how lovely a velvety pureed soup could be. This soup is simple and filling and a great *entrée*, or entrance into a meal.

2 tablespoons olive oil
1 cup chopped onion
1 teaspoon minced garlic
3 cups peeled and cubed butternut squash
1½ cups chopped peeled carrots
2 cups water
1 teaspoon herbes de Provence
¾ teaspoon kosher salt
Freshly ground black pepper to taste

1. In a large stockpot, heat the oil over medium-high heat until shimmering. Add the onion and garlic and cook for 5 minutes.

2. Add the squash, carrots, and water and simmer until the vegetables are very tender, 45 to 50 minutes.

3. Blend the mixture with an immersion blender until very smooth. Alternatively, you can puree it in a blender or a food processor fitted with a metal blade. Be sure to vent the lid according to the manufacturer's directions.

4. Season with the herbes de Provence, salt, and pepper.

MAKE IT AHEAD: Let the soup cool, then store it in an airtight container in the refrigerator for up to 3 days or in the freezer for up to 2 months. If frozen, thaw completely in the refrigerator before reheating in the microwave or on the stovetop.

Versatile Vegetable Tart

Serves 4

MEATLESS | MAKE-AHEAD | FREEZER-FRIENDLY

You can use whatever vegetables you have on hand for this quiche-like tart, making it a great way to use up small bits of leftovers. It's packed with flavor and allows you untold combinations.

1 (8-inch) unbaked Versatile Buttery Pie Crust (page 37)
2 cups cooked vegetables, such as corn, green beans, or peas,
   or sliced potatoes, peppers, onions, or zucchini
⅓ cup crumbled feta or shredded cheddar, Comte, or Gruyère
3 large eggs
⅔ cup half-and-half
Kosher salt and freshly ground black pepper

1. Preheat the oven to 375°F.

2. Place the pie plate on a rimmed baking sheet to catch any drips. Layer the vegetables over the bottom of the pie crust. Sprinkle the cheese over the vegetables.

3. In a small bowl, beat the eggs with the half-and-half. Season to taste with salt and pepper. Pour this mixture into the pie shell.

4. Bake until set and golden brown, 40 to 50 minutes. Serve warm or at room temperature.

MAKE IT AHEAD: Place the unbaked tart in the freezer and freeze until firm, about 2 hours. Wrap the unbaked tart tightly and store in the freezer for up to 1 month. Bake directly from the freezer, adding 10 to 15 minutes to the baking time. The baked tart can be refrigerated for up to 2 days; reheat before serving.

GOOD TO THE LAST DROP

Use that almost empty jar of mustard, garlic, jam, or vinegar as a mixing vessel for dressings or marinades. You will be able to use every last bit of the condiment as well as save on dishwashing. You also get a pretty handy storage vessel for free.

Michèle's Salade

Serves 4

`MEATLESS` `DAIRY-FREE` `GLUTEN-FREE`

During my time in France, I was "adopted" by longtime friends of my high school French teacher. Michèle became my "French mom," taking me under her wing, answering my silly questions, and teaching me about French cooking. I loved to eat the French way, with its multiple courses that ended with a salad followed by a bit of cheese and bread. This is a salad I well remember enjoying *chez Durieux*.

1 tablespoon red wine vinegar
1 teaspoon Dijon mustard
Pinch of kosher salt
Freshly ground black pepper
3 tablespoons vegetable oil
2 tablespoons finely chopped red onion
1 head butter lettuce, torn into bite-size pieces

1. In a large salad bowl, whisk the vinegar, mustard, salt, and pepper to taste until well blended. Whisk in the oil in a thin stream. Stir in the onion.

2. Add the lettuce and toss to combine with the dressing. Serve immediately.

Spinach and
Mushroom Pizza
with Roasted
Tomato Sauce

Baby Greens
with Lemon-Basil
Vinaigrette

Salted Caramel
Affogato

Quality take-out
pizza used to be
go-to cheap eats, but
it seems that pizza
costs have risen dra-
matically in the past
10 years or so. Forget
about going to a
pizza parlor, where
the cost of salads,
drinks, and dessert
will push the bill sky-
high. You can pull
off this elegant pizza
night for a fraction
of the price. Make it
a festive family affair
by letting the kids
help you make the
pizzas.

Spinach and Mushroom Pizza with Roasted Tomato Sauce

Makes 2 (12-inch) pizzas

`MEATLESS`

I try to incorporate vegetables into our main dishes every chance I get. This pizza, doused with a roasted tomato sauce and studded with spinach and mushrooms, fills the bill. The cool avocado goes on after baking, adding a unique twist and rich flavor. It's so good that you'll probably want to make two pizzas instead of just one. Meat lovers can add cooked chicken or sausage.

½ recipe Honey Whole-Wheat Pizza Dough (page 88)
1 cup Roasted Tomato Sauce (recipe follows)
1 cup shredded spinach or kale
1 cup sliced mushrooms
2 cups shredded mozzarella cheese
¼ cup shredded cheddar cheese
Diced avocado, for topping

1. Preheat the oven to 475°F. Grease two 12-inch pizza pans with nonstick cooking spray.

2. Stretch the 2 pieces of dough to fit the pans. Spread half of the tomato sauce over each prepared pizza round. Layer on the spinach and mushrooms. Sprinkle on the mozzarella and cheddar cheeses.

3. Bake until the crust is crisp and the cheese is melted and golden in spots, 8 to 10 minutes.

4. Cool slightly before topping with the diced avocado and slicing.

Twice a year, I set a limited grocery budget and focus on using up what we have. It's like a real-life game of Food Network's *Chopped* as I try to make sense of random ingredients languishing in the cupboard. Not only do I use up what we have, but I learn from my buying mistakes. *I really don't need to buy X, Y, or Z again. It took us forever to use it up!*

roasted tomato sauce

Makes 1½ cups

MEATLESS DAIRY-FREE **GLUTEN-FREE** MAKE-AHEAD FREEZER-FRIENDLY

The flavors of summer are captured in this roasted tomato sauce. Besides pizza, this garlicky sauce is great for pasta or for dipping bread sticks. Roasting the garlic mellows its flavor, but if you prefer a less garlicky flavor, use half a head of garlic.

1 head garlic, separated into cloves and peeled
1½ pounds tomatoes, cored and halved
1 tablespoon olive oil
¾ teaspoon kosher salt
Freshly ground black pepper to taste
1 tablespoon chopped fresh basil or 1 teaspoon dried basil

1. Preheat the oven to 350°F.

2. Place the garlic cloves and tomatoes in a 9 x 13-inch pan. Drizzle with the olive oil and season with the salt and pepper. Toss to coat.

3. Roast until very soft, about 45 minutes. The skins will be wrinkled and darkened in spots.

4. Transfer the tomatoes and garlic to the bowl of a food processor fitted with a metal blade and add the basil. Pulse until the sauce reaches your desired texture. Adjust the seasonings as desired.

MAKE IT AHEAD: Store the sauce in an airtight container in the refrigerator for up to 5 days or in the freezer for up to 1 month.

Baby Greens with Lemon-Basil Vinaigrette

Serves 4

`MEATLESS` `DAIRY-FREE` `GLUTEN-FREE`

A crisp green salad is the perfect accompaniment to hot, cheesy pizza. This salad, reminiscent of a Caesar salad but less complicated, is fresh and tangy.

LEMON-BASIL VINAIGRETTE
1½ tablespoons red wine vinegar
1½ tablespoons freshly squeezed lemon juice
1 tablespoon chopped fresh basil
½ teaspoon minced garlic
Kosher salt and freshly ground black pepper
½ cup olive oil

5 ounces baby salad greens

1. In a small jar or bowl, combine the vinegar, lemon juice, basil, garlic, salt, and pepper. Place the lid on the jar and shake well or whisk until smooth. Add the olive oil and shake or whisk again to emulsify.

2. Place the baby salad greens in a large salad bowl. Toss with the dressing to coat thoroughly. Season to taste with kosher salt and freshly ground black pepper.

FRESH HERBS VERSUS DRIED

I grew up in a household where much of the produce was fresh from the garden, but the herbs were of the dried variety, purchased in a jar and stored in the cupboard. I didn't know any different. That's how my grandmothers had cooked; that's how my parents cooked; that's how I learned to cook. I didn't meet a fresh clove of garlic until college. Prior to that, I thought that garlic was for decoration in Italian restaurants and that a garlic press was for making cool "hair" for Play-Doh people.

In college, while cooking in a catering kitchen, I discovered fresh herbs. I got to know their different flavors and textures. I learned that they "worked" differently than their dried counterparts. I'm still exploring the nuanced differences between fresh and dried herbs and experimenting with new acquaintances.

I've read books by authors who completely eschew the use of dried herbs, claiming that they taste like dust. This may be the case with some of the tins you've had high up in the cupboard for 5 or 10 years, but dried herbs that are used in a reasonable amount of time can be a great, affordable fill-in for fresh.

Fresh herbs have a lot going for them. They are easy to grow and offer a light, fresh flavor to foods. Dried herbs, for their part, have a longer shelf life and don't melt into a weird pile of goo at the bottom of your crisper. I say there's a place for each in your kitchen. Here are some things to keep in mind as you include herbs (fresh or dried) in your kitchen.

Grow your own herbs if you can, either on a kitchen windowsill or steps from your back door so that you have easy access. Growing herbs from seed or buying a potted plant is also a more economical way to buy your herbs than buying a small packet in the produce department.

Store cut fresh herbs in the manner that is most suited to that variety. For instance, store parsley and cilantro in the fridge in cups of water with a plastic bag inverted over the greens. Store mint wrapped in damp paper towels in a bag in the fridge. Basil and dill can be stored using either method.

Dried herbs should be stored in a cool, dry place away from the stove. I buy mine in bulk or on sale to keep costs down, storing larger containers in the freezer. You can also split a bulk-size container with a friend or two to benefit from the bulk pricing without having to store a lot. Dried herbs that have lost their color and scent are too old to be flavorful.

Dried herbs also allow you to mix up custom seasoning blends easily. See page 80 for some ideas to get you started creating your own mixtures.

#12

INDULGE SOMETIMES

Splurge on the things that matter to you. For me, that's good coffee and cheese. You will avoid feeling "deprived," and that will give you the fortitude to keep saving in areas where the brand doesn't really matter to you.

Salted Caramel Affogato

Serves 4

GLUTEN-FREE

Affogato is just a fancy word for a coffee float. A traditional Italian version would, of course, feature gelato, but regular ice cream works just as well. The better quality the ice cream, though, the better your treat. Tradition would also dictate that you use espresso. But in the absence of an espresso machine, feel free to use strong brewed coffee.

4 cups hot espresso or strong brewed coffee
4 large scoops vanilla bean gelato or ice cream
¼ cup caramel sauce, warmed to drizzling consistency
4 large pinches of kosher salt

Divide the hot coffee among four large mugs. Place a scoop of gelato in each mug. Drizzle the caramel sauce over the creamy foam that forms. Sprinkle each serving with a pinch of salt. Serve immediately.

Hot Cheese Dip
with Sun-Dried
Tomatoes

Lemony Linguini
with Broccoli and
Mushrooms

I love to start a meal
with a casual snack-
type appetizer. It
gives folks time to
mingle and unwind
before sitting down
to a larger meal. And
my kids love to have
something to munch
while they wait. Plus,
offering an appetizer
gives the cook time
to put the finishing
touches on the main
dish without feeling
harried. Serve fresh
Italian or French
bread with both
courses of this filling
vegetarian meal.

Hot Cheese Dip with Sun-Dried Tomatoes

Serves 4

MEATLESS **GLUTEN-FREE**

This hot cheese dip flecked with basil and tomatoes is delicious.
Serve it with fresh bread or crackers for dipping.

8 ounces Monterey Jack cheese, cubed
¼ cup julienned sun-dried tomatoes
2 tablespoons chopped fresh basil
1 tablespoon sliced scallion
Freshly ground black pepper to taste
1 tablespoon olive oil

1. Preheat the oven to 375°F. Grease a 4-cup baking dish with
nonstick cooking spray.

2. Combine the cheese cubes, sun-dried tomatoes, basil, scallion,
and pepper in the prepared dish. Drizzle with the oil and toss gently
to coat.

3. Cover with aluminum foil and bake until the cheese is melted
and bubbly, about 25 minutes. Serve immediately.

13

Meal planning saves you on a number of fronts. If you know what you have and what you can serve for dinner, you'll be less likely to eat out, which is guaranteed to be more expensive. The meal plan also allows you to shop more effectively. No forgetting something when you're at the store; no running back; no impulse shopping. Plan meals that build on one another or that share common ingredients. You'll waste less if you've got a plan for everything in your fridge.

Lemony Linguini with Broccoli and Mushrooms

Serves 4

`MEATLESS`

This one-dish dinner provides a vegetable and a starch as well as the umami-rich flavors of mushrooms to take the place of meat. Toss it all together in a large pasta bowl to serve family-style at the table.

2 tablespoons butter or olive oil
8 ounces mushrooms, sliced
1 teaspoon minced garlic
4 cups broccoli florets
½ cup vegetable broth
2 tablespoons freshly squeezed lemon juice
1 teaspoon grated lemon zest
1 pound linguini
Red pepper flakes
Kosher salt and freshly ground black pepper
Grated Parmesan, for garnish
Chopped fresh parsley, for garnish

1. Melt the butter in a large skillet with a lid over medium heat. Cook the mushrooms and garlic in the butter until the mushrooms release their liquid and start to brown, 10 to 12 minutes.

2. Add the broccoli, broth, lemon juice, and zest. Cover and let steam until the broccoli is tender, about 5 minutes.

3. Meanwhile, bring a large pot of salted water to a boil over high heat and cook the linguini according to the package directions. Drain the pasta, reserving some of the cooking water. Place the pasta in a large serving bowl.

4. Add the vegetable mixture to the pasta. Toss to combine, adding a little of the pasta water if the mixture seems dry. Season to taste with red pepper flakes, salt, and black pepper. Garnish with the Parmesan and parsley.

MENU

Potato-Leek Soup

Honey Whole-
Wheat Bread

This hearty yet meat-
less soup and bread
combo will satisfy
the tummy without
emptying the pocket-
book. Serve the bread
warm with lots of
butter alongside the
bubbling-hot potato
soup.

Potato-Leek Soup

Makes about 6 cups

`MEATLESS` `DAIRY-FREE` `GLUTEN-FREE`

Potato-leek soup is ubiquitous throughout France. It was there that
I first tasted it—and fell in love with it. Be sure to rinse the leeks
really well after slicing them. They can hide bits of grit between their
layers. Omit the half-and-half for the dairy-free option. This soup is a
great way to use up leftover mashed potatoes.

2 tablespoons olive oil
2 leeks, halved and thinly sliced
1 teaspoon minced garlic
4 cups vegetable broth
3 cups Smashed Potatoes (page 95) or chopped peeled potatoes
Kosher salt and freshly ground black pepper
½ cup half-and-half (optional)
2 tablespoons chopped fresh parsley

1. In a large stockpot, heat the oil over medium heat until shimmering. Cook the leeks and garlic until tender, 7 to 8 minutes.

2. Add the stock and whisk in the potatoes. Simmer for 15
minutes if using cooked potatoes, 30 minutes if using uncooked
potatoes.

3. Blend the soup with an immersion blender until very smooth.
Alternatively, you can puree it in batches in a blender or food
processor. Be sure to vent the lid according to the manufacturer's
directions. Season the soup with salt and pepper to taste.

4. If you prefer a thinner soup, add some or all of the half-and-
half. Stir in the parsley and serve.

14

Got some heels of a bread loaf or a spare roll left over from a previous meal? Repurpose those random bits into homemade fresh bread crumbs. Whiz them in a food processor or blender and store in a zip-top plastic bag in the freezer until ready to use. Don't spend good money on overly salted or artificially flavored commercial bread crumbs when you can make them for (almost) free.

Honey Whole-Wheat Bread

Makes 1 (5 x 9-inch) loaf

MEATLESS   MAKE-AHEAD   FREEZER-FRIENDLY

Home-baked bread is simple to make yet so satisfying. Using a bread machine to form the dough makes it super easy, but you can mix the dough by hand as well. And yes, I do bake bread machine dough in the oven. Crazy, I know, but I think it turns out better looking that way.

White whole-wheat flour is readily available in most supermarkets and has less of a strongly wheaty flavor while still retaining the nutrients of the whole grain.

1 cup buttermilk
4 tablespoons (½ stick) butter
1 large egg, beaten
¼ cup honey
1½ cups unbleached all-purpose flour
1½ cups white whole-wheat flour
1 teaspoon fine sea salt
2¼ teaspoons active dry yeast

1. Combine the ingredients in the pan of your bread machine according to the manufacturer's directions. Set to the dough cycle and start the machine. (If making the dough by hand: Combine the buttermilk, butter, and honey in a medium-size saucepan and warm slightly over medium heat. Transfer the mixture to a large bowl and add the yeast. Stir and allow the yeast to proof for 5 minutes. Add the flours, beaten egg, and salt. Stir to combine well. Turn the mixture out onto a lightly floured surface and knead for 5 minutes to create a smooth, elastic dough, adding more all-purpose flour as necessary. Transfer to a greased bowl and turn the dough ball to coat. Allow to rise until doubled in bulk, about 1 hour.)

2. Grease a 5 x 9-inch loaf pan with nonstick cooking spray. When the machine beeps or the dough has doubled in bulk, remove the dough from the pan or bowl and form it into a tight loaf. Place it in the loaf pan and allow it to double in bulk, about 1 hour.

3. Meanwhile, preheat the oven to 400°F.

4. Bake the bread until golden brown, 20 to 25 minutes. Cool on a rack before serving.

MAKE IT AHEAD: Wrap the cooled bread in plastic wrap and store on the counter for up to 4 days. Or place the cooled and wrapped bread in a zip-top plastic bag and freeze for up to 2 months. Thaw in the wrappings on the counter.

MEAL PLANNING BASICS

I'm the type of person who is thinking of the next meal while I am enjoying the current one. My mind can't help but think ahead to future deliciousness. My kids are no different, often asking me at bedtime what we'll have for breakfast. Clearly meal planning is a family hobby around here.

Not everyone gets as jazzed as we do about meal planning. It can seem like boring drudgework to some. But the rewards are clear. If you've planned your meals for the week, you'll know what to buy at the store. If you've shopped for groceries and know what to do with them, you'll easily be able to prepare supper. If you prepare supper, you will eat well and spend less money. I'd say meal planning is a game-winning strategy.

So, what are the basics of meal planning?

1. Create a list of meals that your family enjoys and that fit your budget. Look at what's in the cupboard, fridge, and freezer. What meals can you prepare with what you already have? Jot those down or check them off on your list. Check out the store ads. What's on sale that fits your family's tastes? Shoot for seven meals that you know you can make this week.

2. Grab a calendar. You can download some free meal planning printables at http://good-cheapeats.com/printables/.

3. Look at what activities you have scheduled for the week. What days are busiest? Put the simplest meals on those days. If you have a late doctor's appointment or soccer practice, then plan a slow cooker meal. If there is a day with time to cook a more elaborate meal, plug that meal into that day's spot on your weekly grid. If you know you'll be gone all evening, plan a packable meal.

4. Double-check your menus to see that you have the ingredients necessary for each meal. If not, write them on your grocery list. Go shopping just *once*!

Now you shouldn't have to ask yourself at 5:00 p.m., "What am I going to make?" You have a plan. Check it each morning to make sure you've thawed the necessary items. You might even pull out the nonperishable ingredients and place them on the counter so that you're all ready when prep time arrives. If you keep the meal plan list and recipes handy, you can even delegate dinner prep to someone else in the family.

Stretching It

As my kids have learned their scientific classifications of animals and the different characteristics of their eating behavior, they've latched on to the different names for eaters: carnivore, omnivore, herbivore, and dessertivore.

Okay, they made that last one up.

Most of them would choose to be carnivores, if they could. (Dessertivore is in close competition.) When we have grilled meat such as tri-tip, those nearby need to stand back. The FishBoys go after it like a pack of hungry wolves.

Unfortunately, big hunks of meat are kinda pricey. There's no way I could offer them their fill of meat and stay out of debt. So, meat is not always a big menu item. One particular child often asks, "But is there any meat in it?" I've discovered that he is easily appeased if there's even a small amount of meat in a dish. I stock up when it's on sale, and then ration it. We eat well; we stay under budget; everyone's happy.

Mac (and Ham) and Cheese Casserole 56
Pumpkin-Onion-Poppy Rolls. 57
Lemon-Blueberry Crumble. 58

Roasted Beet Salad with Herbed Feta Dressing 59
Shrimp and Cilantro Pasta 60

Fired-Up Chili Bean Soup. 62
Cheesy Jalapeño Cornbread 63

Peanut Butter Chicken and Pasta 64
Sesame Broccoli. 65
Homemade Lemonade. 66

Chicken, Black Bean, and Rice Soup. 67
Sourdough Rolls. 68

Jalapeño Cheese Dip with Homemade Tortilla Chips 72
Arroz con Pollo 75
Cumin-Scented Cabbage Salad 76

Cajun Shrimp and Sausage Rice 77
Buttery Dill Carrots 78
Banana-Walnut Mini Muffins. 79

Sloppy Fo's. 82
ChiChi's Italian Salad 83

Cheesy Beefy Chili Bake 84
Mexican Tossed Salad. 85

Supreme Sausage Pizza. 86
Spinach-Apple Salad with Scallion-Lime Dressing 89

MENU

Mac (and Ham) and Cheese Casserole

Pumpkin-Onion-Poppy Rolls

Lemon-Blueberry Crumble

This meal reminds me of something my Gramma John would have made. She raised eight children on a Minnesota farm, partly as a single mom, between widowhood and remarriage. Six of her kids were boys, so she knew how to feed hungry folks well. She was big on baking and passed that love on to me. This homey meal is just the kind of fare Gramma might have served, along with a variety of steamed veggies, fresh from the garden patch.

Mac (and Ham) and Cheese Casserole

Serves 4

MAKE-AHEAD　**FREEZER-FRIENDLY**

This casserole, an easy adaptation of traditional macaroni and cheese, gets a boost from chunks of ham and aromatic dill. It's freezer-friendly, so feel free to make a double batch and freeze half for later use. The FishKids prefer broccoli to peas in this dish, but both are tasty.

9 ounces wide egg noodles (about 4 cups)
4 tablespoons (½ stick) butter
¼ cup chopped onion
¼ cup unbleached all-purpose flour
2 cups milk
1½ teaspoons chopped fresh dill or ½ teaspoon dried dill
¼ teaspoon freshly ground black pepper
Kosher salt
2 cups diced ham
1 cup cubed cheddar cheese
1 cup small broccoli florets or peas

1. Preheat the oven to 350°F. Grease an 8-inch square baking pan with nonstick cooking spray.

2. Bring a large pot of salted water to a boil over high heat and cook the noodles according to the package directions. Drain.

3. Meanwhile, in a medium-size saucepan over medium heat, melt the butter. Cook the onion until translucent, 5 to 7 minutes. Add the flour and stir until well combined. Cook, stirring, for 2 minutes more.

4. Slowly whisk in the milk and simmer until thickened, about 5 minutes. Stir in the dill and pepper. Season to taste with salt.

5. In a large bowl, combine the noodles, white sauce, ham, cheese, and broccoli. Spoon the mixture into the prepared dish and cover with aluminum foil.

6. Bake until hot and bubbly, about 20 minutes.

MAKE IT AHEAD: The unbaked casserole can be stored in the refrigerator for up to 1 day or in the freezer for up to 1 month. If frozen, thaw completely in the refrigerator before baking. In either case, add 5 to 10 minutes to the baking time since the dish will be cold.

15

Scratch and dent stores offer discounted food products that might have slightly damaged boxes but that are perfectly good and usable. Check the expiration dates to make sure you've got time to enjoy the product before it goes bad.

Pumpkin-Onion-Poppy Rolls

Makes 16 rolls

MEATLESS **MAKE-AHEAD** **FREEZER-FRIENDLY**

Making your own bread is not difficult, though our generation seems intimidated by the process. It's liberating to know that you can make something from scratch, just like Gramma did. It's also a great way to economize compared with purchasing commercial baked goods.

These rolls are fabulous served warm with butter, but they also work well with any number of sandwich fillings.

1⅓ cups buttermilk
⅓ cup vegetable oil
1 large egg, beaten
½ cup canned pumpkin puree (not pumpkin pie filling)
3 cups unbleached all-purpose flour
1 cup whole-wheat flour
3 tablespoons sugar
3 tablespoons dried onion flakes
2 teaspoons fine sea salt
1 teaspoon poppy seeds
2¼ teaspoons active dry yeast

1. Combine the ingredients in the bread pan of your bread machine according to the manufacturer's instructions. Set to the dough cycle and start the machine. (If making the dough by hand: Combine the buttermilk, oil, and sugar in a medium-size saucepan and warm slightly over medium heat. Transfer the mixture to a large bowl and add the yeast. Stir and allow the yeast to proof for 5 minutes. Add the flours, egg, pumpkin puree, onion flakes, salt, and poppy seeds. Stir to combine well. Turn the mixture out onto a lightly floured surface and knead for 5 minutes to create a smooth, elastic dough, adding more all-purpose flour as necessary. Transfer to a greased bowl and turn the dough ball to coat. Allow to rise until doubled in bulk, about 1 hour.)

2. Line a baking sheet with parchment or a silicone baking mat. When the machine beeps or the dough has doubled in bulk, turn the dough out onto a floured surface and divide into 16 portions. Form each portion into a tight round and place them, evenly spaced, on the prepared baking sheet. Allow the rolls to rise for 30 minutes.

3. While the rolls rise, preheat the oven to 350°F. Bake the rolls until golden brown, 15 to 20 minutes. Cool the rolls slightly on a rack before serving.

MAKE IT AHEAD: Store the rolls in an airtight container at room temperature for up to 2 days or in the freezer for up to 1 month.

Lemon-Blueberry Crumble

Serves 4 to 6

`MAKE-AHEAD`

Growing up, the only blueberries I ever encountered were the disappointing canned variety that came in packaged muffin mixes. It wasn't until adulthood that I first tasted them in all their fresh, sun-kissed glory. Wow! Since they often go on sale during the summer, we enjoy them fresh in fruit salads and yogurt, or baked into strudel or this fabulous lemon-scented crumble.

4 cups blueberries (12 to 16 ounces)
1 cup granulated sugar
⅓ cup cornstarch
2 teaspoons grated lemon zest
1 cup unbleached all-purpose flour
½ cup rolled oats
8 tablespoons (1 stick) cold butter, cubed
¼ cup light brown sugar

1. Preheat the oven to 375°F. Grease an 8-inch square baking pan with nonstick cooking spray.

2. In a large bowl, combine the blueberries, granulated sugar, cornstarch, and lemon zest. Toss gently to coat. Spoon the mixture into the prepared baking dish.

3. In a food processor fitted with a metal blade, combine the flour, oats, and butter. Pulse until coarse crumbs form. You can also do this in a bowl with a pastry blender or two knives. Stir in the brown sugar.

4. Sprinkle the crumb mixture over the blueberries.

5. Bake until the filling is bubbly and the topping is lightly browned, 30 to 35 minutes. Cool slightly before serving.

MAKE IT AHEAD: The crumble can be made up to 2 days ahead, covered, and refrigerated.

MENU

Roasted Beet
Salad with
Herbed Feta
Dressing

Shrimp and
Cilantro Pasta

Salad and pasta is
a favorite meal at
our house. It's true
comfort food, and
it's easy to stretch to
accommodate bigger
appetites or unex-
pected guests. This
meal comes together
effortlessly.

Roasted Beet Salad with Herbed Feta Dressing

Serves 4

`MEATLESS` `GLUTEN-FREE` `MAKE-AHEAD`

This salad is packed with flavor from the beets and feta dressing.
Roast the beets in advance if you wish; they taste great hot or cold.

ROASTED BEETS
4 small beets, peeled and sliced ¼ inch thick
2 tablespoons olive oil
1 tablespoon white wine vinegar
Kosher salt and freshly ground black pepper

HERBED FETA DRESSING
¼ cup red wine vinegar
1 tablespoon crumbled feta cheese
½ teaspoon dried oregano
½ teaspoon dried parsley
¼ teaspoon dried dill
¼ teaspoon kosher salt
⅛ teaspoon freshly ground black pepper
⅓ cup olive oil

1 head red or green leaf lettuce, washed and torn into bite-size
   pieces

1. Preheat the oven to 400°F.

2. In an 8-inch square baking dish, combine the beets, oil, white
wine vinegar, and salt and pepper to taste. Roast the beets for 25
minutes or until tender. Cool slightly.

3. In a small jar or bowl, combine the red wine vinegar, feta
cheese, oregano, parsley, dill, salt, and pepper. Place the lid on the
jar and shake well or whisk to combine. Whisk in the olive oil in a
thin stream.

4. Place the lettuce in a large salad bowl. Toss with enough
dressing to coat. Divide the salad among serving plates. Divide the
beets among the salads. Serve the remaining dressing on the side.

MAKE IT AHEAD: The beets and dressing can be prepared and stored separately
in airtight containers in the refrigerator for up to 4 days, then tossed with the
lettuce just before serving.

#16

SAVING CILANTRO

Fresh cilantro, parsley, and dill are fairly inexpensive to purchase, but they often end up in a gooey mess in the bottom of the crisper if not used quickly enough. Save your herbs from such a sorry fate! Store the bouquet in the refrigerator in a glass of water with a plastic bag tented over the top.

Shrimp and Cilantro Pasta

Serves 4

`MEATLESS`

This pasta dish is rich and flavorful thanks to the shrimp. Look for frozen shrimp on sale in the months of March and April, when Lenten dietary guidelines encourage supermarkets to offer seafood at a discount. Stock up so you can enjoy shrimp dishes all year long.

12 ounces spaghetti
2 tablespoons olive oil
1 teaspoon minced garlic
1 pound medium shrimp (thawed if frozen), peeled and deveined
½ teaspoon ground cumin
⅛ teaspoon freshly ground black pepper
⅛ teaspoon red pepper flakes
Juice of 1 lime
½ cup chopped fresh cilantro
1 large tomato, chopped
Grated Parmesan cheese, for serving

1. Bring a large pot of salted water to a boil over high heat and cook the spaghetti according to the package directions. Drain.

2. Meanwhile, heat the olive oil in a large skillet over medium heat. Add the garlic and cook until fragrant, about 2 minutes.

3. Add the shrimp to the pan and cook until opaque and almost pink, 7 to 10 minutes.

4. Add the cumin, black pepper, and red pepper to the pan. Stir to combine. Squeeze the lime juice all over the shrimp and stir. Add the cilantro and tomato and the hot cooked pasta and stir until well combined. Serve immediately, with Parmesan on the side.

MENU

Fired-Up Chili
Bean Soup

Cheesy Jalapeño
Cornbread

I'm always surprised when folks tell me they've never considered soup to be a meal. For centuries, folks around the world have devoted their evening meal to a bowl of soup and a morsel of bread. It's filling and comforting all at once.

Fired-Up Chili Bean Soup

Makes about 12 cups

MEATLESS | **DAIRY-FREE** | **GLUTEN-FREE** | **SLOW COOKER** | **MAKE-AHEAD** | **FREEZER-FRIENDLY**

This soup is meatless, but you can certainly add cooked ground beef, pork, or turkey or leftover roast meats if you'd like to beef it up. It's delectable on its own, though, and features a mystery ingredient (cinnamon) that adds warmth and flavor. Use whatever beans you have if you don't have the varieties listed. Chill and freeze any leftovers for quick lunches and dinners another day.

5 cups cooked or canned pinto beans (rinsed and drained if canned)
3 cups cooked or canned black beans (rinsed and drained if canned)
2 cups vegetable broth
1 (14.5-ounce) can diced fire-roasted tomatoes with green chiles, undrained
2 tablespoons chopped dried onion flakes
2 tablespoons chili powder
1 tablespoon dried parsley
½ teaspoon ground cinnamon
Kosher salt and freshly ground black pepper

1. Combine the beans, broth, tomatoes with their juices, onion, chili powder, parsley, cinnamon, and salt and pepper to taste in a 4-quart slow cooker. Stir gently to combine.

2. Cover and cook on High for 4 hours or on Low for 6 to 8 hours.

MAKE IT AHEAD: Let the soup cool to room temperature and chill in the refrigerator for up to 4 days. Or divide into desired portions and freeze for up to 2 months. If frozen, thaw completely in the refrigerator before reheating in the microwave or on the stovetop.

#17

GOT MILK?

Milk about to expire? Use it up before it's no good. Make home-made yogurt, freeze pancake batter, stir up a homemade pud-ding, or whisk up a white sauce or gravy. In a pinch, you can even freeze it until you have time to deal with it. Just be sure to thaw it completely and shake to recom-bine. Being mindful of expiration dates will help you save money.

Cheesy Jalapeño Cornbread

Serves 4 to 8

MEATLESS **MAKE-AHEAD** **FREEZER-FRIENDLY**

This spicy cornbread is a huge hit, especially when served with but-ter. Make up several bags of the dried ingredients so that you can prepare a quick side dish any night of the week.

1⅓ cups unbleached all-purpose flour
⅔ cup cornmeal
1 tablespoon baking powder
½ teaspoon fine sea salt
½ cup shredded pepper Jack cheese
½ to 1 jalapeño, seeded and diced
1 cup milk
2 large eggs
½ cup honey
¼ cup vegetable oil

1. Preheat the oven to 350°F. Grease a 9-inch pie plate with non-stick cooking spray.

2. In a large bowl, combine the flour, cornmeal, baking powder, and salt. Add the shredded cheese and jalapeño and toss to coat.

3. In another bowl, whisk together the milk, eggs, honey, and oil. Add the wet ingredients to the dry and fold to combine.

4. Spoon the mixture into the prepared pie plate and bake until a tester inserted comes out with a few crumbs attached, about 30 minutes.

MAKE IT AHEAD: Combine the flour, cornmeal, baking powder, and salt in a zip-top plastic bag. Label the bag with the other ingredients to add as well as the baking directions. Store the bag in the freezer. Baked and cooled cornbread can also be wrapped in aluminum foil and frozen. Thaw completely at room tempera-ture, then warm in a 350°F oven for 5 minutes before serving.

Peanut Butter
Chicken and
Pasta

Sesame Broccoli

Homemade
Lemonade

This is a perfect budget meal: a little meat, pasta, veg, and homemade lemonade. It's packed with flavor and economical ingredients, and it's easy to pull together in a short amount of time. Sometimes I skip the broccoli and make a double batch of the chicken and pasta—the FishKids go crazy for it.

Peanut Butter Chicken and Pasta

Serves 4

DAIRY-FREE **MAKE-AHEAD** **FREEZER-FRIENDLY**

My friend Julie originally gave me this recipe, which I've tweaked over the years. The original contained Paul Newman's salad dressing, a bit more chicken, and a lot less pasta. I eliminated the expensive bottled dressing and stretched the chicken with more pasta. There are rarely leftovers, but if you have them, they are good cold, at room temperature, or reheated.

Scant ⅓ cup rice vinegar
Generous ⅓ cup plus 2 tablespoons vegetable oil
2 tablespoons peanut butter
2 tablespoons reduced-sodium soy sauce
1 tablespoon honey
1 tablespoon toasted sesame oil
1 teaspoon grated fresh ginger
½ teaspoon red pepper flakes
1 medium carrot, peeled and shredded
1 pound boneless, skinless chicken breasts, chopped
1 cup chopped scallions
1 pound linguini or thin spaghetti
2 tablespoons chopped fresh cilantro

1. In a small bowl, whisk together the vinegar, generous ⅓ cup of the oil, peanut butter, soy sauce, honey, sesame oil, ginger, and red pepper. Set aside.

2. In a large skillet, heat the remaining 2 tablespoons oil until very hot. Cook the carrot for 1 minute, stirring. Add the chicken and scallions to the pan and cook, stirring constantly, until the chicken is cooked, about 10 minutes.

3. Meanwhile, bring a large pot of salted water to a boil over high heat and cook the linguini according to the package directions. Drain the pasta and toss it with the sauce and cilantro. You may toss the chicken in as well, but we like to serve it atop the noodles—otherwise, the chicken pieces drop to the bottom and are not evenly distributed. Serve hot or at room temperature.

MAKE IT AHEAD: Prepare through step 2 and cool slightly. Package the sauce and chicken mixture separately and store in the refrigerator for up to 3 days or in the freezer for up to 1 month. If frozen, thaw completely in the refrigerator. Reheat the chicken briefly and let the sauce come to room temperature before continuing with step 3.

18

WASTE NOT, WANT NOT

Rinse empty cans and jars with a tablespoon or two of water or other cooking liquid to grab the last bits, wasting less and prepping the vessel for recycling all at once.

Sesame Broccoli

Serves 4

`MEATLESS` `DAIRY-FREE` `GLUTEN-FREE`

This broccoli dish, scented with sesame and soy sauce, is a huge hit among the FishKids. There's no need for a reminder to "Eat your veggies"; they gobble it down. As my 11-year-old food critic says, "This broccoli is amazing." You can substitute other vegetables, like green beans or frozen Asian mixed vegetables, if that's what you have on hand.

6 cups broccoli florets
1 cup water
2 tablespoons vegetable oil
1 garlic clove, sliced
1 to 2 tablespoons reduced-sodium soy sauce
1 tablespoon toasted sesame oil
Toasted white sesame seeds, for sprinkling (optional)

1. Place the broccoli and water in a large skillet. Cover and cook over medium-high heat for 5 minutes. Drain the broccoli and return it to the skillet, pushing it to one side.

2. Add the oil and garlic to the skillet and raise the heat to high. Cook, stirring, until the garlic is fragrant, 2 to 3 minutes. Toss the broccoli with the garlic and oil in the skillet. The broccoli should be tender but not too soft.

3. Drizzle the broccoli with the soy sauce and sesame oil. Sprinkle with the sesame seeds, if you like, and serve hot.

Homemade Lemonade

Serves 8

DAIRY-FREE **GLUTEN-FREE** **MAKE-AHEAD**

If you have a backyard lemon tree or know someone who does, this is the best way to make use of nature's bounty. This homemade lemonade is super flavorful, so serve it over lots of ice.

1½ cups freshly squeezed lemon juice
1½ cups sugar
5 cups water

In a large pitcher, combine the lemon juice and sugar. Stir until the sugar has dissolved. Stir in the water. Serve chilled over crushed ice.

MAKE IT AHEAD: Store the lemonade in the refrigerator for up to 2 days.

We have soup night about once a week from fall to spring. Soup is an economical—and versatile—way to stretch ingredients to feed a crowd. You could probably make a different soup every night for a year and not repeat yourself; there are so many possible combinations.

Chicken, Black Bean, and Rice Soup

Makes about 12 cups

DAIRY-FREE **GLUTEN-FREE** MAKE-AHEAD FREEZER-FRIENDLY

My husband's childhood and bachelor years were spent living in Santa Barbara. He still waxes eloquent about one of his favorite Mexican restaurants, Little Alex's, where they served a delicious chicken and rice soup with a Mexican twist. This is my re-creation of it.

This makes a big pot of soup, leaving you free to take a night off from cooking later in the week or to pack the leftovers for lunches.

1 tablespoon olive oil
1½ cups chopped onion
1 teaspoon minced garlic
8 cups Homemade Chicken Stock (page 97)
2 to 3 cups shredded or chopped cooked chicken
2 cups cooked or canned black beans (rinsed and drained if canned)
1 (14.5-ounce) can diced tomatoes, undrained
1 cup shredded zucchini
1 cup sliced peeled carrots
1 cup white rice
Juice of 1 lime
1 teaspoon ground cumin
½ teaspoon dried oregano
⅛ teaspoon cayenne pepper
Kosher salt and freshly ground black pepper
Chopped fresh cilantro, for garnish

1. In a large stockpot over medium heat, heat the olive oil until shimmering. Cook the onion and garlic until tender, about 6 minutes.

2. Add the chicken stock, cooked chicken, beans, tomatoes with their juices, zucchini, carrots, rice, lime juice, cumin, oregano, cayenne, and salt and pepper to taste. Simmer until the rice and vegetables are tender, about 20 minutes.

3. Garnish the soup with chopped cilantro.

MAKE IT AHEAD: Once the soup is cooked, cool it to room temperature and refrigerate until ready to serve, up to 2 days. Or divide into desired portions and freeze for up to 1 month. If frozen, thaw completely in the refrigerator before reheating in the microwave or on the stovetop.

19

BAKE SOMEONE HAPPY

Bread loaves from the store cost $2 to $3 or more per loaf and are often filled with preservatives and other dubious ingredients. Bake your own bread to customize the ingredients as well as save money. I bake homemade baguettes and boules for as low as 25 cents per loaf.

Sourdough Rolls

Makes 12 rolls

`MEATLESS` `DAIRY-FREE` `MAKE-AHEAD` `FREEZER-FRIENDLY`

Our family loves sourdough rolls, but it's proven not to be the most economical of purchased breads, unless I can find it marked down. Instead, I've learned the very basic art of making my own sourdough starter. It takes no special equipment or ingredients: just flour, water, and a little patience.

1 cup Sourdough Starter (recipe follows)
½ cup water
3 tablespoons olive oil
3 cups unbleached all-purpose flour
1 tablespoon sugar
1½ teaspoons fine sea salt
2¼ teaspoons active dry yeast

1. Combine the ingredients in the pan of your bread machine according to the manufacturer's directions. Set to the dough cycle and start the machine. (If making the dough by hand: Combine the water, oil, and sugar in a small saucepan and warm slightly over medium heat. Transfer the mixture to a large bowl and add the yeast. Stir and allow the yeast to proof for 5 minutes. Add the starter, flour, and salt. Stir to combine well. Turn the mixture out onto a lightly floured surface and knead for 5 minutes to create a smooth, elastic dough, adding more flour as necessary. Transfer to a greased bowl and turn the dough ball to coat. Allow to rise until doubled in bulk, about 1 hour.)

2. Line a baking sheet with parchment paper or a silicone baking mat. When the machine beeps or the dough has doubled in bulk, remove the dough from the pan and divide it into 12 equal parts. Form each portion into a tight round and place on the prepared baking sheet. Allow the rolls to rise 30 minutes.

3. While the rolls rise, preheat the oven to 375°F.

4. Slash the tops of the rolls with a sharp knife and bake until golden brown, 15 to 20 minutes. Cool slightly on a rack before serving.

MAKE IT AHEAD: The baked and cooled rolls can be stored in an airtight container at room temperature for up to 2 days or in the freezer for up to 1 month. Thaw them on the counter before serving. Rolls can be reheated in a 350°F oven for 5 minutes to warm.

sourdough starter

This sourdough starter should be used up or "fed" once a week. You can feed it by mixing in 1 cup flour, 1 cup water, and a pinch of sugar. After feeding, allow it to "work" at room temperature for 24 hours before using or refrigerate, loosely covered. A starter, properly cared for, can keep indefinitely; pay careful attention to the notes in step 2.

2 cups water
2 cups unbleached all-purpose flour
1 tablespoon active dry yeast
2 teaspoons sugar

1. In a large bowl, combine the water, flour, yeast, and sugar. Whisk until a smooth batter is formed. Cover it loosely with cheesecloth or plastic wrap and allow it to sit at room temperature for 2 to 5 days, stirring at least once a day.

2. At that point, the starter should be bubbly and have a distinct yeasty scent. If any gray or yellow liquid rises to the top, you can just stir this "hooch" back in. (If the starter turns orange or pink or grows mold, it's bad, so chuck it and start over.)

3. The starter is ready to use at this point or can be refrigerated in a quart-size canning jar, loosely covered with plastic wrap.

HOW TO HAVE A PANTRY CHALLENGE

A pantry challenge—cooking what's already in your fridge, freezer, or pantry—is a great way of eating on the cheap as well as wasting less. This isn't rocket science, but you'd be surprised to learn how many people have cupboards and freezers bursting at the seams, yet can't figure out what to make for supper.

Believe it or not, cooking at home is easier when you've got a blank canvas to work from. If you can see what's in the fridge, if you can count how many jars and cans you have, if you know what proteins you have in the freezer, then you are less likely to be overwhelmed, you'll have a sense of what cooking resources you have at your disposal, and the cooking experience will be a lot more fun.

A pantry challenge is a focused, but limited, effort to "eat down the pantry." Rather than buying groceries as I normally would, I focus on what we already have. I build my menus around the ingredients I've been avoiding using. It might be something that is cumbersome to prepare or something that I've been too lazy to be creative with. The pantry challenge helps me deal with those items—and teaches me not to buy them again if they weren't good or were too much of a pain to prepare. I end up saving money because I'm not buying more; rather, I'm using up what I've already purchased. And I'm learning from experience.

Savvy home cooks probably do a regular, everyday-type pantry challenge once a week. However, an extended pantry challenge, like the one I do for a month twice a year and post on my blog Good Cheap Eats, allows for a much greater turnover in your food storage, helping you to weed out items that may be close to their expiration dates as well as make the most of what you already have squirreled away for winter. Often we save things "for a rainy day" and then forget to use them!

A pantry challenge can save you money and at the same time expand your cooking horizons. Here's how:

1. **Eating what you have means you don't have to buy something new.**

2. **You will learn what *not* to buy in the future.**

3. **You waste less.**

4. **You must get creative in the kitchen and try new recipes.**

5. **Purging the kitchen makes it a more fun place to cook in.**

Jalapeño
Cheese Dip with
Homemade
Tortilla Chips

Arroz con Pollo

Cumin-Scented
Cabbage Salad

This menu, inspired
by the flavors of
Mexico and Mexican-
American culture,
is a feast for the
senses. Spicy pep-
pers, crunchy chips,
the homey flavors of
corn and rice—what
a meal! It's perfect
for entertaining on
a budget. And kids
love it, too.

Jalapeño Cheese Dip with Homemade Tortilla Chips

Serves 4 to 8

MEATLESS   GLUTEN-FREE   MAKE-AHEAD

Try this easy, homemade alternative to canned processed queso dip. Even if you prefer store-bought chips (as in the photo) to homemade, you'll find that the dip is still very much worth making.

1 tablespoon olive oil
1 jalapeño, seeded and sliced
½ cup chopped red bell pepper
½ teaspoon minced garlic
8 ounces cream cheese
1 cup shredded cheddar cheese
¼ cup sour cream
1 tablespoon chopped scallions
Homemade Tortilla Chips, for serving (page 74)

1. Preheat the oven to 400°F. Grease a 4-cup baking dish with nonstick cooking spray.

2. In a small skillet, heat the oil over medium heat until shimmering. Add the jalapeño, bell pepper, and garlic. Sauté until the peppers and garlic are soft, 3 to 4 minutes. Allow to cool.

3. In the bowl of a food processor fitted with a metal blade, combine the pepper mixture, cream cheese, and ½ cup of the shredded cheese. Blend until smooth. Stir in the sour cream and scallions.

4. Transfer the mixture to the greased baking dish. Top with the remaining ½ cup shredded cheese.

5. Bake until hot and bubbly, about 20 minutes. Serve with tortilla chips.

MAKE IT AHEAD: Wrap the unbaked dish and store in the refrigerator for up to 2 days. Add 5 to 10 minutes to the baking time since the dish will be cold.

MENU

Cajun Shrimp and
Sausage Rice

Buttery Dill
Carrots

Banana-Walnut
Mini Muffins

Before we had children, Bryan and I often frequented the Palace Café, a Cajun-inspired restaurant in Santa Barbara. It holds a place of honor in our hearts, since we dined there on the night he proposed. A hallmark of the Palace was the basket of muffins, both savory and sweet, that they served while you waited for your meal.

This shrimp and sausage rice is a more economical take on the Palace's jambalaya. I like to serve it with the Herb-and-Spice Green Beans on page 232, but Bryan prefers it with these oh-so-yummy Buttery Dill Carrots. Be sure to pass a basket of Banana-Walnut Mini Muffins and pretend you're at the Palace.

Cajun Shrimp and Sausage Rice

Serves 4 to 6

`DAIRY-FREE` **GLUTEN-FREE**

This rice dish comes together easily on the stovetop. The Cajun spice blend gives it a nice kick; for more heat, simply increase the amount. My kids absolutely devour this dish.

1 tablespoon olive oil
8 ounces sweet Italian sausage links
1 cup chopped onion
½ cup chopped red or green bell pepper
½ cup chopped celery
2 cups white rice
2 tablespoons Cajun Spice Blend (page 80)
4 cups Homemade Chicken Stock (page 97)
8 ounces medium shrimp (thawed if frozen), peeled and deveined

1. In a large stockpot over medium heat, heat the oil until shimmering. Cook the sausages until browned and cooked through. Transfer them to a plate and tent with aluminum foil.

2. Add the onion, pepper, and celery to the stockpot and cook for 5 minutes, stirring and scraping up any brown bits. Add the rice and cook until the rice starts to appear opaque, 3 to 5 more minutes.

3. Stir in the spice blend and then add the stock, scraping up any brown bits. Bring the mixture to a low boil. Reduce the heat to low, cover, and simmer for 15 minutes.

4. Meanwhile, slice the sausages. Add the shrimp and sausages to the pot. Cover and cook until the rice is tender and the shrimp are pink, another 10 to 15 minutes.

Buttery Dill Carrots

Serves 4

MEATLESS GLUTEN-FREE

My mom often made this dish when I was a child. I'm not sure, but she might have added sugar or honey. I prefer to let the sweet carrots speak for themselves.

6 medium carrots, peeled and sliced thickly on the bias
2 tablespoons butter
¼ teaspoon dried dill
Kosher salt and freshly ground black pepper
Pinch of cayenne pepper

1. Place the carrots in a steamer basket in a medium-size stockpot with 1 inch of water. Bring the water to a boil, cover, and steam the carrots until tender, about 10 minutes.

2. Drain the carrots and transfer them to a serving dish. Add the butter and dill and season to taste with salt, black pepper, and cayenne. Toss gently to coat.

#22

GO BANANAS

The grocery produce manager will often mark down ripe bananas to very low prices, sometimes lower than 25 cents per pound. Snatch them up! You can use them right away in baking, or freeze banana slices to use later in smoothies. Just slice up the bananas and place them on a plastic-lined baking sheet in the freezer until very firm. Package in a zip-top plastic bag and return to the freezer immediately. Use just what you need when you want a banana-flavored smoothie.

Banana-Walnut Mini Muffins

Makes 24 mini muffins

`MAKE-AHEAD` `FREEZER-FRIENDLY`

These mini muffins disappear in a bite or two. Their sweetness complements the savory-spicy kick of the shrimp and sausage. They are also perfect for breakfast, snacks, lunches, or as part of a varied bread basket at holidays. Make several batches and freeze the extras so you never run out.

1 cup unbleached all-purpose flour
1½ teaspoons baking powder
¼ teaspoon baking soda
¼ teaspoon fine sea salt
½ cup light brown sugar
¼ cup vegetable oil
1 large egg
½ cup buttermilk
1 ripe banana, peeled and mashed
1 teaspoon pure vanilla extract
½ teaspoon ground cinnamon
¼ cup chopped walnuts

1. Preheat the oven to 400°F. Grease a 24-cup mini muffin pan with nonstick cooking spray.

2. In a large bowl, whisk together the flour, baking powder, baking soda, and salt.

3. In another bowl, combine the brown sugar and oil. Add the egg and beat until well combined. Stir in the buttermilk, mashed banana, vanilla, cinnamon, and walnuts.

4. Add the wet ingredients to the dry ingredients and fold to combine.

5. Divide the batter among the 24 muffin cups. Bake until a tester comes out clean, about 12 minutes.

6. Cool the muffins on a rack.

MAKE IT AHEAD: The baked and cooled muffins can be stored in an airtight container at room temperature for up to 2 days or in the freezer for up to 1 month. Thaw them on the counter before serving.

MAKE-YOUR-OWN SPICE BLENDS

I prefer to make my own seasoning blends rather than buy packaged mixes. I control the ingredients and save money at the same time. I buy the individual spices in bulk and store excess in the freezer for the longest shelf life. This allows me quick and easy access to seasonings without paying an arm and a leg for them. If you don't want to buy large containers, go in with a friend or two to split up the investment.

Here are three of my favorite blends:

cajun spice blend
Makes about 5 tablespoons

I used to pay an exorbitant price for commercial Cajun spice blends. No longer. This mélange goes well on baked chicken or grilled meats, and mixed into vegetables, pasta, or casseroles. I've even used it to flavor homemade vinaigrettes. Try it in Cajun Grilled Chicken Salad with Creamy Scallion Dressing (page 276) or Cajun Turkey Meatloaf (page 101).

1 tablespoon onion powder
1 tablespoon garlic powder
1 tablespoon kosher salt
2 teaspoons paprika
2 teaspoons dried thyme
1 teaspoon freshly ground black pepper
½ teaspoon dried oregano
¼ teaspoon cayenne pepper

Combine all of the ingredients in a small bowl. Transfer the mixture to an airtight plastic container or zip-top plastic bag and store in the cupboard.

mexican spice blend

Makes about ½ cup

This all-purpose taco seasoning mix can be used in place of any commercial blend. I use it to season meat and rice dishes as well as chilis and casseroles. The cinnamon adds a unique flavor twist; omitting it will give you a more traditional "taco" flavor. Try it in Cheesy Beefy Chili Bake (page 84), Spicy No-Bean Chili (page 167), Easy Shredded Pork Tacos with Two Salsas (page 220), Paso Mom Tacos (page 109), or Confetti Rice (page 123).

3 tablespoons chili powder
1 tablespoon fine sea salt
1 tablespoon onion powder
1 tablespoon garlic powder
1 tablespoon dried oregano
1 teaspoon ground cumin
1 teaspoon ground cinnamon (optional)
½ teaspoon cayenne pepper

Combine all of the ingredients in a small bowl. Transfer the mixture to an airtight plastic container or zip-top plastic bag and store in the cupboard.

greek spice blend

Makes about 6 tablespoons

Admittedly, I've never been to Greece, but I love the flavors associated with the Mediterranean islands. This all-purpose seasoning goes great on grilled meats and in dressings and dips. Try it in Orzo with Tomatoes and Basil (page 228) or Chicken Kabobs with Mint-Yogurt Sauce (page 128).

1 tablespoon garlic powder
1 tablespoon onion powder
1 tablespoon dried parsley
2 teaspoons dried oregano
2 teaspoons fine sea salt
1 teaspoon freshly ground black pepper
1 teaspoon dried thyme
1 teaspoon grated lemon zest
½ teaspoon ground cinnamon
½ teaspoon ground nutmeg

Combine all of the ingredients in a small bowl. Transfer the mixture to an airtight plastic container or zip-top plastic bag and store in the cupboard (if using dried lemon zest) or in the freezer (if using fresh).

Over time, I've found that the simplest and most inexpensive ingredients can be combined into untold flavor combinations. So while your grocery list might vary only a little from week to week, there's no reason to be bored. This menu is a perfect example: lots of flavor without getting too exotic or pricey.

Sloppy Fo's

Serves 4

MAKE-AHEAD

Since we serve this Italian-style sloppy joe on focaccia bread, we've dubbed it a Sloppy Fo'. If you can't find focaccia bread, simply sub in your favorite kind of sandwich roll. We enjoy these sandwiches open-faced.

1 pound bulk Italian sausage
1 cup chopped bell pepper (any color)
1 cup chopped onion
1 (15-ounce) can tomato sauce
¼ cup chopped fresh basil or 1 teaspoon dried basil
Kosher salt and freshly ground black pepper
1 round focaccia bread or 4 focaccia rolls
1 cup shredded mozzarella or Monterey Jack cheese

1. In a large skillet over medium heat, cook the sausage, bell pepper, and onion until the vegetables are tender and the meat is cooked through, 10 to 15 minutes.

2. Add the tomato sauce, basil, and salt and black pepper to taste. Simmer for 15 minutes.

3. Slice the focaccia round horizontally and then again into 4 pie-shaped sections so that you have eight pieces total.

4. Place 2 pieces of focaccia on each plate. Divide the sausage mixture among the plates, covering the bread generously. Top with the mozzarella cheese.

MAKE IT AHEAD: Prepare through step 2. Cool the filling and store in an airtight container in the refrigerator for up to 3 days. Reheat the filling in the microwave or on the stovetop until hot, and then proceed with step 3.

23

See a great sale on canned beans, tomatoes, or another pantry staple? If you know it's something that you will use, stock up! Great sales can cut the price of an item by 50 to 75 percent. Just watch expiration dates to make sure you're not buying more than you can use in time.

ChiChi's Italian Salad

Serves 4

`MEATLESS` `GLUTEN-FREE` `MAKE-AHEAD`

My favorite childhood restaurant growing up was an Italian place called ChiChi's. Their salad was a must-have every time we visited. Since I've become an adult and realized that the current establishment is overpriced, I've learned to make the equivalent of my favorite salad at home. To make this a dinner salad that can stand alone, add sliced salami and pepperoni.

1 head romaine lettuce, torn into bite-size pieces
1 large tomato, cut into wedges
½ cup cooked or canned chickpeas (rinsed and drained if canned)
½ cup shredded mozzarella cheese
½ cup shredded Monterey Jack cheese
¼ red onion, thinly sliced
½ cup sliced pepperoncini
¼ cup red wine vinegar
½ teaspoon minced garlic
¼ teaspoon dried oregano
¼ teaspoon dried basil
¼ teaspoon fine sea salt
⅛ teaspoon freshly ground black pepper
Pinch of sugar
¼ cup vegetable oil
Grated Parmesan cheese, for garnish (optional)

1. Combine the lettuce, tomato, chickpeas, cheeses, onion, and pepperoncini in a large salad bowl.

2. In a small jar or bowl, combine the vinegar, garlic, oregano, basil, salt, pepper, and sugar. Put on the lid and shake well or whisk until smooth. Add the oil and shake or whisk again to emulsify.

3. Toss the salad with enough of the dressing to coat and serve the extra dressing on the side. Sprinkle with Parmesan cheese, if desired.

MAKE IT AHEAD: Store the salad and dressing in separate airtight containers in the refrigerator for up to 3 days. Toss together right before serving.

Cheesy Beefy
Chili Bake

Mexican Tossed
Salad

A good make-ahead casserole can be both filling and convenient. Knowing that you've got tasty comfort food waiting at home means that you're less likely to choose a more expensive option when you're stuck in traffic after work or hockey practice.

Cheesy Beefy Chili Bake

Serves 4

GLUTEN-FREE **MAKE-AHEAD** **FREEZER-FRIENDLY**

This kid-pleasing oven-baked chili casserole can be easily doubled, allowing you to bake one and freeze the other, reaping twice the rewards from one stint in the kitchen.

- 1 pound ground beef
- ½ cup chopped onion
- 1 teaspoon minced garlic
- 1 cup cooked or canned black beans (rinsed and drained if canned)
- 1 cup enchilada sauce
- ¾ cup canned or fresh diced tomatoes (drained if canned)
- ½ tablespoon Mexican Spice Blend (page 81)
- 3 cups crushed tortilla chips (about half of a 12-ounce bag)
- 2 cups shredded pepper Jack or cheddar cheese

1. Preheat the oven to 350°F. Grease an 8-inch square baking pan with nonstick cooking spray.

2. In a large skillet over medium heat, cook the beef, onion, and garlic until the meat is cooked through and the onion is translucent, about 10 minutes. Add the black beans, enchilada sauce, tomatoes, and spice blend. Simmer for 5 minutes.

3. Place half of the crushed chips in the bottom of the prepared baking dish. Spoon half of the chili mixture over the chips. Sprinkle with half of the cheese. Repeat the layering process with the remaining chips, chili, and cheese.

4. Bake the casserole until bubbly and hot throughout, 20 to 25 minutes.

MAKE IT AHEAD: The unbaked dish can be covered and stored in the refrigerator for up to 1 day or in the freezer for up to 1 month. If frozen, thaw it completely in the refrigerator before baking. In either case, add 5 to 10 minutes to the baking time since the dish will be cold.

24

Leftovers don't need to be something you dread. If you enjoyed the meal but have lots left over, wrap it for freezing. In this way, you've bought yourself a "free" lunch or dinner without any extra work.

Mexican Tossed Salad

Serves 4

MEATLESS | **GLUTEN-FREE** | **MAKE-AHEAD**

This salad is a fun riff on your typical tossed salad. Instead of croutons, we've got tortilla chips. Jicama and cilantro continue the Latin theme. You can easily make this into a main-dish salad by adding grilled chicken or steak.

3 cups baby spinach
3 cups green leaf lettuce, torn into bite-size pieces
2 medium carrots, peeled and sliced
1 medium bell pepper (any color), seeded and sliced
½ cup julienned jicama
½ cup chopped fresh cilantro
½ cup broken tortilla chips
2 tablespoons red wine vinegar
2 tablespoons crumbled feta cheese
1 garlic clove, minced
¼ teaspoon kosher salt
⅛ teaspoon freshly ground black pepper
¼ cup olive oil

1. Combine the spinach, lettuce, carrots, bell pepper, jicama, cilantro, and tortilla chips in a large salad bowl.

2. In a small jar or bowl, combine the vinegar, feta cheese, garlic, salt, and pepper. Place the lid on the jar and shake well or whisk until smooth. Add the oil and shake or whisk again to emulsify.

3. Toss the salad with enough of the dressing to coat. Serve the extra dressing on the side.

MAKE IT AHEAD: Store the salad and dressing in separate containers in the refrigerator for up to 3 days. Toss together right before serving.

Supreme
Sausage Pizza

Spinach-Apple
Salad with
Scallion-Lime
Dressing

Pizza night is typically how our family starts the weekend. I get some music going, pour a glass of wine, and start tinkering in the kitchen. My kiddos love to help with the assembly, but it always starts off with my chopping up a bunch of pizza toppings.

One night I realized how well those same toppings fit into a brunch frittata to enjoy on a lazy weekend morning. Ta-da! Another great two-for-one meal. You'll find the frittata menu on page 261.

Supreme Sausage Pizza

Makes 2 (12-inch) pizzas

At our house the ultimate pizza is loaded with veggies and juicy bits of sausage. Consider making more if you've got big pizza fans at your house—any leftovers can be served for lunch the next day.

1 pound Italian sausage links
½ recipe Honey Whole-Wheat Pizza Dough (page 88)
1 cup favorite tomato sauce, such as Roasted Tomato Sauce (page 43)
2 cups shredded mozzarella cheese
1 cup chopped bell pepper (any color)
1 cup sliced button or cremini mushrooms
½ cup chopped yellow or red onion
½ cup sliced black olives

1. In a large skillet over medium heat, cook the sausages until cooked through, about 15 minutes. When cool enough to handle, slice the sausages thinly.

2. Preheat the oven to 475°F. Grease two 12-inch pizza pans with nonstick cooking spray. Stretch the dough to fit the pans.

3. Spread half of the tomato sauce over each prepared pizza round. Layer on each round ¾ cup of the cheese and half of the sausage, peppers, mushrooms, onions, and olives. Sprinkle on the remaining mozzarella.

4. Bake until the crust is crisp and the cheese is melted and golden in spots, 8 to 10 minutes. Cool slightly before slicing.

Forget paying the high price of pizza parlor pizza. What they charge ten to twenty bucks for at a restaurant, you can make for about three dollars at home. You can even make individual-size pizzas so that each person in the family can have his or her favorite toppings.

honey whole-wheat pizza dough

Makes enough dough for 4 (12-inch) thin-crust pizzas or 4 (8-inch) thick-crust pan pizzas

I've been making pizza dough from scratch for about 17 years, all the while with little kids underfoot. If I can do it, so can you. (How can you talk back to that?)

It's really not that hard, so please don't be intimidated. Just plan ahead and start your dough a few hours before you want to shape and bake your pizzas.

Since this dough is generous in its use of whole wheat and honey, it will brown faster than traditional pizza crust. Keep an eye on it, especially if your oven runs hot. You can use all or mostly unbleached all-purpose flour if you prefer. The dough can also be used for rolls or bread sticks.

1½ cups water
¼ cup olive oil
¼ cup honey
2 cups unbleached all-purpose flour
2 cups whole-wheat flour
2 tablespoons cornmeal
1½ teaspoons fine sea salt
2¼ teaspoons active dry yeast

1. Combine the ingredients in the pan of your bread machine according to the manufacturer's directions. Set to the dough cycle and start the machine. (If making the dough by hand: Combine the water, oil, and honey in a small saucepan and warm slightly over medium heat. Transfer the mixture to a large bowl and add the yeast. Stir and allow the yeast to proof for 5 minutes. Add the flours, cornmeal, and salt. Stir to combine well. Turn the mixture out onto a lightly floured surface and knead for 5 minutes to create a smooth, elastic dough, adding more all-purpose flour as necessary. Transfer to a greased bowl and turn the dough ball to coat. Allow to rise until doubled in bulk, about 1 hour.)

2. When the machine beeps or the dough has doubled in bulk, remove the dough from the pan or bowl and divide it into quarters. Shape each piece into a round ball. Proceed with the pizza recipe.

Spinach-Apple Salad with Scallion-Lime Dressing

Serves 4

MEATLESS DAIRY-FREE **GLUTEN-FREE**

This scallion-lime dressing has plenty of flavor and plays nicely with the fruit and nuts in the salad. Save the leftover dressing to make the cucumber salad on page 262.

SCALLION-LIME DRESSING
Juice of 1 lime
2 tablespoons red wine vinegar
1 tablespoon finely chopped scallions
1 tablespoon finely chopped fresh parsley
1 teaspoon minced garlic
Kosher salt and freshly ground black pepper
⅓ cup olive oil

5 ounces baby spinach
1 apple, cored and chopped
¼ cup dried cranberries
¼ cup sliced almonds

1. In a small jar or bowl, combine the lime juice, vinegar, scallions, parsley, garlic, and salt and pepper to taste. Place the lid on the jar and shake well or whisk until smooth. Add the olive oil and shake or whisk again to emulsify.

2. Place the spinach in a large salad bowl. Toss with enough of the dressing to coat.

3. Divide the salad among serving plates. Top with equal portions of the apple, cranberries, and almonds. Serve the extra dressing on the side.

STONE SOUP

Soup is a wonderfully frugal, delicious meal to serve your family. And it can successfully be made from leftovers. What a great way to exercise the "waste not, want not" mentality that will keep us all in the black these days!

Now, don't go thinking you're gonna throw everything into a pot, à la Pippi Longstocking. There's a method here.

Use wisdom when making soup from leftovers. If your family didn't like the meal the first time, chances are slim that they will like it better in its new form. You can make a good soup from what you have, provided what you have is still fresh and something you liked the first time.

I typically make soup once a week from fall to spring. And often, it seems as if I'm making it from virtually nothing. A handful of rice, an onion, a cup of this, a smidgen of that: It all turns out delicious. It really is like that folk tale of three soldiers making soup from a stone; little contributions from different quarters produce a veritable feast!

My method for stone soup is pretty standard:

1. Heat oil in a stockpot and add a chopped onion and some minced garlic. Once that is browning nicely, add other chopped vegetables, like carrots, celery, or potatoes.

2. Add broth or stock as well as a small can of tomato sauce, if you're feeling tomato-y.

3. Next add the starch. If you have leftover cooked rice, quinoa, or noodles, add those; otherwise, add one of those items uncooked.

4. Throw in some herbs and seasonings.

5. Last, add chopped leftover meat and vegetables. These might be steamed broccoli, a bit of roast chicken, some sausage, or a handful of peas.

6. Cook until everything is tender. The cooking time will vary depending on whether your starch is cooked or uncooked.

Soup is never exactly the same each time I do it this way, but it's always flavorful and filling. While the possibilities are endless, here are some suggestions to get you started:

- **CHICKEN NOODLE SOUP:** Bake a few extra breasts when you're making chicken and save the drippings to make Homemade Chicken Stock (page 97). Shred the chicken into the stock, add noodles of your choice, and simmer until the noodles are cooked. Any leftover cooked vegetables can be added as well.

- **CHILI BEAN SOUP:** Got only one or two portions of chili left? Add a quart of beef, vegetable, or chicken broth and a can of hominy or corn and simmer together. Serve with tortilla chips, salsa, and grated cheese.

- **VEGETABLE CHOWDER:** Whisk together leftover mashed potatoes and gravy with chicken broth. Stir in leftover cooked vegetables and simmer until hot. Season with dried dill and add salt and pepper at the end.

- **BEEF STROGANOFF SOUP:** Thin leftover beef stew with beef broth and bring almost to a boil. Stir in egg noodles and cook until the noodles are tender. Add a little cream or milk at the end.

- **BEAN AND RICE SOUP:** Combine last night's leftover beans and rice into a soup with broth, salsa, and chopped vegetables. Serve with a sprinkle of shredded cheese.

Something Meatier

I've never forgotten that old commercial that said, "Move over, bacon, now there's something meatier." I don't think that supposedly leaner bacon product is still on the market, but the message stuck: We're a culture that likes its meat. I know I do. And my kids, as I've mentioned, are self-proclaimed carnivores.

The menus in this chapter feature meaty proteins as the star of each show. My typical MO to make this happen budget-wise is to stock up on the supermarket "loss leaders." Each week, stores offer one to three meat department items at a super low price, anywhere from $0.69 to $2.99 per pound. Every six weeks or so the cycle repeats, so if you missed the boneless, skinless chicken breasts last week, it will likely be back on special within the next two months. I buy enough of those proteins to last us a month or two, grabbing them at their low prices and freezing them until I'm ready to cook.

Classic Roast Chicken 94
Smashed Potatoes 95
Spicy Creamy Chicken Gravy 98

Gussied-Up Sausage and Vegetables. 99
Curried Roasted Potatoes 100

Cajun Turkey Meatloaf. 101
Brown Rice Pilaf. 102
Creamy Kale with Sun-Dried Tomatoes 103

"Shake and Bake" Chicken 104
Buttery Orzo Pilaf 105
Mix-It-Up Vegetable Stir-Fry 106

Avocado and Black Bean Salsa. 107
Paso Mom Tacos. 109

Pot Roast with Mushrooms and Root Vegetables 110
Pear and Spinach Salad with Raspberry Vinaigrette 112

Salisbury Steak with Mushroom Gravy 114
Roasted Green Beans 115

Ale-Braised Pork Roast. 118
Fransconi Potatoes 119
Maple Fried Apples. 120

Grilled Cumin Chicken Legs 121
Sautéed Corn with Thyme. 122
Confetti Rice 123

MENU

Classic Roast Chicken

Smashed Potatoes

Spicy Creamy Chicken Gravy

Roast chicken with all the trimmings is probably one of the FishKids' favorite meals. If I bust out the cranberry sauce, they are over the moon. Even in July. Since whole chickens go for as low as 69 cents a pound at my local store, it makes it easy for me to be a yes-mom. Serve this with any steamed vegetables you like. After supper's over, I simmer what's left of the chicken to make homemade stock (see page 97).

Classic Roast Chicken

Serves 4 to 6

GLUTEN-FREE

Whether you buy a whole chicken, an eight-piece "picnic pack," or a combination of your favorite pieces, bone-in chicken is typically less expensive and more flavorful than boneless. This roast chicken can easily turn into three meals. Enjoy roast chicken one night, prepare a casserole or salad with the leftover meat the next night, and then make homemade stock to turn into soup for a third night.

2 tablespoons butter, softened
1½ teaspoons favorite seasonings (Use your imagination, or try one of my spice blends on pages 80 and 81.)
1 (4-pound) whole chicken or 4 pounds bone-in chicken pieces
1 onion, quartered

1. Preheat the oven to 425°F.
2. In a small bowl, combine the butter and seasonings.
3. Place the chicken in a roasting pan. Loosen the skin of the chicken and spread the seasoned butter all over the chicken, under the skin. Stuff the onion quarters into the cavity of a whole chicken or arrange around the chicken pieces in the pan.
4. Roast in the oven until an internal temperature of 165°F is achieved, 1¼ to 1½ hours. If cooking pieces, they should be done in 45 to 60 minutes.

#26

A whole chicken is remarkably inexpensive to buy, often as low as 59 cents per pound, and can yield many meals. Cook a whole chicken and enjoy several pieces for dinner, then use the other bits and pieces for a casserole or pasta dish, and make stock for soup from the carcass and drippings. You will eat well and spend less.

Smashed Potatoes

Serves 4 to 6

`MEATLESS` `GLUTEN-FREE`

These rustic potatoes are full of flavor and take just minutes to prepare. They're supposed to have some lumps, so you don't have to worry about "perfectly smooth" potatoes.

    4 pounds red-skinned potatoes, peeled and cubed
    4 tablespoons (½ stick) butter, softened
    2 tablespoon chopped scallions
    Kosher salt and freshly ground black pepper

1. Bring a large pot of salted water to a boil over high heat. Cook the potatoes until tender and a chunk easily falls apart when pierced with a fork. Drain well.

2. Smash the potatoes with a potato masher, leaving some bite-size chunks. Add the butter, scallions, and salt and pepper to taste and carefully fold to melt the butter and blend everything together. Serve immediately.

HOMEMADE CHICKEN STOCK

Makes 8 to 10 cups

Making homemade chicken stock is a must for the frugal kitchen. It is one of the easiest ways to make something from nothing. If you've roasted a whole chicken or chicken pieces, save the bones, skin, and drippings to make a delicious stock to use in soups, gravies, or pilafs. The resulting golden-brown goodness will taste much better than anything you could buy in a package. This is also a great way to use up bits of vegetables that might be getting a little wilted in the crisper. If you don't want to mess with the bones right away, you can package them in a zip-top plastic bag and store in the freezer until you're ready to make stock.

You can also make a couple of batches in quick succession from one set of trimmings. The first round, which has the richest flavor, is like the "extra-virgin olive oil" of chicken stock. Once you've drained off that batch of broth, add 8 cups of water to the pot and make stock from a second "press." This second batch won't have as concentrated a flavor as the first batch, but it will still be quite good.

The basic recipe can be adjusted for vegetable or beef stock as well.

8 to 10 cups water
Bones/carcass of 1 (4-pound) cooked chicken or 4 pounds chicken pieces
5 or 6 small inner celery stalks with leaves
2 carrots, cut into chunks
1 onion or leek, sliced
2 garlic cloves, peeled
10 black peppercorns
3 whole cloves
2 sprigs fresh thyme, rosemary, or oregano
2 bay leaves

1. Place all of the ingredients in a 5-quart slow cooker and cook on High for 4 hours or on Low for 8 hours or overnight. Alternatively, place all of the ingredients in a large stockpot and bring to a gentle boil over medium heat. Reduce the heat, cover, and simmer for about 3 hours.

2. Strain the stock and discard the solids; or reserve the solids and add water to repeat the process for a second batch of stock.

3. Use the stock in your recipe as needed or pour it into containers and allow it to cool. Cover the containers tightly and store in the refrigerator for up to 3 days or in the freezer for up to 3 months.

#27

SPICE IT UP

Spice blends can be
pricey, especially
those that come in
individual packets or
bottles. It's amaz-
ing how simple it is
to make your own.
Buy spices in bulk
and mix up your
own favorite blends,
or try the recipes
on pages 80 and 81.
Store excess spices
in the freezer for the
longest shelf life.

Spicy Creamy Chicken Gravy

Makes 2 cups

This gravy is rich and creamy, perfect for a roast chicken dinner, but
it's also good in potpies and casseroles, or served over biscuits.

4 tablespoons (½ stick) butter
¼ cup unbleached all-purpose flour
1½ cups Homemade Chicken Stock (page 97)
½ cup milk
1½ teaspoons Cajun Spice Blend (page 80)

1. In a large stockpot over medium heat, melt the butter. Add the
flour and whisk to combine; the mixture will start to bubble. Cook
until the mixture is light brown and fragrant, 1 to 2 minutes.

2. Whisk in the broth, milk, and Cajun spices. Bring to a low boil,
stirring constantly.

3. Reduce the heat and simmer until the gravy is thickened, 5 to
10 minutes. Taste and adjust the seasoning as desired.

Gussied-Up
Sausage and
Vegetables

Curried Roasted
Potatoes

We're Hobbits here,
so the idea of eating
sausages and taters
is quite the happy
one for our bunch.
One dish is prepped
on the stovetop while
another roasts in the
oven. Accompanied
by a tossed green
salad I made earlier
and chilled in the
fridge, this makes for
a delicious meal that
Bilbo would be happy
to partake of.

Gussied-Up Sausage and Vegetables

Serves 4

DAIRY-FREE **GLUTEN-FREE**

The addition of zucchini and a bit of wine turns classic sausages
with peppers and onions into something special. If there's anything
left over, which is doubtful, it goes great on a pizza or folded into
an omelet. You might even want to make extra so you can have the
best of both worlds.

1¾ pounds Italian sausage links
1 tablespoon olive oil
1 small onion, sliced
1 medium zucchini, sliced
1 green bell pepper, seeded and sliced
½ teaspoon dried thyme
2 tablespoons Marsala
Kosher salt and freshly ground black pepper

1. Place the sausages in a skillet and cover them halfway with
water. Simmer until cooked through, 20 to 25 minutes, making sure
that the water doesn't evaporate before the sausages are done.
Once cooked, drain off any remaining liquid and sauté the sausages
until browned. Remove from the skillet.

2. Add the oil to the skillet. Add the onion and cook until translucent, scraping up any brown bits, about 5 minutes. Add the zucchini,
bell pepper, and thyme. Cook the vegetables until they are tender
and lightly browned in spots, another 5 minutes.

3. Add the Marsala to the pan, stirring to distribute the wine. Add
the sausage back in to reheat. Season to taste with salt and pepper.

THIS SPUD'S FOR YOU

Potatoes are good cheap eats. Cook a double batch of mashed potatoes and use leftovers to thicken soup, top a shepherd's pie, or fry into potato cakes. Use sliced fried potatoes as the base for nachos instead of chips, or serve baked potatoes stuffed with any number of fillings to make a tasty and inexpensive supper.

Curried Roasted Potatoes

Serves 4

`MEATLESS` `DAIRY-FREE` `GLUTEN-FREE`

My mom used to make a family-favorite dish she called curried potatoes. I've simplified its preparation, taking it off the stove and into the oven, for easy, hands-free cooking. The potatoes will take on a bright yellow hue, thanks to the curry powder.

5 large russet potatoes, cut into ⅛-inch wedges
2 tablespoons vegetable oil
1½ teaspoons curry powder
1 teaspoon kosher salt
⅛ teaspoon freshly ground black pepper

1. Preheat the oven to 450°F. Grease a 9 x 13-inch baking pan with nonstick cooking spray.
2. Place the potatoes in the prepared baking pan and toss them with the oil to coat.
3. In a small bowl, combine the curry powder, salt, and pepper. Sprinkle the mixture over the potatoes.
4. Bake the potatoes until fork-tender, 30 to 40 minutes.

MENU

Cajun Turkey
Meatloaf

Brown Rice Pilaf

Creamy Kale
with Sun-Dried
Tomatoes

Meatloaf, rice, and
creamed kale—
sounds like a vintage
style of meal, doesn't
it? This one has
plenty of modern
twists, though, with
a Cajun spice blend,
brown rice, and a
kiss of sun-dried
tomatoes.

Cajun Turkey Meatloaf

Serves 4

`DAIRY-FREE` `MAKE-AHEAD` `FREEZER-FRIENDLY`

My people sometimes balk at ground turkey, claiming it doesn't
have the flavor of its beefier—and fattier—counterpart. However,
this zingy meatloaf has them fooled. There are seldom any leftovers
to speak of, which is a shame, because it makes for awesome
sandwiches the next day. You might want to make extra just for
tomorrow's lunch.

1 tablespoon vegetable oil
½ cup chopped onion
¼ cup chopped bell pepper (red, green, or mixed)
1 pound ground turkey
1½ cups fresh bread crumbs
1 large egg, beaten
2 tablespoons Cajun Spice Blend (page 80)

1. Preheat the oven to 350°F. Grease a 9-inch square baking dish
with nonstick cooking spray.

2. In a small skillet over medium heat, heat the oil until shimmering. Add the onion and bell pepper and cook until softened. Cool to
room temperature.

3. In a large bowl, combine the turkey, bread crumbs, egg, Cajun
spice blend, and cooked vegetables. Mix well, just until the ingredients are evenly distributed.

4. Form the mixture into a 4 x 9-inch loaf and place in the prepared baking dish.

5. Bake until an internal temperature of 165°F is achieved, 45 to
60 minutes.

MAKE IT AHEAD: Prepare the recipe through step 4, cover, and refrigerate up to
1 day ahead. Or wrap the prepared loaf in aluminum foil, place in a zip-top plastic bag, and store in the freezer for up to 2 months, then thaw in the refrigerator
overnight on a plate to catch the drips. In either case, add a few minutes to the
baking time since the pan will be cold.

Brown Rice Pilaf

Serves 4

MEATLESS **GLUTEN-FREE**

My husband can eat a whole pan of rice when it's prepared this way. We try not to let him, since the rest of us want some, too. You can make it with white rice as well; just reduce the cooking time to 20 minutes.

2 tablespoons butter
¼ cup finely chopped onion
1 cup long-grain brown rice
2 cups vegetable broth
1 teaspoon dried parsley
Kosher salt and freshly ground black pepper

1. In a large skillet with a lid, melt the butter over medium heat. Add the onion and rice. Sauté until the rice becomes opaque and the onion becomes translucent, about 5 minutes.

2. Add the broth and parsley and bring to a low boil. Cover and reduce the heat to low. Cook until the liquid is absorbed, about 40 minutes. Fluff with a fork and season to taste with salt and pepper.

BUDGET GOURMET

The clearance section is the ideal place to find gourmet items that might not otherwise fit your budget. I've found sun-dried tomatoes, excellent wines, cedar planks for grilling, and expensive condiments marked down by 75 percent. What a fun treat for just pennies!

Creamy Kale with Sun-Dried Tomatoes

Serves 4

MEATLESS **GLUTEN-FREE**

Creamy kale was another of those adulthood revelations, as in, *Wow! This is good! Why have I never tried this?* I'd never cooked greens until a few years ago. Now it's an easy and nutritious side dish that makes a regular appearance on our table.

I prepare this same recipe with chard or spinach, so if you've "kaled over," feel free to make that substitution. This sauté contains just a hint of cream and sun-dried tomatoes, enough to add richness but not to bump the price point too high.

2 tablespoons olive oil
2 garlic cloves, minced
8 cups chopped curly kale
⅓ cup heavy cream
¼ cup sun-dried tomatoes
Kosher salt and freshly ground black pepper

1. In a large skillet over medium-high heat, warm the oil and then cook the garlic until fragrant, about 1 minute. Add the kale, lower the heat, and cook until wilted, about 10 minutes.

2. Stir in the cream and sun-dried tomatoes. Season to taste with salt and pepper.

"Shake and
Bake" Chicken

Buttery Orzo
Pilaf

Mix-It-Up
Vegetable
Stir-Fry

Chicken is a hearty
protein that pleases
practically everyone.
Bone-in chicken is
typically the most
economical option,
sometimes less than
$1 per pound. A bowl
of pasta and some
seasonal veggies
round out the menu,
making a simple and
delicious meal that
everyone will love.

"Shake and Bake" Chicken

Serves 4

`DAIRY-FREE`

Oven-fried chicken is a great substitute for pricier take-out chicken.
This is a tribute to my childhood, when Shake 'n Bake was what
all the cool moms were making. My version is a tasty update with
panko crumbs and a custom spice blend. The kids tell me I am the
best mom ever when I make this chicken. If you want to use drum-
sticks, which the FishKids absolutely love, adjust the baking time to
about 30 minutes, depending on their size.

2 cups panko bread crumbs
1 tablespoon sweet paprika
1 teaspoon kosher salt
½ teaspoon dried thyme
¼ teaspoon freshly ground black pepper
⅛ teaspoon cayenne pepper
3 pounds bone-in chicken breasts or legs or 1½ pounds boneless,
   skinless chicken breasts

1. Preheat the oven to 375°F. Line a rimmed baking sheet with
parchment paper.

2. In a gallon-size zip-top plastic bag, combine the panko, paprika,
salt, thyme, black pepper, and cayenne.

3. Working in batches, place a few pieces of chicken in the bag
and shake until well coated. Place on the prepared baking sheet,
leaving space between the pieces. Discard any leftover panko
mixture.

4. Bake until the chicken's internal temperature reaches 165°F,
about 1 hour for bone-in breasts or legs or 45 minutes for boneless
breasts.

#31

CUT TO THE BONE

Bone-in roasts and chops are often cheaper and more flavorful than their boneless counter-parts. Not only can you serve the meat as a hearty main dish, but you can also include little bits of leftover meat in cas-seroles and stir-fries and then use what's left on the bones to make broth.

Buttery Orzo Pilaf

Serves 4

`MEATLESS`

Orzo, a rice-shaped pasta, cooks up amazingly well into a pilaf. This side dish goes with any number of dishes.

2 tablespoons butter
2 tablespoons finely chopped onion
8 ounces orzo
3½ cups vegetable broth
Kosher salt and freshly ground black pepper

1. In a large skillet with a lid, melt the butter over medium heat. Cook the onion and orzo until the orzo starts to brown and the onion starts to turn translucent, about 10 minutes.

2. Add the broth and bring to a low boil. Cover and turn the heat to low. Simmer until all the liquid has been absorbed, about 12 minutes.

3. Let the pilaf sit, covered, for 5 minutes. Fluff with a fork and season to taste with salt and pepper.

32

Don't throw away those bits and pieces of cooked vegetables left over from dinner. Let them cool and then save them in a container in the freezer. When the container is full, make a pot of soup. You'll be amazed at the rich flavor.

Mix-It-Up Vegetable Stir-Fry

Serves 4

MEATLESS **DAIRY-FREE** **GLUTEN-FREE**

This sauté can change depending on the season or whatever you have in the fridge. Steamed broccoli is seasoned and then joined by stir-fried vegetables of your choosing.

12 ounces broccoli florets
2 tablespoons olive oil
1 teaspoon minced garlic
⅛ teaspoon red pepper flakes
2 cups mixed vegetables, such as chopped bell peppers, chopped
   onions, sliced zucchini, sliced mushrooms, or sliced celery
½ teaspoon kosher salt
⅛ teaspoon freshly ground black pepper

1. Place the broccoli in a steamer basket in a medium-size stockpot with 1 inch of water. Bring the water to a boil, cover, and steam the broccoli until tender but still bright green, 8 to 10 minutes. Remove from the heat and drain.

2. Heat the oil in a large skillet or wok over medium-high heat until shimmering. Add the garlic and red pepper flakes and cook until fragrant, about 1 minute. Add the mixed vegetables and stir-fry until tender and starting to brown, about 10 minutes.

3. Add the broccoli to the skillet and toss to combine. Season the vegetables with the salt and pepper.

Avocado and
Black Bean Salsa

Paso Mom Tacos

Taco night makes
for really good cheap
eats that please
everyone. Bryan
and I, both SoCal
kids, grew up on
homemade tacos.
I remember travel-
ing to the Midwest
to visit family and
being stunned at
how difficult it was
to find tortillas at the
grocery store.

Times have
changed, and it's
easy to make a fun
taco night at home
no matter where you
live. We typically
throw in some chips
and salsa for good
measure.

Avocado and Black Bean Salsa

Serves 4

MEATLESS   DAIRY-FREE   GLUTEN-FREE   MAKE-AHEAD

My mom's cactus and avocado salsa was one of my favorite foods
when I was growing up. Talk about weirding out the Minnesota rela-
tives! You can certainly add a drained jar of *nopales* to this dish
instead of beans, but this combination is a little more mainstream
and kid-friendly. Serve with tortilla chips.

2 cups cooked or canned black beans (rinsed and drained if canned)
3 medium tomatoes, chopped
2 avocados, pitted, peeled, and diced
¼ cup chopped fresh cilantro
¼ cup chopped red onion
1 jalapeño, seeded and chopped
Juice of 1 lime
Kosher salt and freshly ground black pepper
Homemade Tortilla Chips (page 74), for dipping

Combine the beans, tomatoes, avocados, cilantro, onion, jalapeño, lime juice, and salt and pepper to taste in a medium-size
bowl. Toss gently to combine. Serve immediately with tortilla chips.

MAKE IT AHEAD: The salsa can be made up to 2 hours ahead of time and stored
in a covered container in the refrigerator.

33

Ground meats have been getting pricier. It's usually cheaper for me to buy a nice cut of beef, pork, or chicken and grind it myself. Place cubed pieces of meat in the freezer until they start to firm up. You don't want to grind solidly frozen meat; just freeze it until firm to the touch. Pulse it quickly in a food processor fitted with a metal blade. If you've got a meat grinding attachment for your stand mixer, so much the better.

Paso Mom Tacos

Serves 4

GLUTEN-FREE **MAKE-AHEAD**

Simple home-fried tortilla shells filled with seasoned ground beef and topped with whatever suits your fancy, these tacos are certainly not complicated. But they are filling. And good.

And for these reasons, they were the "all you can eat" Thursday noontime special at a diner we used to frequent in our small town of Paso Robles years ago. These are the kinds of tacos we grew up on, too. Not exactly authentic Mexican fare, but truly delicious.

One of FishPapa's coworkers at the time had grown up in Paso Robles, and when we told Jim about the all-you-can-eat tacos, he said, "Oh yeah, Paso Mom tacos." Apparently lots of moms re-created these tacos at home. I have no idea if anyone besides Jim ever called them that, but we do now. And now, of course, so do *you*.

1 pound ground beef
2 tablespoons Mexican Spice Blend (page 81)
Oil, for frying the tortillas
12 corn tortillas
2 cups shredded cheese (cheddar, Monterey Jack, or a mixture)
2 cups shredded lettuce
1 cup chopped tomatoes
Salsa or taco sauce, for topping (optional)
Sour cream, for topping (optional)

1. In a large skillet over medium heat, brown the beef. Once it starts to change color, stir in the spice blend. Drain off the drippings and tent the skillet with aluminum foil to keep warm.

2. Add oil to a second large skillet to reach a depth of 1 inch. Heat the oil over medium-high heat until a bit of tortilla sizzles. Fry the tortillas into taco shell shapes: Fry on one side for about 20 seconds, flip, and fold, holding with tongs. Fry until crisp, about 1 minute total. Flip and fry the other side until crisp, for another 45 seconds. Drain the cooked shells on paper towels.

3. Once the shells are fried, fill with seasoned beef and add other toppings such as cheese, lettuce, tomatoes, salsa, and sour cream.

MAKE IT AHEAD: While the taco shells really need to be fried right before serving, you can certainly prep the toppings in advance and store them in the refrigerator. The seasoned beef can be cooked, cooled, and stored in an airtight container in the refrigerator for up to 3 days or in the freezer for up to 1 month.

MENU

Pot Roast with
Mushrooms and
Root Vegetables

Pear and
Spinach Salad
with Raspberry
Vinaigrette

What could be more
welcoming than to
come home from
a long day to the
aroma of pot roast
and veggies cook-
ing? You can pull
off this meal easily
by getting the slow
cooker fired up
before you leave for
the day. No tempta-
tion from the drive-
through tonight!

Pot Roast with Mushrooms and Root Vegetables

Serves 4

`DAIRY-FREE` **GLUTEN-FREE** `SLOW COOKER`

This heavenly pot roast dinner is practically a one-dish dinner. The ale contributes a rich depth of flavor, but you can use beef broth if you prefer.

2 tablespoons olive oil
1 (2-pound) boneless chuck, cross rib, or rump roast
Kosher salt and freshly ground black pepper
1 cup chopped onion
½ cup chopped button or cremini mushrooms
1 (12-ounce) bottle brown ale or 1½ cups beef broth
1 teaspoon fresh thyme
6 medium carrots, peeled and halved
1 large sweet potato, peeled and cut into 1-inch slices
2 medium potatoes, peeled if desired and quartered

1. In a large skillet, heat the oil over medium heat until shimmer-ing. Season the roast generously with salt and pepper. Brown the roast on all sides, 5 to 7 minutes. Transfer the roast to a 6-quart slow cooker.

2. Turn the heat under the skillet to medium-high, add the onion and mushrooms to the drippings, and cook until the onion turns translucent and the mushrooms release their liquid, 5 to 7 minutes. Stir in the ale and thyme, scraping up any brown bits. Simmer for 1 minute. Add this mixture to the slow cooker.

3. Place the carrots, sweet potato, and potatoes around the roast. Cover and cook on High for 4 hours or on Low for 6 to 8 hours.

4. Remove the roast and vegetables from the cooking liquid. Skim off any fat and adjust the seasonings of the *jus* as desired. Serve the roast and vegetables with the *jus* on the side.

CATEGORY	FOOD	TEMPERATURE	REST TIME
ground meat and meat mixtures	beef, pork, veal lamb	160°	none
	turkey, chicken	165°	none
beef, veal, and lamb	steaks, roasts, chops	145°	3 minutes
poultry	chicken and turkey, whole	165°	5 minutes
	poultry breasts, roasts	165°	none
	poultry thighs, legs, wings	165°	none
	duck, goose	165°	none
	stuffing (cooked alone or in bird)	165	none
pork and ham	fresh pork	145°	3 minutes
	fresh ham (raw)	145°	3 minutes
	precooked ham (to reheat)	140°	none
egg dishes	egg dishes	160°	none
leftovers and casseroles	leftovers and casseroles	165°	none
seafood	fin fish	145° or until flesh is opaque and separates easily with a fork	none
	shrimp, lobster, crabs	until flesh is pearly opaque	none
	clams, oysters, mussels	until shells open during cooking	none
	scallops	until flesh is milky white or opaque and firm	none

Source: U.S. Department of Health and Human Services

MENU

Ale-Braised
Pork Roast

Fransconi
Potatoes

Maple Fried
Apples

Set the slow cooker
to work on the roast
before you leave for
the day and come
home to a delicious
aroma. Slide the pan
of potatoes in the
oven and set some
seasonal vegetables
on the stove to steam
while you check
messages and sort
the mail. End the
evening with fried
apples spooned over
ice cream. Life could
be a dream, after all.

Ale-Braised Pork Roast

Serves 4

`DAIRY-FREE` `SLOW COOKER`

Pork roasts are one of the lowest-priced meats available, often $1 to $2 per pound, making for good cheap eats that cook up beautifully in the slow cooker. The gravy boasts a rich flavor thanks to the ale and spices, but feel free to use chicken broth instead of ale if you prefer.

    1 tablespoon olive oil
    2 pounds boneless pork butt roast or pork sirloin roast, tied
    Kosher salt and freshly ground black pepper
    1 medium onion, sliced
    1 teaspoon minced garlic
    1 (12-ounce) bottle brown ale or beer or 1½ cups chicken broth
    1 teaspoon ground mustard
    1 teaspoon smoked paprika
    ½ teaspoon ground marjoram
    ¼ teaspoon dried thyme
    1 bay leaf
    ¼ cup unbleached all-purpose flour
    ½ cup water

   1. In a large skillet, heat the oil over medium heat. Season the roast generously with salt and pepper. Brown the roast in the hot pan on all sides, about 5 minutes. Transfer to a 6-quart slow cooker.
   2. Turn the heat under the skillet to medium-high, add the onion and garlic to the drippings, and cook until the onion starts to turn translucent, about 5 minutes. Season to taste with salt and pepper.
   3. Add the ale, mustard, paprika, marjoram, thyme, and bay leaf, scraping up any browned bits. Simmer for 2 minutes. Add this mixture to the slow cooker. Cover and cook on High for 4 hours or on Low for 6 to 8 hours.
   4. Remove the roast from the crock and allow to rest, tented with aluminum foil, for 10 minutes.
   5. Meanwhile, remove the bay leaf and turn the slow cooker to High. In a small bowl, whisk together the flour and water into a thin paste. Add this to the *jus* in the pot and whisk until combined. Allow the gravy to thicken slightly before serving with chunks of the pork roast.

Have a target price
for things that you
regularly buy. Some
folks keep track of
their target prices
in a price book. My
price book is always
in my head: $1 per
pound for produce;
$2.50 per pound for
butter; $2.50 per
pound for meat, $5
per pound for fish.
I try to buy things
only when they
are at or below my
target prices. I stock
up when it hits the
target and thus can
avoid paying higher
prices at those times
when I really want
that particular item.

Fransconi Potatoes

Serves 4

MEATLESS **GLUTEN-FREE**

Recipe sharing is much like playing a game of telephone. As the
recipe changes hands and each cook makes changes, the recipe
morphs and sometimes even experiences a name change. Such is
the case with these potatoes, a recipe handed to my mom from a
cousin, who got it from who knows where. We call them Fransconi
Potatoes, but you might know them as Franconia Potatoes. Tradi-
tionally, they are cooked with a roast and basted with drippings, but
these tender spuds are cooked on their own and basted with butter.
They're so easy to make that you'll wonder why you haven't been
making them for years.

6 medium potatoes, peeled if desired and quartered
8 tablespoons (1 stick) butter, melted
½ teaspoon minced garlic
1 teaspoon dried parsley
Kosher salt and freshly ground black pepper

1. Preheat the oven to 375°F.

2. Place the potatoes in a 9 x 13-inch baking dish. Pour in the
melted butter and add the garlic, parsley, and salt and pepper to
taste. Toss to coat.

3. Bake, basting the potatoes with the butter two or three times,
until tender, about 45 minutes.

Dollar stores can be a surprising place to find grocery deals. While a dollar may not be a great price for a can of beans, it is for a loaf of whole-grain bread. Find out what your local discount store offers so that you can grab some good deals.

Maple Fried Apples

Serves 4

GLUTEN-FREE

These warm fried apples are delicious served over ice cream or as a topping for oatmeal in the morning. They're tasty all by themselves, too.

- 1 tablespoon butter
- 3 Granny Smith apples, peeled, cored, and chopped
- 1 tablespoon pure maple syrup
- ½ teaspoon ground cinnamon
- 2 tablespoons sliced almonds, toasted

In a large skillet over medium heat, melt the butter. Add the apples and sauté, stirring frequently, until tender, 7 to 10 minutes. Add the maple syrup and cinnamon and stir to combine. Right before serving, stir in the almonds.

MENU

Grilled Cumin
Chicken Legs

Sautéed Corn
with Thyme

Confetti Rice

Chicken, corn, and rice was a common meal when I was growing up, but the meal was typically created through a variety of boxed mixes and cans. I've taken a childhood favorite and made it healthier and tastier—not to mention cheaper!— by using fresh, whole ingredients. You won't notice much of a difference in preparation time making it from scratch. Promise.

Grilled Cumin Chicken Legs

Serves 4

`DAIRY-FREE` `GLUTEN-FREE`

This dish comes together in a snap with a custom spice rub and a family-size pack of chicken legs.

1½ teaspoons onion powder
1½ teaspoons chili powder
½ teaspoon ground cumin
½ teaspoon kosher salt
¼ teaspoon freshly ground black pepper
4 pounds chicken legs

1. Prepare a medium-hot fire in a charcoal or gas grill.

2. In a small bowl, combine the onion powder, chili powder, cumin, salt, and pepper.

3. Place the chicken legs on a platter or baking sheet and sprinkle generously with the seasoning mix, rubbing it in evenly.

4. Cook on the hot grill, turning occasionally, until the chicken's internal temperature reaches 165°F, 45 minutes to 1 hour.

38

INSPECT YOUR GADGETS

You don't need a kitchen full of gadgets and appliances to prepare an array of great meals. Good knives and cookware are worth the investment, as well as a set of cutting boards and measuring tools. Beyond that, other gadgets may or may not help you do the job faster or more gracefully. Don't think that you "have to have" the latest doodad to be successful in the kitchen.

Sautéed Corn with Thyme

Serves 4

MEATLESS **GLUTEN-FREE**

Simple, fresh ingredients are the cornerstones of a great meal. Corn, butter, and thyme combine quickly and easily in this tasty side dish. Because there are so few ingredients, fresh thyme will shine here, but if all you have is dried, use ½ teaspoon of that instead.

3 cups frozen corn kernels
½ cup water
2 tablespoons butter
1½ teaspoons fresh thyme leaves
Kosher salt and freshly ground black pepper

1. In a large skillet with a lid, combine the corn and water over medium heat. Cover and cook until the corn is hot, 7 to 10 minutes.

2. Drain off the liquid and add the butter, thyme, and salt and pepper to taste. Cook, stirring, until the butter has melted and the seasonings are blended. Serve hot.

Confetti Rice

Serves 4

MEATLESS **DAIRY-FREE** **GLUTEN-FREE**

Boxed rice mixes seem like a great idea, but a pilaf is not that difficult to make from scratch! This confetti rice, packed with flavor, comes together quickly—without the sodium, preservatives, or high price tag of a packaged mix.

2 tablespoons olive oil
¼ cup chopped onion
2 tablespoons diced peeled carrot
2 tablespoons diced bell pepper (any color)
2 tablespoons diced celery
1 cup white rice
1 teaspoon Mexican Spice Blend (page 81)
½ teaspoon grated lemon zest
2 cups vegetable broth
Kosher salt and freshly ground black pepper

1. In a large skillet with a lid, heat the oil over medium heat. Add the onion, carrot, bell pepper, and celery. Cook for 5 minutes, stirring. Add the rice. Sauté until the rice becomes opaque and the onion becomes translucent, about 5 minutes.

2. Stir in the spice blend and lemon zest, mixing well. Add the broth and bring to a low boil. Cover and reduce the heat to low. Cook until the liquid is absorbed, about 20 minutes. Fluff with a fork, season to taste with salt and pepper, and serve hot.

Grilling and Eating Outdoors

There's something extra delicious about food cooked out-of-doors. Not only does it keep the heat out of the kitchen on a sweltering summer day, but it also offsets the crisp spring evenings or the chill of fall with a little outdoor warmth. It brings out the adventurer in all of us.

The meals in this chapter are designed with the heat of summer in mind. The side dishes can be made ahead or cooked in a manner that doesn't involving heating up the oven. But, summer daze aside, they can be enjoyed any time of the year.

Easy Homemade Hummus 126
Chicken Kabobs with Mint-Yogurt Sauce 128
Curried Couscous 129
Greek Spinach Salad 130

Beer-Marinated Grilled Steak 131
Chopped Vegetable Salad 132
Cranberry-Pesto Pasta Salad 134

Blackened Pork Chops 135
Red and Green Salad with Cilantro-Onion Dressing 136
Favorite Potato Salad 137

Spiced Fish with Garlic-Lemon Butter 138
Rich and Creamy Polenta 139
Balsamic Grilled Peppers and Squashes 140

Grilled Spinach-Pesto Pizza 142
Chocolate-Cinnamon Meringues 145

Basil-Marinated Chicken 146
Grilled Green Beans 147
Fruit and Cream Tart 148

Grilled Chicken with Tangy Pineapple Barbecue Sauce 149
Jack's Best Baked Beans 151
Grilled Corn with Basil Butter 152
Cream Cheese and Nectarine Tart 153

Easy Homemade
Hummus

Chicken Kabobs
with Mint-Yogurt
Sauce

Curried
Couscous

Greek Spinach
Salad

My little girls, ages
5 and 7, have always
been huge fans of
hummus and pita
bread. Their favorite
restaurant is a Greek
café where the kids'
meal includes their
favorite dip and dip-
per. Not surprisingly,
it's more economical
to make the same
meal at home. The
varied flavors and
texture of hummus,
pita bread, grilled
meat on a stick, cous-
cous, and a spinach
salad create a feast
for the senses.

Easy Homemade Hummus

Makes about 2 cups

`MEATLESS` `DAIRY-FREE` `GLUTEN-FREE` `MAKE-AHEAD`

Hummus is a favorite dip at our house. It wasn't until I tried to make
it myself that I realized how easy—and cheap—it is to prepare. It's
also a dip designed to impress. The first time I made it, my husband
asked where I'd gotten the hummus. His jaw dropped when I said
I made it from scratch. Serve this dip with wedges of pita bread or
cut vegetable spears.

2 cups cooked or canned chickpeas (rinsed and drained if canned)
2 garlic cloves, halved
2 tablespoons freshly squeezed lemon juice
2 tablespoons olive oil
½ teaspoon kosher salt
¼ teaspoon cayenne pepper
¼ teaspoon ground cumin
Freshly ground black pepper to taste

Place all of the ingredients in the bowl of a food processor fitted
with a metal blade and blend until very smooth. Adjust the seasonings as desired. Chill for 1 hour to allow the flavors to blend.

MAKE IT AHEAD: Refrigerate the hummus in an airtight container for up to 3 days.

39

Some seasons are better than others for buying certain products. Grilling ingredients go on sale throughout the summer, while baking items are priced lower around the holidays. Buy as much as your budget and your storage space will allow at sale time so that you can save all year long.

Chicken Kabobs with Mint-Yogurt Sauce

Serves 4

`GLUTEN-FREE`

Meat cooked on skewers offers such a lovely presentation. Kids of all ages will light up when you serve these kabobs with a mint-yogurt sauce.

> 1 pound boneless, skinless chicken breasts, cut into bite-size chunks
> 1 tablespoon olive oil
> 2 teaspoons Greek Spice Blend (page 81)
> Mint-Yogurt Sauce (recipe follows)

1. Prepare a hot fire in a charcoal or gas grill.

2. Thread the chicken cubes on metal or soaked bamboo skewers. Brush with the olive oil and sprinkle with the seasoning mix, rubbing it into the chicken.

3. Cook the chicken over the hot fire until cooked through, about 15 minutes, turning once. Serve with the mint-yogurt sauce.

mint-yogurt sauce

Makes a scant 1 cup

`MEATLESS` `GLUTEN-FREE` `MAKE-AHEAD`

> ⅔ cup plain Greek yogurt
> 2 tablespoons olive oil
> 1 tablespoon freshly squeezed lemon juice
> 1 tablespoon chopped fresh mint
> 1 teaspoon minced garlic
> Kosher salt and freshly ground black pepper to taste

In a small bowl, combine all of the ingredients. Taste and adjust the seasonings as desired. Serve immediately or chill until ready to serve.

MAKE IT AHEAD: Refrigerate the sauce in an airtight container for up to 3 days. Stir to recombine.

Curried Couscous

Serves 4

MEATLESS DAIRY-FREE

Couscous is the fastest side dish I know how to prepare. This ingenious method of preparing the couscous in a bowl rather than right on the stovetop is a trick I learned when I worked in catering.

1½ cups boiling water
1 tablespoon olive oil
½ teaspoon ground cumin
½ teaspoon curry powder
1¼ cups couscous
Kosher salt and freshly ground black pepper

In a medium-size heatproof bowl, whisk together the boiling water, olive oil, cumin, and curry powder. Add the couscous and stir quickly. Cover and set aside for 5 minutes so the couscous can absorb the liquid. Fluff with a fork and season to taste with salt and pepper.

40

Plant a garden. Homegrown vegetable plants can yield enough food to more than justify their initial expense. Tomatoes, zucchini, radishes, lettuces, and bell peppers have huge yields and are all easy to grow in a backyard garden.

Greek Spinach Salad

Serves 4

GLUTEN-FREE **MAKE-AHEAD**

This flavorful spinach salad is a great side dish for grilled meats. Or you can make it a main-dish salad on its own by topping it with grilled shrimp or chicken or by adding chickpeas or hard-cooked eggs.

2 cups baby spinach
5 radishes, sliced
3 celery stalks, chopped
1 cucumber, quartered lengthwise and sliced crosswise
½ small red onion, sliced
¼ cup crumbled feta cheese
3 tablespoons red wine vinegar
1 teaspoon minced garlic
½ teaspoon dried oregano
⅛ teaspoon freshly ground black pepper
¼ cup olive oil

1. Combine the spinach, radishes, celery, cucumber, onion, and feta in a large salad bowl.

2. In a small jar or bowl, combine the vinegar, garlic, oregano, and pepper. Place the lid on the jar and shake well or whisk until smooth. Add the oil and shake or whisk again to emulsify.

3. Toss the salad with enough of the dressing to coat. Serve the extra dressing on the side.

MAKE IT AHEAD: Prepare the dressing up to 2 days ahead and the salad several hours ahead and refrigerate them separately until ready to serve.

MENU

Beer-Marinated
Grilled Steak

Chopped
Vegetable Salad

Cranberry-Pesto
Pasta Salad

I'm a steak-and-salad kind of girl. I could easily live on that— if our pocketbook allowed for it. Until that day comes, we enjoy steak dinners from time to time when I can find inexpensive cuts of beef. The salads are easier to come by, especially when there's room for variety in the ingredients, as there are with these two salads.

Beer-Marinated Grilled Steak

Serves 4

`DAIRY-FREE`

Round steak has recently been relabeled as London broil in my neck of the woods. At $2 per pound, it's the lowest-priced cut of beef I can find. It does best when marinated, so it requires a little bit of planning. This steak, doused in beer and spices, tastes great when grilled on the rare side and sliced thinly.

1 cup beer or brown ale
1 teaspoon minced garlic
½ teaspoon dried thyme
¼ teaspoon dried sage
⅛ teaspoon freshly ground black pepper, plus more to taste
1 pound top round steak (London broil), about 1 inch thick
Kosher salt

1. In a zip-top plastic bag or a glass dish with a lid, combine the beer, garlic, thyme, sage, and pepper. Add the steak and flip to coat. Marinate in the refrigerator for 4 to 24 hours.

2. Prepare a medium-hot fire in a charcoal or gas grill. Allow the steak to come to room temperature while the grill heats.

3. Remove the steak from the marinade and discard the marinade. Cook the steak to the desired doneness, about 7 minutes per side for medium-rare (145°F internal temperature).

4. Allow the meat to rest for 10 minutes before cutting against the grain into thin slices. Season to taste with salt and pepper.

#41

STEAK OUT

The supermarket meat department usually has a small section of meats that are marked down in price, sometimes considerably. This is often because the sell-by date is imminent. I've purchased boneless chicken breasts and ground beef for less than a dollar a pound because the store needed to move it quickly. Steak dinners have cost us less than $10. Grab a good deal and make a great supper that night. If you can't use the meat right away, freeze it as is or cook it up and freeze the dish to serve later.

Chopped Vegetable Salad

Serves 4

MEATLESS **GLUTEN-FREE**

With its crunchy vegetables and bright vinaigrette, this refreshing salad goes great with grilled meats. Don't turn up your nose at iceberg lettuce—its light, crisp texture is perfect in a chopped salad. It's also super economical to buy. Feel free to add other vegetables, like green beans or cucumbers.

1 head iceberg lettuce, chopped into bite-size pieces
1 small zucchini, thinly sliced
1 cup halved cherry tomatoes
1 cup cooked or canned chickpeas (rinsed and drained if canned)
½ cup pitted black olives
¼ cup finely shredded Romano or Parmesan cheese
Lemon-Basil Vinaigrette (page 44)

Combine the lettuce, zucchini, tomatoes, chickpeas, olives, and cheese in a large salad bowl. Toss the salad with enough of the vinaigrette to coat. Serve the extra vinaigrette on the side.

#42

PESTO ON DEMAND

Pesto can be expensive, so stretch it to get the biggest bang for your buck. For a burst of flavor without a lot of work, freeze cubes of pesto or other savory sauces in ice cube trays until firm and then store them in a zip-top plastic bag in the freezer. Add a cube to soup or steamed vegetables for instant flavor.

Cranberry-Pesto Pasta Salad

Serves 4 to 6

MAKE-AHEAD

This salad idea comes from my sister, who got the idea from her sister-in-law, who . . . I dunno. Doesn't matter, because just look at it! Pesto, feta, and cranberries? All having a party together with multicolored pasta? Count me in! You can sub in slivered almonds or pumpkin seeds for the sunflower seeds, if you like.

12 ounces rainbow rotini
½ cup basil pesto
½ cup crumbled feta cheese
½ cup dried cranberries
¼ cup sunflower seeds
2 scallions, chopped

1. Bring a large pot of salted water to a boil over high heat. Cook the rotini until al dente according to the package directions. Drain and rinse the pasta to cool it off.

2. In a large bowl, combine the cooked rotini and pesto. Toss well. Add the feta, cranberries, sunflower seeds, and scallions. Toss gently and chill until ready to serve.

MAKE IT AHEAD: Store the pasta salad in an airtight container in the refrigerator for up to 2 days.

MENU

Blackened Pork
Chops

Red and Green
Salad with
Cilantro-Onion
Dressing

Favorite Potato
Salad

This menu is a happy
mélange of flavors
and textures: spicy,
crusty pork; cool,
crisp lettuce; tangy,
creamy potato salad.
The salads are a nice
foil to the hot meat.
Prepare the salads
and the spice rub in
advance so that all
that's left to do at
dinnertime is grill
the meat.

Blackened Pork Chops

Serves 4

`DAIRY-FREE` `GLUTEN-FREE`

Pork loin chops are a great bargain, often available under $2 per pound. These are seasoned with a spicy rub and grilled over a hot flame.

1 teaspoon garlic powder
1 teaspoon kosher salt
½ teaspoon paprika
¼ teaspoon freshly ground black pepper
¼ teaspoon dried thyme
¼ teaspoon dried marjoram
⅛ teaspoon cayenne pepper
4 (1-inch-thick) pork loin chops

1. In a small bowl, combine the garlic powder, salt, paprika, black pepper, thyme, marjoram, and cayenne. Stir well to combine.

2. Prepare a medium-hot fire in a charcoal or gas grill.

3. Season the pork chops with the spice rub. Grill until a crust develops and an internal temperature of 145°F is reached, 6 to 8 minutes, turning once.

Red and Green Salad with Cilantro-Onion Dressing

Serves 4

The flavors of this salad really pop when it's served chilled, so prepare the components several hours in advance and store them in the refrigerator. For a nice touch on a hot day, serve the salad on chilled plates.

1 head butter lettuce, washed and torn into bite-size pieces
1 cup thinly sliced or shredded purple cabbage
½ medium cucumber, cut into half-moons
1 medium tomato, chopped
3 scallions, chopped
Cilantro-Onion Dressing (recipe follows)

Combine the lettuce, cabbage, cucumber, tomato, and scallions in a large salad bowl. Toss the salad with enough of the dressing to coat. Serve the extra dressing on the side.

MAKE IT AHEAD: Prepare the salad several hours ahead and refrigerate until ready to serve.

---

cilantro-onion dressing

Makes about 2 cups

MEATLESS DAIRY-FREE GLUTEN-FREE MAKE-AHEAD

This is a fabulous dressing for salads; it's sweet and tangy without being overpowering.

¼ medium sweet onion (like Vidalia or Walla Walla), cut into chunks
⅓ cup apple cider vinegar
¼ cup fresh cilantro leaves
⅛ teaspoon freshly ground black pepper
⅔ cup olive oil

In a food processor or blender, combine the onion, vinegar, cilantro, and pepper. Blend until smooth. With the machine running, add the oil in a thin stream. Chill until ready to serve. Just before dressing the salad, shake or whisk the dressing to re-emulsify.

MAKE IT AHEAD: Prepare the dressing up to 2 days ahead and store in an airtight container in the refrigerator.

43

DRESS IT UP

Bottled salad dressings are expensive and loaded with preservatives and ingredients you can't pronounce. Yet making your own is so easy—start with a little vinegar, add some Dijon mustard if you like, sprinkle in some kosher salt and freshly ground black pepper, and top it off with olive oil. *Voilà!* A simple vinaigrette for salads and sandwiches. Try the recipes on pages 44 and 112 for more ideas and inspiration.

Favorite Potato Salad

Serves 4

`MEATLESS` `DAIRY-FREE` `GLUTEN-FREE` `MAKE-AHEAD`

This is my go-to potato salad recipe. It's simple, filling, and a favorite with everyone.

6 russet potatoes, peeled and cut into 1-inch chunks
4 hard-cooked eggs, peeled and halved
1 cup mayonnaise
½ cup chopped celery
½ cup chopped red or white onion
2 tablespoons red wine vinegar
1 teaspoon dried dill
Kosher salt and freshly ground black pepper

1. Bring a large pot of salted water to a boil over high heat. Cook the potatoes until tender (a knife should pierce them easily), about 20 minutes. Drain well.

2. In a large bowl, smash the eggs coarsely with a potato masher or the back of a fork. Add the potatoes, mayonnaise, celery, onion, vinegar, dill, and salt and pepper to taste. Stir gently to combine. Adjust the seasonings as desired. Cover and chill until ready to serve.

MAKE IT AHEAD: Refrigerate the potato salad in an airtight container for up to 2 days.

MENU

Spiced Fish with
Garlic-Lemon
Butter

Rich and Creamy
Polenta

Balsamic Grilled
Peppers and
Squashes

This meal looks and tastes like it cost a million bucks, but it doesn't. Grilled fish tops creamy pillows of polenta, placed aside grilled vegetables for a show-stopping meal that doesn't break the bank. Start the polenta a short while before throwing the fish and veggies on the grill.

Spiced Fish with Garlic-Lemon Butter

Serves 4

MEATLESS **GLUTEN-FREE**

Quick-frozen fish is often quite economical and also fresh, since it is typically frozen on the boat as soon as it's caught. You can usually get a good deal on tilapia, but feel free to substitute another flaky white fish if something that looks good is on sale. In this recipe, spice-rubbed fish is topped with a compound butter that melts into an instant sauce.

½ teaspoon onion powder
½ teaspoon garlic powder
½ teaspoon kosher salt
¼ teaspoon paprika
¼ teaspoon ground cumin
4 tablespoons (½ stick) butter, softened
1 tablespoon finely chopped fresh cilantro
1 teaspoon grated lemon zest
1 garlic clove, minced
4 (4-ounce) fish fillets, such as tilapia
Olive oil, for brushing

1. Prepare a medium-hot fire in a charcoal or gas grill.

2. In a small bowl, combine the onion powder, garlic powder, salt, paprika, and cumin. In another bowl, combine the butter, cilantro, lemon zest, and garlic.

3. Brush the fish with oil and season generously with the spice mix. Grill the fish, turning once, until the fish starts to flake, 10 to 15 minutes.

4. Divide the butter among the 4 fish fillets and serve immediately.

MAKE IT AHEAD: Prepare the compound butter up to 2 days ahead of time, wrap in plastic wrap, and store in the refrigerator; let it come to room temperature while the grill heats up.

Many sport fishermen and hunters pursue their hobby for the love of it and not just for the sustenance. They are often thrilled to share their catch—and their spouses are more than happy to empty out the freezer of proteins they've grown weary of preparing. We've been the recipients of amazing fish dinners and wild boar or venison sausage, thanks to the kindness of friends.

Rich and Creamy Polenta

Serves 4

MEATLESS **GLUTEN-FREE**

Polenta feels like a ritzy side dish, but it's inexpensive and incredibly easy to make on the stovetop in about 30 minutes. This recipe is rich and flavorful thanks to the stock, milk, butter, and cheese.

2 cups Homemade Chicken Stock (page 97)
2 cups milk
½ teaspoon fine sea salt
1 cup polenta or cornmeal
3 tablespoons butter
1 cup shredded mozzarella cheese

1. In a medium-size saucepan, bring the stock, milk, and salt to a boil over medium-high heat. Stir in the polenta and reduce the heat to a simmer. Cook for 30 minutes, stirring occasionally to prevent sticking.

2. Stir in the butter and cheese, stirring until the cheese is melted. Serve immediately.

NO VAMPIRES ALLOWED

Got leftover garlic butter from making garlic bread? Use it to season veggies or as a sauce for cooked meats, or drizzle it over popcorn.

Balsamic Grilled Peppers and Squashes

Serves 4

`MEATLESS` `DAIRY-FREE` `GLUTEN-FREE`

Vegetables cook quickly on the grill and take on extra layers of flavor from the smoke and the caramelization of their natural sugars. Cook extra so you have leftovers to layer on pizza or sandwiches or to toss into salads.

¼ cup olive oil
1 tablespoon balsamic vinegar
1 large bell pepper (any color), seeded and quartered
2 yellow summer squash, cut lengthwise into ½-inch-thick slices
2 zucchini, cut lengthwise into ½-inch-thick slices
2 pattypan squash, halved horizontally
1 red onion, sliced (optional)
Kosher salt and freshly ground black pepper

1. Prepare a medium fire in a charcoal or gas grill.
2. In a small bowl, combine the olive oil and balsamic vinegar.
3. Arrange the vegetables on a baking sheet and brush the vegetables with the oil mixture. Season to taste with salt and pepper. Grill until tender, 10 to 15 minutes, turning occasionally. Serve hot or at room temperature.

Grilled Spinach-
Pesto Pizza

Chocolate-
Cinnamon
Meringues

Pizza is always a fun way to celebrate the weekend, and grilled pizza is even more of a novelty. The smoke from the fire adds a lovely taste to the crust, evoking wood-fired restaurant pizza. Add a tossed green salad to round out the meal. Top it all off with easy, make-ahead meringue cookies.

Grilled Spinach-Pesto Pizza

Makes 4 individual pizzas

MEATLESS

One way to save yourself from food boredom is to mix things up a bit. Grilling your pizza instead of baking it is one way to do that. (But if the weather isn't cooperating, you can bake these pizzas on baking sheets for 8 to 10 minutes at 475°F.) If you want to beef up this pizza, add some grilled chicken or steak.

½ recipe Honey Whole-Wheat Pizza Dough (page 88) or other
   favorite dough
¼ cup Spinach Pesto (recipe follows)
1 cup shredded mozzarella cheese
½ cup diced tomato
¼ cup sliced red onion
¼ cup crumbled feta cheese

1. Prepare a hot fire in a charcoal or gas grill.

2. On a lightly floured surface, divide the dough into 4 equal portions. Form each portion into a 6-inch round.

3. Grill the rounds on one side for 5 minutes.

4. Flip the rounds over onto a work surface, grilled sides up. Divide the pesto, mozzarella, tomatoes, onion, and feta among the 4 pizzas.

5. Return the pizzas to the grill and cook until the crust is crisp and the cheese is melted, about 5 minutes more. Not all grills are created equally—you may need to cook this longer to achieve your desired meltiness.

spinach pesto

Makes about 1 cup

MEATLESS **GLUTEN-FREE** **MAKE-AHEAD** **FREEZER-FRIENDLY**

This spinach and basil pesto goes well on pasta and grilled bread as well as pizza. You could even swirl a little into an omelet.

2 cups spinach leaves
½ cup fresh basil leaves
½ cup grated Parmesan cheese
3 garlic cloves, halved
Kosher salt and freshly ground black pepper
⅓ cup olive oil

In a food processor fitted with a metal blade, combine the spinach, basil, cheese, garlic, and salt and pepper to taste. Process until smooth. With the machine running, pour in the olive oil in a slow stream and process until combined.

MAKE IT AHEAD: Divide into portions as desired and store in the refrigerator for up to 3 days or in the freezer for up to 3 months. Thaw in the refrigerator before using.

#46

YOLKING AROUND

When making meringues, plan for another recipe to use the egg yolks, like homemade mayonnaise (page 273), lemon pie (page 36), or pudding.

Chocolate-Cinnamon Meringues

Makes 3 to 4 dozen cookies

`DAIRY-FREE` `GLUTEN-FREE`

Meringues are a delicious gluten-free cookie made from egg whites. Here they get an extra kiss of flavor from mini chocolate chips and vanilla extract; you can also flavor them with different extracts. Make them at night to avoid heating up the kitchen during a hot summer day. The longer they sit in the turned-off oven, the crisper they become, so feel free to leave them overnight.

4 egg whites
¼ teaspoon cream of tartar
¼ teaspoon fine sea salt
1 cup sugar
1 teaspoon pure vanilla extract
¼ teaspoon ground cinnamon
½ cup mini chocolate chips

1. Preheat the oven to 250°F. Line two baking sheets with parchment paper or silicone baking mats.

2. In a large bowl, whip the egg whites until soft peaks form. Beat in the cream of tartar and salt.

3. Add the sugar a little bit at a time, beating until stiff and glossy. Beat in the vanilla and cinnamon. Gently fold in the chocolate chips.

4. Drop rounded teaspoons of the mixture onto the prepared baking sheets and bake for 45 minutes. Turn off the oven and leave the cookies in there for several hours or overnight—they will crisp up further. Store the cooled cookies in an airtight container to preserve their crispness.

Basil-Marinated
Chicken

Grilled Green
Beans

Fruit and Cream
Tart

Make-ahead meals are perfect for summer entertaining. This marinated chicken can be made several weeks in advance and stored in the freezer until you're ready to grill. Bake up the tart crust the night before; assembly is then quick and easy. Throw the chicken and beans on the grill, and dinner is served.

Basil-Marinated Chicken

Serves 4

`DAIRY-FREE` `GLUTEN-FREE` `MAKE-AHEAD` `FREEZER-FRIENDLY`

This bright, fresh herbal marinade comes together quickly in the blender or food processor. It also works nicely with shrimp.

⅓ cup white wine vinegar
⅓ cup coarsely chopped onion
¼ cup loosely packed fresh basil leaves
2 garlic cloves, halved
¼ teaspoon freshly ground black pepper
⅓ cup olive oil
4 boneless, skinless chicken breasts

1. In a blender or food processor fitted with a metal blade, blend the vinegar, onion, basil, garlic, and pepper until smooth. With the machine running, add the oil in a thin stream.

2. Put the chicken breasts in a zip-top plastic bag or a glass dish with a lid. Pour the marinade over the chicken and turn to coat. Marinate in the refrigerator for 2 to 24 hours.

3. Prepare a hot fire in a charcoal or gas grill.

4. Remove the chicken from the marinade and discard the marinade. Grill the chicken, turning once, until cooked through (the internal temperature should reach 165°F), 15 to 20 minutes.

MAKE IT AHEAD: Store the chicken and marinade in an airtight container or zip-top plastic bag in the freezer for up to 2 months. Thaw the chicken completely in the refrigerator before grilling.

#47

CUT DOWN TO SIZE

Industrialized chickens are being bred to be meatier. I recently noted that the boneless, skinless chicken breasts at my local market were weighing in at 1 pound each! One breast is too large for one serving. To stretch your protein dollar, fillet chicken breasts and even divide each cutlet in half, depending on the size. By doing so, you create reasonable portions for two to four people instead of just one.

Grilled Green Beans

Serves 4

MEATLESS **DAIRY-FREE** **GLUTEN-FREE**

A garlicky green bean packet cooks neatly on the grill, keeping the kitchen cool and leaving one less pot for the dishwasher.

12 ounces fresh green beans
2 tablespoons olive oil
3 garlic cloves, minced
Kosher salt and freshly ground black pepper

1. Prepare a hot fire in a charcoal or gas grill.

2. Lay out a large sheet of heavy-duty aluminum foil. Spread the beans on the foil in a single layer. Drizzle the olive oil over the beans. Sprinkle on the garlic. Season to taste with salt and pepper. Fold the foil over and crimp the edges to create a tightly sealed packet.

3. Grill the beans, until tender, 10 to 15 minutes. Take care when opening the packet as it will be filled with hot steam. Serve hot or at room temperature.

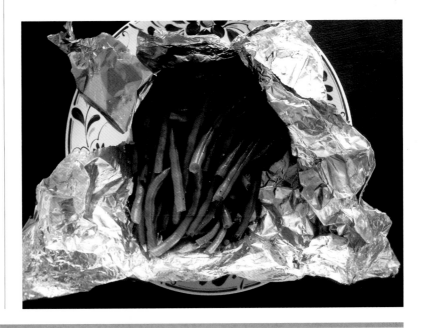

48

Buy fruits and vege-
tables in season. Not
only will they taste
better, but they'll
also be better priced.
We enjoy the arrival
of peaches and nec-
tarines in summer,
apples in fall, or-
anges in winter, and
apricots in spring.

Fruit and Cream Tart

Makes 1 (9-inch) tart

MAKE-AHEAD **FREEZER-FRIENDLY**

The crust of this elegant tart can be used as a platform for whatever fruit is in season. Although assembly should be done at the
last minute, the baked and cooled tart crust can be made well
ahead of time.

1 cup unbleached all-purpose flour
¼ cup plus 2 tablespoons confectioners' sugar
8 tablespoons (1 stick) cold butter
1 to 2 tablespoons cold water
1 cup heavy cream
1 teaspoon pure vanilla extract
3 cups sliced fruit or berries, such as plums, peaches, strawberries, or
    blueberries

1. Preheat the oven to 375°F.

2. In the bowl of a food processor, combine the flour, ¼ cup of
the confectioners' sugar, and the butter. Pulse until coarse crumbs
form. Alternatively, in a medium-size bowl, combine the flour, sugar,
and butter with a pastry blender or two knives. Work these ingredients together until coarse crumbs form.

3. Quickly pulse or stir in the cold water, 1 tablespoon at a time,
and mix until a dough forms. Press the dough into the bottom of a
9-inch springform pan. Pierce it all over with a fork and bake until
lightly golden, about 15 minutes. Cool completely on a rack. Remove the sides of the pan.

4. Right before serving, whip the cream, the remaining 2 tablespoons confectioners' sugar, and the vanilla until stiff peaks form.
Spread the whipped cream over the cooled crust.

5. Arrange the fruit on top of the whipped cream. Serve
immediately.

MAKE IT AHEAD: The baked and cooled tart crust can be wrapped airtight and
stored at room temperature for up to 2 days or in the freezer for up to 1 month.
Thaw, wrapped, on the counter before assembling the tart.

MENU

Grilled Chicken
with Tangy
Pineapple
Barbecue Sauce

Jack's Best
Baked Beans

Grilled Corn with
Basil Butter

Cream Cheese
and Nectarine
Tart

This quintessential
barbecue menu has
it all: chicken with
a smoky pineapple
glaze, baked beans,
corn on the cob, and
a fresh fruit tart for a
light, sweet ending.
Bring on summer!

Grilled Chicken with Tangy Pineapple Barbecue Sauce

Serves 4

DAIRY-FREE **GLUTEN-FREE**

Grilled chicken with barbecue sauce is a favorite everywhere for backyard cookouts. This version features an easy, mouth-wateringly delicious homemade sauce.

2 to 3 pounds bone-in chicken pieces
Kosher salt and freshly ground black pepper
Tangy Pineapple Barbecue Sauce (page 150)

1. Prepare a medium-hot fire in a charcoal or gas grill.

2. Season the chicken pieces generously with salt and pepper. Place the chicken on the grill and close the lid. Cook the chicken, turning once or twice, until done (the internal temperature should reach 165°F), 40 to 50 minutes.

3. Brush the chicken pieces with the sauce. Cook for just a few minutes to allow the sauce to cook and caramelize on the chicken. Serve the chicken with the extra sauce on the side.

tangy pineapple barbecue sauce

Makes about 2 cups

Who would have thought that you could—or should—make barbecue sauce from scratch? I certainly didn't. I didn't know how easy and fun it was until a few years ago. Now I would never consider buying bottled sauces, which are typically full of high-fructose corn syrup and preservatives. I can make my own, better version for about a dollar. And so can you.

1 tablespoon olive oil
¼ cup finely chopped onion
¼ cup finely chopped red bell pepper
1 garlic clove, minced
1 cup pineapple juice
1 (6-ounce) can tomato paste
¼ cup light brown sugar
1 tablespoon smoked paprika
½ teaspoon kosher salt
¼ teaspoon dry mustard
¼ teaspoon freshly ground black pepper
¼ teaspoon cayenne pepper
⅛ teaspoon ground cloves
⅛ teaspoon ground ginger

1. In a medium-size saucepan over medium heat, heat the oil until shimmering. Add the onion, bell pepper, and garlic and sauté until the vegetables are tender, about 5 minutes.

2. Add the pineapple juice, tomato paste, brown sugar, paprika, salt, mustard, black pepper, cayenne, cloves, and ginger. Stir well to combine. Simmer for 15 minutes.

MAKE IT AHEAD: Store in an airtight container in the refrigerator for up to 1 week or in the freezer for up to 3 months.

PICK YOUR BATTLES

When I was growing up, my dad allowed only a certain brand of ketchup in the house. I took this unwritten law with me into adulthood. It felt like blasphemy the first time I bought a competing brand just because it was cheaper. But I discovered that the price mattered more to me than the brand—at least in the case of ketchup.

Jack's Best Baked Beans

Serves 4

DAIRY-FREE **GLUTEN-FREE** **MAKE-AHEAD**

My dad is the bean king. No matter the occasion—Easter, Fourth of July, even Thanksgiving—he can be counted on to mix up a batch of his favorite baked beans. While you can certainly make your own from dried beans, Dad's method is pretty straightforward and easy, using commercially prepared canned baked beans as a base. Dad, of course, has never written down the recipe, but rather just mixes and seasons until the batch suits him. I've recorded it here for posterity and added a few tweaks of my own.

4 strips bacon, chopped
¼ cup chopped onion
1 (28-ounce) can baked beans
2 to 3 tablespoons ketchup
1 tablespoon brown mustard
½ teaspoon garlic powder
⅛ teaspoon red pepper flakes

1. In a large skillet over medium heat, cook the bacon and onion until the bacon is crisp and the onion turns translucent. Pour off the drippings.

2. Add the baked beans and stir in the ketchup, mustard, garlic powder, and red pepper. Bring to a simmer and cook until heated through.

MAKE IT AHEAD: Refrigerate the beans in an airtight container for up to 3 days.

A clean kitchen can save you money? Yes, indeed. By keeping your kitchen and pantry tidy, you'll know better what you have, you'll prevent spoilage, you'll discourage unwanted pests, and you'll have more fun in the kitchen. Having more fun means you'll cook more—which means you'll eat at home and save more money.

Grilled Corn with Basil Butter

Serves 4

MEATLESS **GLUTEN-FREE** **MAKE-AHEAD** **FREEZER-FRIENDLY**

My dad grew 20 rows of sweet corn in the backyard when I was growing up—20 rows! Suffice it to say, we ate a lot of corn on the cob each summer. The make-ahead basil butter here melts into hot, dripping goodness on your ear of corn, but it's also fabulous served over grilled chicken or fish.

8 tablespoons (1 stick) butter, softened
1 garlic clove, minced
¼ teaspoon dried basil
¼ teaspoon kosher salt
⅛ teaspoon freshly ground black pepper
⅛ teaspoon paprika
4 ears corn, husks removed

1. In a small bowl, combine the butter, garlic, basil, salt, pepper, and paprika. Mix well. Serve immediately or wrap in plastic wrap and chill until ready to use.

2. Prepare a hot fire in a charcoal or gas grill.

3. Wrap the corn in aluminum foil or place in a parchment bag. Grill until tender, 7 to 10 minutes. Serve the corn with the basil butter.

MAKE IT AHEAD: Store the basil butter in the refrigerator for up to 3 days or in the freezer for up to 2 months.

Cream Cheese and Nectarine Tart

Makes 1 (8-inch) tart

`MAKE-AHEAD`

I love summer fruits, especially nectarines and peaches. But I'm not a fan of either fruit cooked. This tart is the perfect solution to a glut of stone fruit. It's cool and refreshing for a hot summer night. Out of season, you can use other fruit or berries.

1½ cups graham cracker crumbs
2 tablespoons granulated sugar
5 tablespoons plus 1 teaspoon butter, melted
8 ounces cream cheese, softened
½ cup heavy cream
½ cup confectioners' sugar
Grated zest of 1 lemon
3 or 4 nectarines or peaches

1. Preheat the oven to 350°F.

2. In a medium-size bowl, combine the graham cracker crumbs, granulated sugar, and melted butter. Pat this crumb mixture into an 8-inch pie pan. Bake for 8 minutes. Let cool on a rack.

3. In a large bowl, whip together the cream cheese, heavy cream, confectioners' sugar, and lemon zest. Spoon this mixture into the prepared crust, cover, and chill for several hours, until firm.

4. Thinly slice the nectarines. Top the cream filling with the sliced nectarines. Serve immediately.

MAKE IT AHEAD: Prepare the tart through step 3 and store in the refrigerator for up to 2 days. When ready to serve, proceed with step 4.

Company Dinners

In the old days, home cooks were encouraged to have a "company dinner" in their kitchen repertoire, a no-fail recipe that could be served to guests. While it might have signified something fancy enough to serve to the boss, it mostly had to be a guaranteed success.

The meals in this chapter are easy, economical, and delicious, yet special enough to serve to guests. They can easily be stretched in case you're feeding a crowd, and they can be dressed up or down, allowing you great freedom of presentation.

Broiled Bruschetta. 156
Meaty Lasagna with Asiago Béchamel 158
Curly Endive and Romaine Salad with Meyer Lemon Dressing 159

Zesty Baked Shrimp with Panko 161
Bryan's Broccoli and Onions 162
Colorful Herbed Couscous 163

Hot Dog and Sausage Buffet. 164
Classic Sautéed Peppers and Onions 166
Spicy No-Bean Chili 167

Grilled Pineapple Chicken 168
Asian Vegetable Skewers 170
Lui's Kitchen Almond Cookies 171

Honey-Mustard Baked Ham 174
Seasoned Cauliflower 176
Tastiest-Ever Scalloped Potatoes 177
Mom's Sweet Rolls 178

Almond-Crusted Chicken Tenders 179
Orange-Ginger Carrots 180
Garlicky Quinoa Pilaf 181

Make-Your-Own Burrito Bar 182
From-Scratch Refried Black Beans 183
Chunky Guacamole 184
Smoky Corn Salsa 185

Slow Cooker Pulled Pork Sandwiches 186
Coleslaw with a Kick 187
Corn, Pepper, and Red Onion Salad 188

Asian Chicken Salad with Rice Noodles 189
Ginger-Orange Crisps 191

Sherried Black Bean Tomato Soup 192
Easy-Peasy Popovers 193
Mixed Berry Pie with Cinnamon and Lemon 194

Pot Roast with Herbed Red Wine Sauce 196
Parsleyed New Potatoes 197
Deep-Dish Apple-Cranberry Pie 198

MENU

Broiled
Bruschetta

Meaty Lasagna
with Asiago
Béchamel

Curly Endive
and Romaine
Salad with Meyer
Lemon Dressing

Italian food is one of the most comforting of cuisines, and it's hard to mess up, making it a great menu to share with friends and family. This supper starts with an easy yet impressive bruschetta, followed by a meaty lasagna and salad. No one will leave the table hungry.

Broiled Bruschetta

Serves 4

`MEATLESS` `MAKE-AHEAD`

There's a tiny Italian restaurant not too far from our home that my husband and I discovered a couple of years ago. It's small and quaint; the owner was born in Italy and raised in a family of restaurateurs. While we love to dine there, our budget doesn't like it so much. This bruschetta is similar to one that Rosina serves as a starter and is a favorite to enjoy at home for less. When I make it for the kids, I have to more than double the recipe or else I won't get any!

2 medium tomatoes, diced
1 tablespoon chopped fresh basil
1 garlic clove, minced
1 tablespoon olive oil
Kosher salt and freshly ground black pepper
8 (½-inch-thick) slices bread from a small artisan loaf, toasted
1 cup shredded mozzarella cheese

1. Preheat the broiler.

2. In a medium-size bowl, combine the tomatoes, basil, and garlic. Drizzle with the olive oil and stir gently to coat. Season to taste with salt and pepper.

3. Place the toasted bread slices on a baking sheet. Divide the tomato mixture among them. Top with the cheese.

4. Broil until the cheese is bubbly, watching carefully so that it doesn't burn.

MAKE IT AHEAD: Store the tomato topping in the refrigerator for up to 1 day. Drain off any tomato juice that accumulates before spooning it onto the toasts.

Meaty Lasagna with Asiago Béchamel

Serves 6 to 8

MAKE-AHEAD **FREEZER-FRIENDLY**

American lasagnas are typically filled with cottage or ricotta cheese, which can be fairly expensive. To cut costs but maintain great flavor, this lasagna is made with a cheesy béchamel sauce that you mix quickly on the stove. You'll find that Asiago cheese is an affordable and flavorful alternative to Parmigiano-Reggiano.

4 tablespoons (½ stick) butter
¼ cup unbleached all-purpose flour
2 cups milk
¼ cup finely shredded Asiago or Romano cheese
Kosher salt and freshly ground black pepper
1 pound ground beef
3 cups Roasted Vegetable Marinara Sauce (page 229) or other favorite pasta sauce
2 cups shredded mozzarella cheese
8 lasagna noodles (uncooked)

1. Preheat the oven to 400°F. Grease a 9 x 13-inch baking dish with nonstick cooking spray.

2. In a medium-size saucepan over medium-low heat, melt the butter. Add the flour and whisk for 1 minute. Slowly whisk in the milk and cook, stirring occasionally, until thickened, 5 to 7 minutes. Remove from the heat and stir in the Asiago cheese. Season to taste with salt and pepper and set the béchamel aside.

3. In a large skillet over medium heat, brown the ground beef and season with 1 teaspoon salt. Stir in the pasta sauce.

4. Spread half of the meat sauce across the bottom of the prepared baking dish. Sprinkle half of the mozzarella over the sauce. Lay 4 lasagna noodles across the cheese layer, breaking them to fit as needed.

5. Pour the béchamel sauce over the noodles. Top with the remaining 4 noodles, again breaking to fit as needed. Spread the remaining meat sauce over the noodles and sprinkle with the remaining mozzarella.

6. Bake until bubbly throughout, about 30 minutes. Allow the dish to rest for 10 minutes before slicing and serving.

MAKE IT AHEAD: The unbaked lasagna can be covered and stored in the refrigerator for up to 2 days or in the freezer for up to 2 months. If frozen, thaw completely in the refrigerator before baking. In either case, add 15 minutes of baking time since the dish will be cold.

Shred cheese finely to stretch it for tacos and other uses. It's amazing how it fools the eye.

Curly Endive and Romaine Salad with Meyer Lemon Dressing

Serves 4

MEATLESS **GLUTEN-FREE**

My dad has a 40-year-old Meyer lemon tree in the backyard, which yields a gold mine of sweet, juicy fruit. Thankfully, Meyer lemons are becoming more widely available in grocery stores across the country, especially during the winter months. It's worth the effort to hunt them down, but if you're out of luck, simply substitute a regular lemon.

The sweetness of the Meyer lemon perfectly complements the slight bitterness of the endive in this salad, but if you can't find curly endive, feel free to use frisée. Some may prefer a higher proportion of romaine, too. Suit your fancy.

Juice of ½ Meyer lemon
½ teaspoon minced garlic
¼ teaspoon coarsely ground black pepper, plus more to taste
¼ cup olive oil
1 small head curly endive, chopped
½ head romaine lettuce, torn into bite-size pieces
½ cup shredded Romano or Asiago cheese
Kosher salt

1. In a small jar or bowl, combine the lemon juice, garlic, and pepper. Place the lid on the jar and shake well or whisk until smooth. Add the olive oil and shake or whisk again to emulsify.

2. Place the endive and romaine in a large salad bowl. Toss with enough of the dressing to coat. Sprinkle with the cheese and season to taste with salt and more pepper. Serve the salad with the extra dressing on the side.

PLANNING FOR HOLIDAY DINNERS ON A DIME

There were many times during our debt-fighting years when I breathed a sigh of relief that we had been invited to a holiday dinner instead of having to foot the bill of hosting it. I remember one year spending as much on Thanksgiving dinner as I did in a regular week!

Holiday dinners should be more about breaking bread together than about breaking the bank. Here are some ways to alleviate the expense of holiday dinners without forgoing them altogether.

1. HOST A POTLUCK.

During the holidays, most folks expect to be able to contribute to a big meal, so let them. Make your plan clear and then let family and friends step up.

2. PLAN AHEAD.

Planning can take many forms. You can plan cheaper meals to offset a more expensive one. Or you can plan a fancy dinner and then shop far enough in advance to fund the venture comfortably.

3. SHOP THE SALES.

Let the sales dictate what you serve. That's a sure-fire way to save money.

4. BE CREATIVE.

Don't be brainwashed into thinking that you have to make turkey on Thanksgiving. I made chicken one year because it was easier and we like it better. Use creative license in meal planning—especially if you're the chef!

MENU

Zesty Baked
Shrimp with
Panko

Bryan's Broccoli
and Onions

Colorful Herbed
Couscous

Three dishes make
up this meal: one for
the oven, one for the
stovetop, one for the
bowl. This allows
the cook adequate
space for prepara-
tion. Start the broc-
coli on a burner, slide
the shrimp into the
oven, and mix up the
couscous. Dinner will
be ready in a jiffy.

Zesty Baked Shrimp with Panko

Serves 4

MEATLESS **DAIRY-FREE**

Shrimp used to be considered special-occasion food, but these days it's pretty easy on the budget. This dish comes together quickly, especially if you can find easy-peel shrimp.

1 pound medium shrimp (thawed if frozen), peeled and deveined
2 tablespoons olive oil
2 tablespoons sliced fresh basil
Grated zest of 1 lemon
⅛ teaspoon red pepper flakes
Kosher salt and freshly ground black pepper
½ cup panko bread crumbs

1. Preheat the oven to 450°F. Grease a shallow baking dish with nonstick cooking spray.

2. Place the shrimp in a medium-size bowl. Add the olive oil, basil, lemon zest, and red pepper flakes and toss to coat. Season to taste with salt and pepper. Spread the shrimp in the baking dish. Sprinkle the panko bread crumbs over the top.

3. Bake just until the shrimp turn pink, 10 to 15 minutes. Do not overcook.

Bryan's Broccoli and Onions

Serves 4

MEATLESS DAIRY-FREE **GLUTEN-FREE**

Back in the day, my mother-in-law insisted that her son didn't like vegetables. But I've noticed that when I use a generous hand with seasonings, everyone in my family loves them. They are named in my husband's honor; he really *does* like vegetables.

2 tablespoons olive oil
½ medium yellow or red onion, sliced from blossom to root end
1 tablespoon minced garlic
12 ounces broccoli florets (about 6 cups)
2 tablespoons Marsala
1 teaspoon grated lemon zest
Kosher salt and freshly ground black pepper
½ cup water

1. In a large skillet with a lid, heat the oil over medium heat until shimmering. Add the onion and garlic and cook until soft and starting to brown, 10 to 12 minutes.

2. Add the broccoli florets and Marsala and toss to coat. Increase the heat to medium-high and cook, stirring, until crisp-tender, about 10 minutes.

3. Add the lemon zest and salt and pepper to taste. Add the water, cover, and steam until tender, 7 to 10 minutes. Serve hot.

Colorful Herbed Couscous

Serves 4

`MEATLESS`

Garlic, butter, and herbs give this couscous dish a rich, comforting flavor boost. If you can't find tricolor couscous, regular will work just fine.

1 cup boiling water
1 tablespoon butter
½ teaspoon minced garlic
½ teaspoon dried Italian herb blend
1 cup tricolor couscous
Kosher salt and freshly ground black pepper

1. In a medium-size bowl, combine the boiling water, butter, garlic, and herbs. Whisk to blend.

2. Quickly stir in the couscous. Cover and let rest for 5 minutes so the couscous can absorb the liquid.

3. Fluff with a fork and season to taste with salt and pepper.

MENU

Hot Dog and
Sausage Buffet

Classic Sautéed
Peppers and
Onions

Spicy No-Bean
Chili

Hot dogs and sausages are my go-to casual meal for feeding a crowd. They are easy on the budget, but you can rock the crowd-pleasing standards if you also serve a spectacular array of toppings alongside.

Hot Dog and Sausage Buffet

Serves 4

MAKE-AHEAD

Use whatever kind of sausages you like here, from the precooked chicken variety to uncured beef or pork. Just adjust the cooking time according to the package directions.

8 hot dogs or sausage links, or a combination
8 hot dog buns

TOPPING SUGGESTIONS
Various mustards and bottled condiments
Chopped onions
Classic Sautéed Peppers and Onions (page 166)
Homemade salsa, like Chunky Tomato Salsa (page 35)
    or Roasted Chipotle Salsa (page 221)
Coleslaw with a Kick (page 187)
Chunky Guacamole (page 184)
Spicy No-Bean Chili (page 167)
Pulled Pork (page 186)
Shredded cheese of your choice

1. Cook the hot dogs or sausages on the grill, on the stovetop, or in the slow cooker.

2. Wrap the hot dog buns in aluminum foil and warm on the grill or in a low oven until hot, 5 to 10 minutes.

3. Serve the hot dogs buffet style, with a variety of toppings as desired.

MAKE IT AHEAD: Prepare the different toppings up to 1 day in advance and store in the refrigerator until ready to serve. Right before serving, reheat any items that should be served hot.

TIPS FOR A SUCCESSFUL HOT DOG AND SAUSAGE BUFFET BAR

Pretend you're running the best hot dog truck in town. You've got great meats (no mystery links here) and fresh rolls. Plan a spread to please anybody and everybody. It's really not that hard.

1. **Offer a variety of sausages.** Consider different meats and spice levels, and perhaps a vegan or vegetarian option. Cook them well and keep them hot.

2. **Have plenty of fresh rolls.** You can bake your own or steam store-bought buns to soften them prior to serving. If you've got the grill going, try grilling the rolls.

3. **Let your imagination run wild with the toppings.** Think outside the box and offer lots of choices—you don't need to be limited to bottled condiments!

Classic Sautéed Peppers and Onions

Serves 4

`MEATLESS` `DAIRY-FREE` `GLUTEN-FREE` `MAKE-AHEAD`

This vegetable mixture goes well on hot dogs, sausages, burgers, and sandwiches. It's particularly good on a cheesesteak sandwich or tucked into a vegetarian wrap.

1 tablespoon olive oil
1 red bell pepper, seeded and thinly sliced
1 green bell pepper, seeded and thinly sliced
1 medium onion, thinly sliced
Kosher salt and freshly ground black pepper
1 tablespoon red wine vinegar
½ teaspoon dried oregano

In a large skillet over medium heat, heat the oil until shimmering. Add the bell peppers and onion and sauté quickly until tender but still slightly crisp, 7 to 8 minutes. Season to taste with salt and pepper. Stir in the red wine vinegar and the oregano. Serve hot or warm.

MAKE IT AHEAD: Store in an airtight container in the refrigerator for up to 3 days. Reheat gently on the stovetop or in the microwave.

Eliminate expensive ingredients whenever possible. Back in the old days, I could buy a can of chopped green chiles for a quarter. Now the price is easily five times that. Instead of buying the can, I chop fresh chiles, which I can buy for a few pennies apiece.

Spicy No-Bean Chili

Serves 4

DAIRY-FREE | **GLUTEN-FREE** | **MAKE-AHEAD** | **FREEZER-FRIENDLY**

This meaty chili comes together quickly and easily on the stovetop. It's great for chili dogs but is equally delicious atop baked potatoes, pasta, and nachos, or folded into burritos.

12 ounces ground beef, turkey, pork, or chicken
2 tablespoons finely chopped onion
2 tablespoons finely chopped seeded jalapeño
1 teaspoon minced garlic
1 (8-ounce) can tomato sauce
1 tablespoon Mexican Spice Blend (page 81)

In a large skillet over medium-high heat, cook the meat, onion, jalapeño, and garlic until the meat is browned and the onion is translucent, 10 to 15 minutes. Spoon off any fat. Stir in the tomato sauce and spice blend. Simmer for 10 minutes.

MAKE IT AHEAD: Store the chili in an airtight container in the refrigerator for up to 4 days or in the freezer for up to 2 months.

MENU

Grilled Pineapple
Chicken

Asian Vegetable
Skewers

Lui's Kitchen
Almond Cookies

I have fond memories of the Chinese restaurant Lui's Kitchen in my small hometown. I went to school with the Lui kids, so it was fun to go out to eat on a Friday night and recognize familiar faces. Pineapple chicken was one of our favorite dishes to order, and we all looked forward to the almond cookies served afterward. Though Lui's Kitchen is now long gone, my kids love going out for Chinese—but "staying in for Chinese" is a more affordable alternative. White rice is a classic accompaniment (see page 172).

Grilled Pineapple Chicken

Serves 4

DAIRY-FREE **GLUTEN-FREE**

The pineapple juice keeps this tangy chicken tender and juicy. If you don't want to cook it on the grill, you can get good results cooking it under the broiler.

¼ cup pineapple juice
¼ cup reduced-sodium soy sauce
1 tablespoon toasted sesame oil
1 teaspoon minced fresh ginger
¼ teaspoon red pepper flakes
1 pound boneless, skinless chicken breast fillets
Pineapple Sauce (recipe follows)

1. In a small bowl, combine the pineapple juice, soy sauce, sesame oil, ginger, and red pepper flakes.

2. Place the chicken in a zip-top plastic bag or a glass dish with a lid. Add the marinade and turn to coat. Allow the chicken to marinate in the refrigerator for 4 to 24 hours.

3. Prepare a hot fire in a charcoal or gas grill. Remove the chicken from the marinade (discard the marinade) and grill, turning once, until an internal temperature of 165°F has been reached. This won't take long for boneless fillets—maybe 3 minutes per side—so watch carefully.

4. Serve the chicken with the hot pineapple sauce.

pineapple sauce

Makes about 1½ cups

`MEATLESS` `DAIRY-FREE` `GLUTEN-FREE`

This Asian-inspired sauce is also good served over rice, grilled pork or shrimp, and mini meatballs. You can even serve it on burgers for a teriyaki twist.

1 cup pineapple juice
⅓ cup reduced-sodium soy sauce
1 tablespoon toasted sesame oil
1 tablespoon cornstarch
½ teaspoon minced fresh ginger

In a medium-size saucepan, whisk together all of the ingredients. Bring the sauce to a boil over medium-high heat. Reduce the heat to medium-low and simmer until thickened, about 10 minutes. Serve hot.

Asian Vegetable Skewers

Serves 4

`MEATLESS` `DAIRY-FREE` `GLUTEN-FREE`

These vegetable skewers cook on the grill alongside the chicken as a sweet and savory accompaniment. They can be assembled and refrigerated several hours ahead of time, leaving only the grilling for the last minute.

2 medium zucchini, thickly sliced
1 medium green bell pepper, cut into squares
4 ounces cremini mushrooms
½ large sweet onion (such as Vidalia), cut into chunks
1 cup fresh or canned pineapple chunks
1½ teaspoons reduced-sodium soy sauce
1½ teaspoons vegetable oil
1½ teaspoons toasted sesame oil
⅛ teaspoon red pepper flakes

1. Prepare a hot fire in a charcoal or gas grill.

2. Thread the vegetables and pineapple on metal or soaked bamboo skewers, alternating and mixing up the order.

3. In a small bowl, combine the soy sauce, vegetable oil, sesame oil, and red pepper flakes. Brush the pineapple and vegetables with this mixture.

4. Grill the skewers until tender, 7 to 10 minutes, turning once.

HAM IT UP

Thanksgiving, Christmas, and Easter grocery ads feature hams and turkeys at rock-bottom pricing. Buy several and store them in the freezer. Each one can produce a number of meals. Cook up a ham or turkey, slice or dice the meat, and freeze it in meal-size packages to use throughout the coming months.

Seasoned Cauliflower

Serves 4

MEATLESS **GLUTEN-FREE**

This spicy cauliflower complements the rich sweetness of the ham. Be sure to look for firm, creamy heads of cauliflower, avoiding those that have brown spots. You can prepare broccoli this way as well.

1 head cauliflower, cut into bite-size florets
3 tablespoons butter, melted
1 teaspoon minced garlic
½ teaspoon fine sea salt
½ teaspoon dried thyme
½ teaspoon dried dill
½ teaspoon paprika
⅛ teaspoon freshly ground black pepper

1. Place the cauliflower in a steamer basket in a medium-size stockpot with 1 inch of water. Bring the water to a boil, cover, and steam the cauliflower until tender, about 10 minutes. Drain the cauliflower and transfer it to a serving dish.

2. In a small bowl, combine the butter, garlic, salt, thyme, dill, paprika, and pepper. Drizzle the spiced butter over the cauliflower and toss gently to distribute evenly.

Tastiest-Ever Scalloped Potatoes

Serves 4

MEATLESS **GLUTEN-FREE**

These are the best potatoes. Ever. I found the recipe in a potato cookbook 20 years ago and committed some version of the recipe to memory. I like when there are leftovers for breakfast—but there rarely are. I use a food processor fitted with a slicing disk to make quick work of the potato prep.

3 pounds russet potatoes, peeled and thinly sliced
Kosher salt and freshly ground black pepper
1½ cups half-and-half
2 tablespoons butter, cut into small pieces
½ cup heavy cream

1. Preheat the oven to 325°F. Grease a 9 x 13-inch baking dish with nonstick cooking spray.

2. Overlap the potato slices in the prepared dish, seasoning with salt and pepper every few layers. Pour the half-and-half over the potatoes and dot the surface with the butter. Bake for 45 minutes.

3. Pour the heavy cream over the potatoes and continue baking until golden brown on top and very tender when pierced with a knife, about 45 minutes more.

While it's tempting to buy the loss leaders at every store—trust me, I've done it—it can be inefficient and time-consuming to visit every store each week, particularly if there are many stores in your area. Scan the ads and see who regularly has the best deals on the things that you buy. Make that your regular stop and don't fret over missing a deal elsewhere.

Mom's Sweet Rolls

Makes 12 rolls

MAKE-AHEAD

My mom always pulled out the stops when company came. It was such fun to see her set up the dining room table with the silver and the good dishes and devise an elegant meal plan. I know she didn't spend a lot of money, but she always made her guests feel like a million bucks. These sweet rolls are an adaptation of those she frequently made when I was a child. She liked to serve them in a linen-lined silver basket.

¾ cup milk
2 tablespoons butter, cut into cubes
1½ cups unbleached all-purpose flour
2 tablespoons dark brown sugar
½ teaspoon fine sea salt
½ teaspoon ground cinnamon
1 teaspoon active dry yeast
2 tablespoons raisins

TOPPING
1 tablespoon butter, melted
1 tablespoon granulated sugar

1. Combine the milk, cubed butter, flour, brown sugar, salt, cinnamon, yeast, and raisins in the pan of your bread machine according to the manufacturer's directions. Set to the dough cycle and start the machine. (If making the dough by hand: Combine the milk, cubed butter, and brown sugar in a small saucepan and warm slightly over medium heat. Transfer the mixture to a large bowl and add the yeast. Stir and allow the yeast to proof for 5 minutes. Add the flour, salt, cinnamon, and raisins and stir to combine well. Turn the mixture out onto a lightly floured surface and knead for 5 minutes to create a smooth, elastic dough, adding more flour as necessary. Transfer to a greased bowl and turn the dough ball to coat. Allow to rise until doubled in bulk, about 1 hour.)

2. Grease a 12-cup muffin pan with nonstick cooking spray. When the machine beeps or the dough has doubled in bulk, remove the dough from the pan or bowl and divide it into 12 equal parts. Divide each part into 3 portions, shaping each portion into a ball. Place 3 dough balls in each muffin cup.

3. Preheat the oven to 350°F.

4. Brush the tops of the rolls with the melted butter and sprinkle them with the granulated sugar. Allow to rise for 20 minutes.

5. Bake the rolls until golden brown, about 15 minutes. Cool on a rack before serving.

MAKE IT AHEAD: Store the cooled rolls in an airtight container at room temperature for up to 2 days.

Almond-Crusted
Chicken Tenders

Orange-Ginger
Carrots

Garlicky
Quinoa Pilaf

No one will ever guess that this tasty gluten-free meal fits a "specialty diet." It's a convenient menu for a regular week-night dinner but also special enough for entertaining guests.

Almond-Crusted Chicken Tenders

Serves 4

DAIRY-FREE **GLUTEN-FREE**

This flavorful chicken is a far cry from your typical chicken tenders. My kids gobble it down and ask for more. Instead of purchasing pre-ground almond meal, you can simply pulse whole raw almonds in a food processor until fine (be careful not to overprocess or they will turn into almond butter).

6 tablespoons almond meal
½ teaspoon fine sea salt
½ teaspoon rubbed sage
½ teaspoon paprika
½ teaspoon onion powder
⅛ teaspoon cayenne pepper
2 pounds boneless, skinless chicken tenders

1. Preheat the oven to 425°F. Line a rimmed baking sheet with parchment paper.

2. In a shallow dish, combine the almond meal, salt, sage, paprika, onion powder, and cayenne.

3. Dip the chicken tenders in the nut mixture, pressing down so the crust adheres, and place on the prepared baking sheet.

4. Bake until the juices run clear, 10 to 15 minutes.

Orange-Ginger Carrots

Serves 4

MEATLESS GLUTEN-FREE

These carrots get a boost of sweetness from the orange and some warm spice from the ginger. They make a delicious side dish to any meal.

6 carrots, peeled and thickly sliced on the bias
1 tablespoon freshly squeezed orange juice
1 tablespoon butter
1 teaspoon minced fresh ginger
Grated zest of 1 orange
Kosher salt and freshly ground black pepper

1. Place the carrots in a steamer basket in a medium-size stockpot with 1 inch of water. Bring the water to a boil, cover, and steam the carrots until tender, about 10 minutes.

2. Drain the carrots and return to the pot. Add the orange juice, butter, ginger, zest, and salt and pepper to taste. Toss gently to coat.

#57

TRY IT BEFORE YOU BUY (A TON OF) IT

While I'm a big fan of stockpiling, I don't think it's a good idea to gamble on things that you may or may not like. Don't buy a dozen of something unless you know you love it. Buy one, try it that day, and go back for more if it's a screaming deal. Otherwise, you will be stuck with 11 cans of something you hate. (Ask me how I know!) Some stores offer samples of certain items (like produce or deli items) so that you can taste-test it *before* buying.

Garlicky Quinoa Pilaf

Serves 4

MEATLESS **GLUTEN-FREE**

I first heard about quinoa 10 years ago. I knew it was healthy, but it sounded weird, so I didn't mess with it. I've come to love it for its high protein content and speedy cooking, which makes it an ideal side dish for busy evenings. It also just happens to be absolutely delicious.

2 tablespoons butter
1 cup quinoa, rinsed and drained
1 teaspoon minced garlic
2 cups vegetable broth
½ teaspoon dried parsley
Kosher salt and freshly ground black pepper

1. In a large skillet with a lid, heat the butter over medium heat. Add the quinoa and garlic and sauté until the quinoa starts to brown, about 5 minutes.

2. Add the vegetable broth and parsley and bring to a low boil. Cover and reduce the heat. Cook until all of the liquid is absorbed, about 12 minutes.

3. Fluff with a fork, cover again, and set aside for 10 minutes. Season to taste with salt and pepper.

MENU

Make-Your-Own
Burrito Bar

From-Scratch
Refried Black
Beans

Chunky
Guacamole

Smoky Corn
Salsa

A burrito buffet bar is a fun, crowd-pleasing supper because folks can prepare their burritos exactly the way they like them. It's filling, festive, and frugal.

Make-Your-Own Burrito Bar

Serves 4

`MEATLESS`

The key to success for any type of buffet is to make sure to offer a variety of options. Here are my suggestions for a burrito buffet; feel free to add more fillings depending on your preferences.

8 burrito-size flour tortillas
From-Scratch Refried Black Beans (recipe follows)
3 cups cooked rice (Zesty Mexican Rice, page 21, or plain cooked rice, page 172)
2 cups shredded cheese of your choice
2 cups shredded lettuce
Chunky Guacamole (page 184)
Smoky Corn Salsa (page 185)

Wrap the tortillas in aluminum foil and warm them in a low oven until hot, about 15 minutes. Arrange bowls of the fillings and allow diners to make their own burritos. (If necessary, show your guests how to roll a proper burrito: Lay out the tortilla. Place the fillings in a line in the bottom third of the tortilla. Fold up that third, fold in the sides, and continue rolling. All the fillings should be well contained inside the tortilla.)

58

Club warehouse stores can be the source of great deals. We rely on our club membership to get us the lowest prices on milk, cheese, breads, pasta, honey, maple syrup, and dried beans. Use caution, though: Much of what they carry is overpriced. Compare prices and buy only what you'll really use.

From-Scratch Refried Black Beans

Serves 4

MEATLESS · **DAIRY-FREE** · **GLUTEN-FREE** · **MAKE-AHEAD** · **FREEZER-FRIENDLY**

Canned refried beans are convenient, but they're typically overly seasoned and overpriced. Homemade beans taste better and are healthier for you, too, since you probably won't add as much fat or salt as the factory. Commercially prepared refried beans are usually pinto beans, so the black beans in this recipe make for a nice twist. Reduce your costs even more by using home-cooked beans (see page 38).

1 tablespoon vegetable oil
¼ cup chopped onion
1 teaspoon minced garlic
4 cups cooked or canned black beans (rinsed and drained if canned)
½ teaspoon ground cumin
Kosher salt and freshly ground black pepper

1. In a large skillet over medium heat, heat the oil until shimmering. Add the onion and garlic and sauté until tender, 5 to 7 minutes, stirring occasionally.

2. Add half of the beans to the skillet, mashing them with a potato masher and mixing them into the onion mixture.

3. Stir in the remaining beans, the cumin, and salt and pepper to taste. If the beans are too dry, add a bit of water to achieve the texture you like. Cook until heated through. Adjust the seasonings to taste.

MAKE IT AHEAD: Store the refried beans in an airtight container in the refrigerator for up to 4 days or in the freezer for up to 2 months.

#59

FRESHEN UP

If you purchase bunches of fresh herbs from the produce department, use them up quickly before they wilt. Blend them into pesto or chop and store them in zip-top plastic bags in the freezer. They may darken in color, but the flavor will remain intact. Be sure to label them so you don't forget what you have.

Chunky Guacamole

Serves 4

`MEATLESS` `DAIRY-FREE` `GLUTEN-FREE`

My favorite trick for making delicious guacamole is to chill the avocados before mixing the dip. The flavors blend quickly and the taste is out of this world.

3 medium avocados, pitted and peeled
1 jalapeño, seeded and finely chopped
¼ cup finely chopped fresh cilantro
¼ cup finely chopped red onion
Juice of 1 lime
¼ teaspoon ground cumin
Kosher salt and freshly ground black pepper

1. In a medium-size bowl, mash 2 of the avocados until smooth. Chop the third avocado. Fold the chopped avocado into the mashed avocado mixture.

2. Gently fold in the jalapeño, cilantro, onion, lime juice, cumin, and salt and pepper to taste. Adjust the seasonings as desired. Serve immediately.

Smoky Corn Salsa

Serves 4

MEATLESS DAIRY-FREE GLUTEN-FREE MAKE-AHEAD

Salsas can be custom-made by varying spiciness, texture, and ingredients—the combinations are practically endless. This salsa gets its smoky flavor from the roasted corn as well as the chipotle chile powder. If you can't find roasted corn, feel free to quickly roast kernels in a hot oven or to use regular corn.

2 cups frozen roasted corn, thawed
¼ cup chopped fresh cilantro
1 jalapeño, seeded and chopped
Juice of 1 lime
1 teaspoon minced garlic
¼ teaspoon ground chipotle chile powder
Kosher salt and freshly ground black pepper

In a medium-size bowl, combine the corn, cilantro, jalapeño, lime juice, garlic, and chile powder. Season to taste with salt and pepper and adjust the other seasonings as desired. Serve immediately or cover and chill until ready to serve.

MAKE IT AHEAD: Store the salsa in an airtight container in the refrigerator for up to 3 days.

MENU

Slow Cooker
Pulled Pork
Sandwiches

Coleslaw with
a Kick

Corn, Pepper,
and Red Onion
Salad

Since pork roasts
are one of the most
inexpensive of pro-
teins, you can easily
feed a crowd with
this hearty supper
of pulled pork, spicy
slaw, and corn salad.
Gild the lily with
Homemade Sour-
dough Hamburger
Buns (page 218).

Slow Cooker Pulled Pork Sandwiches

Serves 4 to 8

DAIRY-FREE **SLOW COOKER** **MAKE-AHEAD** **FREEZER-FRIENDLY**

My slow cooker is one of my best friends, especially when it makes
this dish. Oh my! What a feast, yet so easy. And the homemade
buns take it over the top in terms of impressing your guests.

PULLED PORK
1 tablespoon onion powder
1 teaspoon smoked paprika
1 teaspoon dry mustard
1 teaspoon kosher salt
½ teaspoon freshly ground black pepper
1 (3- to 4-pound) boneless pork butt or shoulder roast

Homemade Sourdough Hamburger Buns (page 218)

1. In a small bowl, combine the onion powder, paprika, mustard,
salt, and pepper.

2. Place the roast in a 6-quart slow cooker. Sprinkle the seasoning all over the roast.

3. Cover and cook on High for 4 hours or on Low for 6 to 8 hours.
The meat should be tender and falling apart.

4. Remove the meat from the crock and shred with two forks.
(Save the drippings for soup or stew.) Pile the pork into the buns
and serve.

MAKE IT AHEAD: Cool the shredded meat and store in an airtight container in
the refrigerator for up to 3 days or in the freezer for up to 2 months.

DIY CONVENIENCE

Make your own convenience items by preparing your favorite dishes, like burritos, taquitos, or sandwich fillings, and storing them in the freezer. If there's something quick to reheat and serve, you'll be less likely to make a run for pricey takeout.

Coleslaw with a Kick

Serves 4

`MEATLESS` `DAIRY-FREE` `GLUTEN-FREE` `MAKE-AHEAD`

Cabbage is so inexpensive, so healthy, and so tasty in salads and slaws that I'd rank it in my top 10 of good cheap eats ingredients. This slaw gets a nice kick from the Dijon and garlic. It's a refreshing departure from traditional, mayonnaise-laden slaws. You can serve it alongside the sandwiches or pile it in the buns on top of the pork.

1 small head cabbage, sliced
2 carrots, peeled and shredded (about 1 cup)
¼ cup chopped fresh chives or scallions
½ cup unseasoned rice vinegar
2 teaspoons light brown sugar
1½ teaspoons chopped fresh dill or ½ teaspoon dried dill
½ teaspoon Dijon mustard
½ teaspoon minced garlic
¼ teaspoon freshly ground black pepper
¼ teaspoon poppy seeds
½ cup olive oil

1. In a large bowl, combine the cabbage, carrots, and chives.
2. In a small jar or bowl, combine the rice vinegar, brown sugar, dill, mustard, garlic, pepper, and poppy seeds. Place the lid on the jar and shake well or whisk until smooth. Add the olive oil and shake or whisk again to emulsify.
3. Toss the dressing with the salad mixture.

MAKE IT AHEAD: Prepare the salad mixture and the dressing and store separately in the refrigerator. Toss just before serving if you prefer a very crisp slaw. Otherwise, the mixed slaw can be stored in the refrigerator for up to 2 days.

BE FLEXIBLY FRUGAL

If it doesn't have a sale price, don't buy it. Unless it's a special occasion, like a birthday, I rarely buy an ingredient at its regular price. If chicken breast is not on sale, we eat something else. If sugar carries an outrageous price, I put off baking and wait until I find a better price.

Corn, Pepper, and Red Onion Salad

Serves 4

`MEATLESS` `DAIRY-FREE` `GLUTEN-FREE` `MAKE-AHEAD`

This corn salad is a great way to use up an abundance of sweet corn, especially when your dad grows 20 rows of it in the backyard. (Ahem.) You can use frozen corn kernels as well.

4 ears grilled corn (page 152) or 3 cups frozen corn kernels, thawed
1 red bell pepper, seeded and chopped
¼ cup chopped red onion
2 tablespoons apple cider vinegar
1 garlic clove, minced
1 tablespoon chopped fresh basil or 1 teaspoon dried basil
Kosher salt and freshly ground black pepper
¼ cup olive oil

1. Cut the corn kernels away from the cobs. In a large bowl, combine the corn, bell pepper, and onion.

2. In a small jar or bowl, combine the vinegar, garlic, basil, and salt and pepper to taste. Place the lid on the jar and shake well or whisk until smooth. Add the olive oil and shake or whisk again to emulsify.

3. Toss the dressing with the salad mixture.

MAKE IT AHEAD: Prepare the salad mixture and the dressing and store separately in the refrigerator for up to 3 days. Toss before serving.

MENU

Asian Chicken
Salad with Rice
Noodles

___

Ginger-Orange
Crisps

___

Asian foods are some
of our favorites.
Simple, fresh ingre-
dients, uncompli-
cated preparations,
and plenty of flavor
make for healthy and
refreshing meals. For
this pairing, perfect
for casual summer
entertaining, you'll
need to allow some
time for the chicken
to marinate. I like
to marinate it over-
night, cook it early in
the day, and allow it
to chill. Then, enlist
your guests to help
chop the vegetables
while you fry up
the rice sticks. The
resulting salad is
"superyum," as we
say in my house. And
the cookies are a
sweet way to cap off
the meal.

Asian Chicken Salad with Rice Noodles

Serves 4

DAIRY-FREE **GLUTEN-FREE**

This is one of our favorite summer meals. I cook the chicken early
in the day so that it has time to chill. Frying up the rice sticks is fun!
You can pretend you're Michael Keaton in *Mr. Mom* when you cook
Chinese food like a boss.

½ cup reduced-sodium soy sauce
1 tablespoon toasted sesame oil
1 teaspoon minced garlic
¼ teaspoon red pepper flakes
1 pound boneless, skinless chicken breasts or thighs, cut into
    ¼-inch strips
½ (6.75-ounce) package rice sticks
Vegetable oil, for frying the rice sticks
½ head napa cabbage, chopped
2 cups spinach leaves, torn into bite-size pieces
1 cup sliced peeled carrots
1 cup daikon radish matchsticks
½ cup chopped fresh cilantro
½ cup cashews
1 orange, peel and pith removed, sliced
4 scallions, sliced
Honey-Ginger Dressing (page 190)

1. In a small bowl, combine the soy sauce, sesame oil, garlic, and
red pepper flakes.

2. Place the chicken in a zip-top plastic bag or a glass dish with a
lid. Add the marinade and toss to coat. Marinate in the refrigerator
for 4 to 24 hours.

3. Remove the chicken from the marinade and discard the marinade. Cook the chicken in a large skillet over medium-high heat
until cooked through, 10 to 15 minutes, stirring often. Transfer to a
plate to cool.

4. Fry the rice sticks in oil according to the package directions.
Drain on paper towels.

5. In a large salad bowl, combine the cabbage, spinach, carrots, radishes, cilantro, cashews, orange, and scallions. Toss with
enough of the dressing to coat well.

6. Divide the salad among serving plates. Top with the chicken
and rice sticks. Serve extra dressing on the side.

62

LOSS LEADERS ARE YOUR FRIEND

Loss leaders are those very low-priced items that the store knows it will take a loss on. (They're usually listed on the front of the sales circular.) The store doesn't mind taking a loss on those items because they figure you'll spend other money while you're there. Beat them at their own game. Stock up on the loss leaders, but resist the full-price items that you don't need.

honey-ginger dressing

Makes about 1 cup

`MEATLESS` `DAIRY-FREE` `GLUTEN-FREE` `MAKE-AHEAD`

This dressing is fabulous on any salad where you crave a little sweet and spicy at the same time.

½ cup rice vinegar
¼ cup reduced-sodium soy sauce
1 tablespoon honey
1½ teaspoons chopped fresh ginger
1 teaspoon minced garlic
½ teaspoon red pepper flakes
½ cup vegetable oil
2 tablespoons toasted sesame oil

In a small jar or bowl, combine the rice vinegar, soy sauce, honey, ginger, garlic, and red pepper flakes. Place the lid on the jar and shake well or whisk until smooth. Add both oils and shake or whisk again to emulsify. Serve immediately or chill until ready to serve.

MAKE IT AHEAD: Store the dressing in the refrigerator for up to 3 days.

Ginger-Orange Crisps

Makes 3 dozen cookies

MAKE-AHEAD   FREEZER-FRIENDLY

These cookies are like a snickerdoodle turned on its head—what with the ginger instead of the cinnamon, and the lovely scent of orange zest. Yum!

2 cups sugar
1 cup (2 sticks) butter, softened
2 large eggs
1 teaspoon pure vanilla extract
2½ cups unbleached all-purpose flour
2 teaspoons cream of tartar
2 teaspoons ground ginger
1½ teaspoons baking soda
Grated zest of 1 orange
½ teaspoon fine sea salt

1. In a large bowl, cream together 1½ cups of the sugar and the butter until light and fluffy. Add the eggs and vanilla. Beat until well combined, scraping down the sides.

2. Stir in the flour, cream of tartar, 1 teaspoon of the ground ginger, baking soda, orange zest, and salt. Mix well. Cover and chill the dough for 1 hour.

3. Preheat the oven to 400°F. Line two baking sheets with parchment paper or silicone baking mats.

4. In a small bowl, combine the remaining ½ cup sugar and the remaining 1 teaspoon ground ginger.

5. Form the dough into walnut-size balls and roll them in the ginger-sugar mixture. Place on the prepared baking sheets, about 2 inches apart.

6. Bake the cookies until set and very lightly brown, 8 to 10 minutes. Cool on a rack before serving.

MAKE IT AHEAD: Store the cooled cookies in an airtight container at room temperature for up to 3 days or in the freezer for up to 1 month.

MENU

Sherried Black
Bean Tomato
Soup

Easy-Peasy
Popovers

Mixed Berry Pie
with Cinnamon
and Lemon

Soup night can be a
company-worthy af-
fair. Serve this black
bean soup in big
mugs, pass a piping-
hot bread basket
and butter, and dish
up slices of pie at
the end. No one will
know this was a bud-
get dinner. Let's hope
your guests bring a
nice bottle of wine
with them!

Sherried Black Bean Tomato Soup

Makes 10 cups

MEATLESS DAIRY-FREE GLUTEN-FREE MAKE-AHEAD FREEZER-FRIENDLY

Many black bean soups rely on smoky bacon or hot spices for flavor. This one is different (and a bit more elegant) with its accent on tomatoes and sherry.

1 tablespoon vegetable oil
1 cup chopped onion
1 cup chopped celery
1 tablespoon minced garlic
8 cups cooked or canned black beans (rinsed and drained if canned)
4 cups vegetable broth
1 (15-ounce) can tomato sauce
¼ cup dry sherry
1 teaspoon kosher salt
½ teaspoon dried oregano
½ teaspoon dried thyme
⅛ teaspoon freshly ground black pepper

1. In a large stockpot, heat the oil over medium heat until shimmering. Sauté the onion, celery, and garlic until the onion is starting to brown, about 10 minutes. Add the beans, broth, tomato sauce, sherry, salt, oregano, thyme, and pepper. Bring the soup to a low boil and simmer for 20 minutes.

2. Blend the soup to your desired consistency with an immersion blender. Alternatively, you can blend the soup in batches in a food processor or blender. Be sure to vent the lid according to the manufacturer's directions. Adjust the seasonings as desired.

MAKE IT AHEAD: Cool, cover, and store in the refrigerator for up to 3 days or in the freezer for up to 2 months.

Easy-Peasy Popovers

Makes 12 popovers

MEATLESS

I first read about popovers in a 1950s children's book about a girl named Ginnie who entered a cooking contest and won. I always remembered those popovers, so when I grew up I made some myself. My kids devour these! I have to make a double batch so everyone gets their fill. We love them on soup night, but they are also delicious for breakfast when served with butter and jam.

I've healthified these a bit with whole-wheat pastry flour. It might be a little harder to find, but I think it's worth the effort for adding more fiber to delicate baked goods. If you can't find it or it's too pricey, simply use additional all-purpose flour.

3 large eggs
1 cup milk
½ cup water
1 cup unbleached all-purpose flour
½ cup whole-wheat pastry flour
½ teaspoon fine sea salt

1. Preheat the oven to 425°F. Grease a 12-cup muffin pan with nonstick cooking spray.

2. In a large bowl, beat the eggs with a handheld blender until thick and frothy, about 3 minutes. Stir in the milk and water. Beat in the flours and salt until a smooth batter is formed.

3. Divide the batter among the prepared muffin cups, pouring about ¼ cup of the mixture in each.

4. Bake for 20 minutes. Slice a small hole in each with a sharp knife and continue baking for another 10 minutes. Serve warm.

Get to know the
prices of your favor-
ite items. That way,
you'll be able to rec-
ognize a great deal
when you see one.
Buy when the price
is low and store it in
the pantry or freezer
until you need it.

Mixed Berry Pie with Cinnamon and Lemon

Makes 1 (9-inch) pie

FREEZER-FRIENDLY

This berry pie is packed with flavor from top to bottom. The crust is scented with cinnamon and lemon, while the filling is bursting with berries. Grab the frozen berries when they're on sale in order to keep your price point in check. If you want to get fancy, cut the top crust into strips and place them atop the pie in a lattice formation.

2 cups unbleached all-purpose flour
1 cup (2 sticks) plus 2 tablespoons cold butter, cut into cubes
1 teaspoon fine sea salt
1 teaspoon ground cinnamon
Grated zest of 1 lemon
¼ cup cold water
1 cup granulated sugar
¼ cup cornstarch
4 cups frozen mixed berries (raspberries, blackberries, and blueberries; do not thaw)
1 tablespoon freshly squeezed lemon juice
1 tablespoon cream or milk
1 teaspoon turbinado sugar

1. Preheat the oven to 425°F.

2. In a medium-size bowl, combine the flour, 1 cup of the cubed butter, salt, cinnamon, and lemon zest with a pastry blender or two knives. You can also use a food processor fitted with a metal blade. Work these ingredients together until they form pea-size crumbs. Quickly stir in the cold water and combine until a dough forms.

3. Form the dough into 2 round disks. Wrap in plastic wrap and refrigerate for 30 minutes.

4. On a lightly floured surface, roll each disk into a circle about 10 inches in diameter. Fit one into the bottom and up the sides of a 9-inch pie plate.

5. In a large bowl, whisk together the granulated sugar and corn-starch. Add the frozen berries and toss to combine. Sprinkle in the lemon juice and combine well.

6. Spoon the berry mixture into the pie crust and sprinkle any remaining sugar mixture over the top. Dot with the remaining 2 tablespoons butter cubes.

7. Place the top crust over the filling, sealing and crimping the edges. Cut a few slits in the top for steam to escape. Place the dish on a rimmed baking sheet to catch any drips.

8. Brush the top crust with the cream and sprinkle with the turbinado sugar.

9. Bake until the crust is golden and the filling bubbles, 45 to 60 minutes. If the crust begins to brown too much, cover the edges with aluminum foil.

10. Cool completely on a rack before serving.

MAKE IT AHEAD: Once you assemble the pie (but before you cut the venting slits), you can freeze it for baking later. Wrap the pie securely with heavy-duty aluminum foil and freeze for up to 1 month. Unwrap the pie, cut the slits, brush the top with milk and sprinkle with sugar, and bake it frozen until the filling bubbles and the crust is golden, 1 hour to 1 hour and 15 minutes.

MENU

Pot Roast with
Herbed Red
Wine Sauce

Parsleyed New
Potatoes

Deep-Dish
Apple-Cranberry
Pie

A pot roast is a cozy, hearty meal for cold nights, yet it's also impressive enough to serve to guests. This pot roast dinner, followed up by a freshly baked pie, will get you rave reviews and subtle requests to be invited over again.

If you can, save some of the roast, carrots, and potatoes to make a potpie for another meal (see page 206). And when you make the pie crust for the apple-cranberry pie, make the crust to top the potpie at the same time.

Pot Roast with Herbed Red Wine Sauce

Serves 4 to 8

DAIRY-FREE **GLUTEN-FREE** **SLOW COOKER**

Succulent beef and sweet carrots cook in a red wine sauce. If you prefer, you can use reduced-sodium beef broth instead of the wine. It will be equally tasty but with a slightly different flavor.

> 1 tablespoon vegetable oil
> 1 (3-pound) chuck or sirloin tip roast
> Kosher salt and freshly ground black pepper
> ¾ cup dry red wine, such as Merlot or Cabernet Sauvignon
> 1 teaspoon minced garlic
> 1 teaspoon herbes de Provence
> ½ teaspoon dry mustard
> 1 bay leaf
> 6 medium carrots, peeled and halved
> 2 teaspoons balsamic vinegar

1. In a large skillet over medium heat, heat the oil until shimmering. Season the roast generously with salt and pepper. Brown the roast on all sides, 5 to 7 minutes. Transfer the roast to a 6-quart slow cooker.

2. Add the wine, garlic, herbes de Provence, mustard, and bay leaf to the skillet, scraping up any browned bits. Simmer for 1 minute. Transfer this mixture to the slow cooker. Add the carrots.

3. Cover and cook on High for 4 hours or on Low for 6 to 8 hours.

4. Remove the roast and carrots from the cooking liquid. Season to taste with salt and pepper. Tent with foil to keep warm.

5. Meanwhile, remove the bay leaf and turn the slow cooker to High. Let the *jus* reduce slightly, skimming any fat. Stir in the balsamic vinegar. Serve the *jus* alongside the roast and carrots.

64

NO REASON TO WHINE

While wine is certainly a luxury item, it can add great flavor and elegance to our meals. It's important not to let the bottle go to waste. If your group doesn't typically finish a bottle in one sitting—we don't—stop it up and store it in the fridge (whether it's red or white). Use up what's left over the next few days, adding to soups and sauces for a little boost of flavor—and have a glass to sip while you cook!

Parsleyed New Potatoes

Serves 4 to 6

MEATLESS **DAIRY-FREE** **GLUTEN-FREE**

Small or "new" potatoes are elegant and tasty, adding a nice touch to this meal. If you can't find new potatoes or if they are too pricey, substitute regular-size waxy potatoes cut into chunks.

2 pounds new or baby potatoes
2 tablespoons olive oil
1 tablespoon chopped fresh parsley
⅛ teaspoon paprika
Kosher salt and freshly ground black pepper

1. Put the potatoes in a medium-size skillet with a lid and add about 1 inch of water. Cover and cook over medium-high heat until tender, about 25 minutes.
2. Drain the water. Drizzle on the oil and toss to coat. Add the parsley, paprika, and salt and pepper to taste. Serve hot.

Deep-Dish Apple-Cranberry Pie

Makes 1 (9-inch) deep-dish pie

MAKE-AHEAD   FREEZER-FRIENDLY

This pie is a departure from my traditional crumb-topped apple pie. I'd always wondered, why mess with perfection? That is, until I did. This pie, with the tartness from the cranberries offsetting the sweetness of the apples, is a nice twist on a traditional favorite.

1 Versatile Buttery Pie Crust for a double-crust pie (page 37; double the recipe)
7 cups cored and sliced apples, such as Jonathan or Braeburn
1 cup fresh cranberries
1 cup sugar
2 tablespoons unbleached all-purpose flour
1 tablespoon freshly squeezed lemon juice
1 teaspoon ground cinnamon
¼ teaspoon ground nutmeg
2 tablespoons butter, cut into small pieces

1. Preheat the oven to 425°F.

2. Line a 9-inch deep-dish pie pan with 1 pie crust. Chill the crust in the refrigerator while you make the filling.

3. In a large bowl, combine the apples, cranberries, sugar, flour, lemon juice, cinnamon, and nutmeg. Pile this filling into the prepared pie shell. Dot with the butter.

4. Fit the top crust over the filling, sealing and crimping the edges. Cut a few slits in the top for steam to vent. Place the pie plate on a rimmed baking sheet to catch any drips.

5. Bake the pie for 15 minutes. Reduce the oven temperature to 375°F and bake until the crust is browned and the filling bubbles, about 45 minutes more. If the crust begins to brown too much, cover the edges with aluminum foil.

6. Allow the pie to cool a bit before serving. Serve warm or at room temperature.

MAKE IT AHEAD: Once you assemble the pie (but before you cut the venting slits), you can freeze it for baking later. Wrap the pie securely with heavy-duty aluminum foil and freeze for up to 1 month. Unwrap the pie, cut the slits, and bake it frozen until the filling is bubbly and the crust is brown, 1 hour to 1 hour and 15 minutes.

WHAT TO DO WITH LEFTOVERS?

Waste not, want not. That's what our grandmothers used to say, and it still makes sense today. If you use up what you have, you won't find yourself in need. While I am not sure that one *always* follows the other, it is true that avoiding waste is good stewardship and will save you money.

Using up leftover food is a great way to conserve. If your family can consume extra meal items before they go bad, you will avoid throwing money away. It's that simple. And no, *leftover* does not mean *bad*. The USDA says that cooked and properly stored food is good for up to 4 days in the refrigerator. You've got plenty of time to enjoy a meal twice.

Here are some guidelines to using up leftovers:

1. THE FOOD MUST BE FRESH.
Label the container that you're storing in the fridge with the date so that you know your own use-by date.

2. TAKE IT FOR LUNCH.
Save some lunch money by brown-bagging last night's dinner.

3. CHILL OUT.
Freeze the leftover part of the meal to enjoy a different day—next month! As soon as dinner is over, package up meal-size portions, wrap, and label them. Chill well before freezing.

4. HELP LEFTOVERS FIND NEW LIFE.
Lots of delicious meals can be made from a previous meal's components. Leftover veggies and meats can be incorporated into casseroles, omelets, quiches, soups, and stews. They can fill sandwiches, tacos, burritos, or quesadillas. They can be added to fried rice or used to top a pizza. Leftover fruit salad can be blended into a smoothie or chopped and stirred into muffin batter. See page 263 for ideas on "Werewolf Meals" that turn into something new the next night.

Think through what your family likes to eat and chances are you can find a way to make last night's dinner new again.

Make-Ahead Meals

One of the biggest roadblocks that can divert us from our budgeting and healthy eating goals is the desire for instant gratification. We're hungry on the way home from soccer practice, so we grab takeout. We're too tired at the grocery store, so we grab frozen entrées. We can't think of what to make for supper, so we head to a restaurant instead of cooking what we have.

Make-ahead meals fool us into thinking that we're getting instant gratification. We did make them ourselves—this morning or last night or last week. But we're enjoying them when it's more convenient for us not to cook.

All of the main dishes in this chapter can be made in advance, though they vary in the length of advance preparation time. While not every side dish is freezer-friendly or make-ahead, they are all easy enough to prep while you reheat the main dish.

Turkey and Spinach Lasagna with Feta Cheese 202
Herbed Garlic Cornbread 204
Tossed Salad with Mediterranean-Spiced Dressing 205

Beef Potpie with Flaky Cheddar Crust 206
Winter Greens and Citrus Salad 207

Beef Stew with Pumpkin and Hominy 210
Garlic-Parmesan Texas Toast 211
Double-Chocolate Oatmeal Cookies 212

Spready Cheese 213
Dilly Dip for Vegetables and Chips 214
Armchair Quarterback Chili 215

Spiced Hamburgers with Lemon–Blue Cheese Butter 216
Homemade Sourdough Hamburger Buns 218
Seasoned Sweet Potato Oven Fries 219

Easy Shredded Pork Tacos with Two Salsas 220
Roasted Chipotle Salsa 221
Homemade Corn Tortillas 222

No-Egg Spinach Meatballs 223
Herbed Onion Gravy 224
Garlic Mashed Potatoes 225

Grilled Vinaigrette Chicken Fillets 226
Summer Vegetable Kabobs 227
Orzo with Tomatoes and Basil 228

Pasta with Roasted Vegetable Marinara Sauce 229
Buttery Italian Bread Sticks 231
Herb-and-Spice Green Beans 232

MENU

Turkey and
Spinach Lasagna
with Feta Cheese

Herbed Garlic
Cornbread

Tossed Salad with
Mediterranean-
Spiced Dressing

This satisfying meal features the flavors of the Mediterranean. Lasagna and cornbread may appear to be an unlikely pairing, but I've been serving them together for more than 20 years. If you prefer, make the Garlic-Parmesan Texas Toast (page 211) or Cloverleaf Garlic Rolls (page 29) instead.

Turkey and Spinach Lasagna with Feta Cheese

Serves 6 to 8

`MAKE-AHEAD` `FREEZER-FRIENDLY`

Full of lean turkey, flavorful feta, and plenty of vegetables, this lasagna can stand on its own if you don't want to make the suggested cornbread and salad as accompaniments. Make several casseroles at once and store them in the freezer for homemade convenience food.

1½ teaspoons olive oil
12 ounces ground turkey
1 cup chopped onion
½ cup finely chopped button or cremini mushrooms
½ teaspoon minced garlic
1 (8-ounce) can tomato sauce
1 (6-ounce) can tomato paste
¾ cup water
1 teaspoon dried oregano
¼ teaspoon ground cinnamon
¼ teaspoon freshly ground black pepper
1 (10-ounce) package frozen chopped spinach, thawed and drained
1 cup small-curd cottage cheese
1 cup crumbled feta cheese
8 lasagna noodles (uncooked)
1 cup shredded mozzarella cheese

1. Preheat the oven to 375°F. Grease a 9 x 13-inch baking dish with nonstick cooking spray.

2. In a large skillet, heat the oil over medium heat until shimmering. Sauté the turkey, onion, mushrooms, and garlic until the meat is browned and the onions are translucent, about 10 minutes.

3. Add the tomato sauce, tomato paste, water, oregano, cinnamon, and pepper. Cover and simmer for 10 minutes.

4. In a large bowl, combine the spinach, cottage cheese, and feta cheese.

5. Spread half of the meat sauce in the bottom of the prepared baking dish. Lay 4 noodles over the sauce, breaking them to fit as needed.

6. Spread the cheese-spinach filling over the noodles. Lay the remaining 4 noodles over the cheese filling, again breaking to fit as needed.

7. Spread the remaining meat sauce over the noodles and sprinkle on the mozzarella cheese. Cover with aluminum foil.

8. Bake for 35 minutes. Uncover and bake until the filling is hot and bubbly and the cheese is browned in spots, about 10 minutes more.

MAKE IT AHEAD: The unbaked lasagna can be covered and stored in the refrigerator for up to 1 day or in the freezer for up to 2 months. If frozen, thaw completely in the refrigerator before baking. In either case, add 15 minutes to the (covered) baking time since the dish will be cold.

65

I have a favorite shop with clearance sections in every department. I make the circuit around the perimeter, checking for markdowns. Through the aisles, I know which kind of tag to look for that indicates items that are being discontinued. If you're familiar with your store, you'll be more likely to spot the great deals.

Herbed Garlic Cornbread

Serves 4 to 8

`MEATLESS` `MAKE-AHEAD` `FREEZER-FRIENDLY`

This cornbread is more savory than sweet, a nice departure from typical sweet cornbread. Make several bags of the dry ingredients to store in the freezer for cornbread whenever you want it. This cornbread tastes best the same day you bake it.

1½ cups unbleached all-purpose flour
½ cup cornmeal
½ cup sugar
1 tablespoon baking powder
½ teaspoon fine sea salt
¼ cup shredded Parmesan cheese
1 cup milk
2 large eggs
½ cup olive oil
2 garlic cloves, minced
½ teaspoon dried basil
⅛ teaspoon cayenne pepper

1. Preheat the oven to 375°F. Grease an 8-inch square baking dish with nonstick cooking spray.

2. In a large bowl, combine the flour, cornmeal, sugar, baking powder, and salt. Add the shredded cheese and toss to coat.

3. In another bowl, whisk together the milk, eggs, oil, garlic, basil, and cayenne. Add the wet ingredients to the dry ingredients and fold to combine.

4. Spoon the mixture into the prepared baking dish and bake until a tester inserted in the center comes out with a few crumbs attached, about 35 minutes.

MAKE IT AHEAD: Combine the flour, cornmeal, sugar, baking powder, and salt in a zip-top freezer bag. Label the bag with the other ingredients to add as well as the baking directions. Store the bag in the freezer.

Tossed Salad with Mediterranean-Spiced Dressing

Serves 4

MEATLESS DAIRY-FREE GLUTEN-FREE

This simple tossed salad is loaded with flavor thanks to crisp lettuce, juicy tomatoes, rich olives, and a tangy dressing that can be made 4 days ahead of time.

1 head romaine lettuce, torn into bite-size pieces
1 cup grape tomatoes
1 cup pitted black olives
¼ cup red wine vinegar
1 teaspoon Dijon mustard
1 teaspoon Greek Spice Blend (page 81)
⅓ cup olive oil

1. In a large salad bowl, combine the lettuce, tomatoes, and black olives.

2. In a small jar or bowl, combine the vinegar, mustard, and Greek spice blend. Place the lid on the jar and shake well or whisk until smooth. Add the olive oil and shake or whisk again to emulsify.

3. Toss the salad with enough of the dressing to coat. Serve extra dressing at the table.

MAKE IT AHEAD: The salad and dressing can be made and stored separately in the refrigerator for up to 4 days.

Beef Potpie
with Flaky
Cheddar Crust

Winter Greens
and Citrus Salad

When I was a kid,
buying a frozen
potpie was a big
highlight of any trip
to the store. They
were cheap, so Mom
didn't mind toss-
ing them in the cart.
Nowadays, they
contain all kinds of
dubious additives. I
was pleasantly sur-
prised to learn that
I could make a great
potpie at home just
as inexpensively, but
with a boost in flavor
as well as nutrition.
Paired with a refresh-
ingly crisp salad, it
makes the perfect
winter meal and has
become a family
favorite.

Beef Potpie with Flaky Cheddar Crust

Serves 4

MAKE-AHEAD **FREEZER-FRIENDLY**

Instead of a traditional double-crust potpie, this potpie is baked in a 9 x 13-inch pan with a single crust on top. You can use any kind of cooked meat—chicken, turkey, or pork—and its complementary gravy. You can also substitute 3½ cups cooked vegetables of your choice for those specified in the recipe, making this an extremely versatile template recipe.

2 cups cooked beef pot roast, cubed
2 cups Herbed Onion Gravy (page 224)
2 cups diced cooked potatoes
1 cup diced cooked carrots
½ cup frozen petite peas (no need to thaw)
1½ cups unbleached all-purpose flour
¾ cup (1½ sticks) cold butter, cut into cubes
½ cup shredded cheddar cheese
½ teaspoon fine sea salt
¼ teaspoon herbes de Provence
Up to ¼ cup ice water

1. Preheat the oven to 375°F. Grease a 9 x 13-inch baking pan with nonstick cooking spray.

2. In a large bowl, combine the meat, gravy, potatoes, carrots, and peas. Spoon the mixture into the prepared dish.

3. In a food processor fitted with a metal blade, combine the flour, butter, cheese, salt, and herbes de Provence. Pulse until coarse crumbs form, 10 to 15 seconds. With the machine running, add the ice water tablespoon by tablespoon, just until the dough comes together.

4. On a lightly floured surface, roll out the pastry into a 10 x 14-inch rectangle. Fit the pastry over the top of the meat mixture in the baking pan. Tuck the edges inside the edge of the pan. Cut a few slits on top to allow steam to escape.

5. Bake until the crust is browned and the filling is bubbly, 30 to 40 minutes.

MAKE IT AHEAD: The potpie can be wrapped in aluminum foil and frozen (just prior to cutting the venting slits) for up to 1 month. Unwrap the pie, cut the slits, and bake it directly from the freezer as follows: Bake for 15 minutes at 425°F. Reduce the heat to 375°F and continue to bake until the crust is browned and the filling is bubbly, about 30 minutes more.

#66

DO YOUR HOMEWORK FIRST

Scan the ads, check what you already have, and plan your meals. Then, make a grocery list of what you need. Stick to the list, veering off only if you find a great markdown that you know you can use.

Winter Greens and Citrus Salad

Serves 4

MEATLESS **DAIRY-FREE** **GLUTEN-FREE**

This wintry salad makes use of what's available in the cooler months: lettuce, citrus, dried fruit, and seeds. Make the dressing up to a day ahead, if you like. To accommodate my daughter's nut allergies, I often use pumpkin seeds (*pepitas*) as an alternative to nuts in recipes to add crunch without the allergens. If you can't find an economical source for pumpkin seeds, feel free to use your favorite chopped nut, toasted in the oven or a dry skillet for a few minutes.

1 head red leaf lettuce, torn into bite-size pieces
2 oranges, peel and pith removed, sliced
¼ cup dried cranberries
¼ cup toasted pumpkin seeds (*pepitas*)
1 scallion, chopped
¼ cup balsamic vinegar
½ teaspoon minced garlic
½ teaspoon herbes de Provence
⅛ teaspoon freshly ground black pepper, plus more to taste
⅓ cup olive oil
Kosher salt

1. In a large salad bowl, combine the lettuce, orange slices, cranberries, pumpkin seeds, and scallion.

2. In a small jar or bowl, combine the vinegar, garlic, herbes de Provence, and pepper. Place the lid on the jar and shake well or whisk until smooth. Add the olive oil and shake or whisk again to emulsify.

3. Toss the salad with enough of the dressing to coat. Season to taste with salt and more pepper. Serve with the extra dressing on the side.

MAKE IT AHEAD: The salad and dressing can be made and stored separately in the refrigerator for up to 4 days.

STRATEGIES FOR AVOIDING TAKEOUT

As much as I love to cook, I also love to have someone else do the cooking for me. I love coming home from a restaurant with a full belly and seeing a clean kitchen. After a hard day, the siren song of takeout and restaurant meals is hard to resist. Takeout is easy, it's convenient, it's tasty, and there's no mess to clean up.

Yet everyone knows that cooking at home is almost always a better way to spend your money. So how do we ignore the siren's temptation?

1. HAVE A MEAL PLAN.

If you take a few minutes each week to plan meals and shop for them, you're more likely to eat at home. It's as simple as that.

2. JUST EAT SOMETHING.

Every meal does not have to be "an event." I know. It's *me* saying that. But really, if it fills the tummy and satisfies the soul, does it matter if there were three courses? Be sure to eat real food and then call it a meal.

3. CRUNCH THE NUMBERS.

An order of burgers and fries for my family costs about $25, without drinks. It's a great value and good food. However, that same money could make about three meals at our house. Three meals for the price of one?

Every little bit counts toward reaching your financial goals. Be farsighted and make the better choice.

4. USE DISPOSABLES.

I know that *disposable* is a despicable word to use in our culture, but the burger joint uses disposables, too. I'm not advocating their use for every meal, but if it makes the difference between eating a healthier, home-cooked meal and eating expensive restaurant fare, I choose paper plates. We can't have things perfect. So, just shoot for 80 percent. Keep a stock of paper plates and napkins on hand for those desperate time-starved evenings. Cook a great meal and then skip that whole dishwashing gig.

5. PLAN FOR NO-BRAINER MEALS.

Consider stocking a few convenience items that come together for quick meals. While they may not be as good as from-scratch meals, they'll fill the gap when you're tempt-ed to make a run for the border.

6. LEARN TO MAKE YOUR RESTAU-RANT FAVORITES.

It's fair to say that my family would unani-mously agree that the best pizza place in town is our house. Since learning to make pizza at home, we've realized that there's no way that pizzeria pizza is worth the cost. We know we can have an equal or superior meal at home for less money.

There are plenty of take-out favorites that you can re-create yourself. Consider reading *Make the Bread, Buy the Butter,* by Jennifer Reese. I don't agree with every conclusion she reaches, but she gives a great cost and work analysis of your favorite takeout foods.

7. TAKE THE MEAL OUT.

Sometimes it's merely the change of pace or atmosphere that we desire, and not the restaurant's food. Consider packing a picnic and heading somewhere else to eat it. Check out the last chapter, "Meals on the Run," for delicious portable dinners.

8. JUST DESSERTS.

One easy compromise is to eat dinner at home but go out for dessert. We've often done this for special occasions when money was too tight to have a full restaurant meal. We prepare a favorite meal at home and then go out for dessert and coffee, often sharing the dessert.

Above all, be realistic with yourself and with your family. If you can afford eating out, there's no rule that says you can't. But there are a wealth of benefits to be had from eating at home, including money saved, relation-ships nourished, and bodies well fed.

My heart is with homemade. Eat at home when you can. Cook the best that you can afford. And enjoy good food with the people you love.

MENU

Beef Stew with
Pumpkin and
Hominy

Garlic-Parmesan
Texas Toast

Double-
Chocolate
Oatmeal Cookies

This is the perfect
supper for a cold fall
evening. The flavors
all shout "Autumn!"
Everything can be
made in advance and
stored in the freezer,
if you're so inclined.

Beef Stew with Pumpkin and Hominy

Serves 4

`DAIRY-FREE` `GLUTEN-FREE` `SLOW COOKER` `MAKE-AHEAD` `FREEZER-FRIENDLY`

Thinking about this stew makes my mouth water. The pumpkin combines with the Southwest spices for a rich and flavorful broth.

2 tablespoons vegetable oil
1 cup chopped onion
1 pound chuck steak, cubed
2 tablespoons unbleached all-purpose flour
¾ cup beef broth
1 (8-ounce) can tomato sauce
½ cup canned pumpkin puree (not pumpkin pie filling)
2 tablespoons chopped canned green chiles
1 tablespoon chili powder
1 teaspoon ground cumin
1 teaspoon kosher salt
½ teaspoon dried oregano
⅛ teaspoon cayenne pepper
3 cups chopped potatoes, peeled if desired
2 cups thickly sliced peeled carrots
1 cup sliced celery
1 (15-ounce) can hominy, drained

1. In a large skillet, heat 1 tablespoon of the oil over medium heat until shimmering. Add the onion and cook until translucent, 5 to 7 minutes. Transfer to a 5-quart slow cooker.

2. Toss the meat cubes with the flour to coat. Heat the remaining 1 tablespoon oil in the skillet and add the meat cubes. Brown the meat on all sides and transfer to the slow cooker.

3. Deglaze the pan by pouring the broth into the hot pan and scraping up any browned bits. Add the tomato sauce, pumpkin puree, green chiles, chili powder, cumin, salt, oregano, and cayenne. Stir until well blended. Add this mixture to the slow cooker along with the potatoes, carrots, celery, and hominy. Stir gently to coat.

4. Cook on High for 4 hours or on Low for 6 to 8 hours.

MAKE IT AHEAD: Store the cooled stew in an airtight container in the refrigerator for up to 4 days or in the freezer for up to 1 month. Thaw completely in the refrigerator before reheating.

67

Fresh herbs add
an elegant and
aromatic touch
to many dishes.
The small packets
of fresh herbs in
the produce sec-
tion of the grocery
store, however, are
pretty pricey for the
amount that you get.
For the same price,
you can buy a potted
herb that will keep
on giving long after
you've prepared that
first recipe. Potted
herbs grow well in a
lighted window and
will give you fresh
flavors all year long.

Garlic-Parmesan Texas Toast

Makes 8 slices

MEATLESS **MAKE-AHEAD** **FREEZER-FRIENDLY**

Commercially frozen Texas toast is undeniably tasty, but it's far
healthier and more cost-effective to make your own. I bet you'll find
it more delicious as well.

½ loaf "Texas toast" bread (8 thick slices), thick-sliced white sand-
    wich bread, or 2 sub rolls, split lengthwise
4 tablespoons (½ stick) butter, softened
¼ cup shredded Parmesan cheese
½ teaspoon minced garlic
1½ teaspoons chopped fresh parsley or ½ teaspoon dried parsley
Pinch of cayenne pepper

1. Preheat the broiler. Lay out the bread slices on a baking sheet.
2. In a small bowl, combine the butter, Parmesan, garlic, parsley,
and cayenne. Spread the butter in a thick layer over the surface of
each bread slice.
3. Broil until golden, 3 to 5 minutes.

MAKE IT AHEAD: Place the baking sheet of buttered bread in the freezer until
the butter is solid. (That way they won't stick together when stacked.) Stack the
frozen buttered bread and wrap with foil. Store in the freezer for up to 1 month.
When ready to serve, place the frozen slices on a baking sheet. Allow to thaw at
room temperature before broiling.

#68

SET A BUDGET

Having a budget was a top strategy for us to get out of debt. We allocated every dollar, including those that would be assigned to feeding us. It was hard to gauge at first; we were so used to just spending. Over time we've settled on a monthly goal. The USDA issues a monthly report of average food costs nationwide and divides this into thrifty, low-cost, moderate-cost, and liberal spending categories. This is a good starting point if you're not sure what number to shoot for. Keep in mind that most frugal folks I know are able to get their spending well below even the thrifty plan estimated costs. So can you!

Double-Chocolate Oatmeal Cookies

Makes 3 to 4 dozen cookies

`MAKE-AHEAD` `FREEZER-FRIENDLY`

These double-chocolate cookies are full of fiber thanks to the oats and full of flavor thanks to two kinds of chocolate. They get a little south-of-the-border kick from the cinnamon and cayenne pepper.

    1 cup light brown sugar
    ¾ cup (1½ sticks) butter
    2 large eggs
    2 teaspoons pure vanilla extract
    2 cups unbleached all-purpose flour
    1¾ cups rolled oats
    ½ cup unsweetened cocoa powder
    1½ teaspoons baking powder
    ½ teaspoon fine sea salt
    ⅛ teaspoon ground cinnamon
    ⅛ teaspoon cayenne pepper
    1 cup semisweet or bittersweet chocolate chips

1. Preheat the oven to 375°F. Line two baking sheets with parchment paper or silicone baking mats.

2. In a large bowl, cream together the brown sugar and butter. Add the eggs and vanilla and beat until well combined. Stir in the flour, oats, cocoa powder, baking powder, salt, cinnamon, and cayenne. Stir in the chocolate chips.

3. Form the dough into rounded tablespoons and place the dough balls 2 inches apart on the prepared baking sheets. Flatten each ball with a wet glass.

4. Bake until set, 8 to 10 minutes. Cool on a rack.

MAKE IT AHEAD: Store the cooled cookies in an airtight container at room temperature for up to 5 days or in the freezer for up to 1 month.

MENU

Spready Cheese

Dilly Dip for
Vegetables and
Chips

Armchair
Quarterback
Chili

Ready for a tailgate
party? This menu is
perfect for game day.
Prep the Spready
Cheese, homemade
dip, and veggie tray
the night before.
Get the slow cooker
going with the fra-
grant chili. You're all
set to relax and play
armchair quarter-
back.

Spready Cheese

Serves 4 to 8

`MEATLESS` `GLUTEN-FREE` `MAKE-AHEAD`

For years I paid a high price for soft herbed cheese from the deli.
Finally I started experimenting to make my own, and I easily cut the
price in half. This goes great on any variety of crackers, bagels, and
sandwiches.

8 ounces Neufchâtel cheese, softened
2 tablespoons grated Parmesan cheese
1 teaspoon minced garlic
¼ teaspoon dried basil
¼ teaspoon dried oregano
¼ teaspoon dried thyme
¼ teaspoon dried dill
¼ teaspoon dried tarragon
¼ teaspoon rubbed sage
¼ teaspoon kosher salt
⅛ teaspoon ground marjoram
⅛ teaspoon freshly ground black pepper
Pinch of paprika

Combine all of the ingredients in a food processor fitted with a
metal blade. Blend until smooth.

MAKE IT AHEAD: Store in an airtight container in the refrigerator for up to 4 days.

Dilly Dip for Vegetables and Chips

Makes 1 cup

MEATLESS GLUTEN-FREE MAKE-AHEAD

My 9-year-old begs me to make this dip. It's healthier and tastier than the one I used to love at his age, which was made from a dry, overly salted mix packet. For an extra health boost, make it with Greek yogurt instead of sour cream. This dip goes with practically any veggie dippers or crisp chips.

1 cup sour cream
1 tablespoon dried onion flakes
1 teaspoon dried dill
1 teaspoon minced garlic
½ teaspoon kosher salt
½ teaspoon paprika
⅛ teaspoon freshly ground black pepper

In a small bowl, combine all of the ingredients, stirring well.

MAKE IT AHEAD: Store in an airtight container in the refrigerator for up to 4 days.

70

Have a plan for
leftovers like cooked
vegetables, meats,
and cheeses. Little
bits that might not
be big enough for
a single portion
can add flavor and
texture to soups,
stir-fries, fried rice,
quesadillas, omelets,
and savory crepes.

Seasoned Sweet Potato Oven Fries

Serves 4

`MEATLESS` `DAIRY-FREE` `GLUTEN-FREE`

These fries have made sweet potato fans out of some kiddos I
know. FishBoy 17 makes this recipe on a weekly basis. Seasoned
and baked in the oven, they are a delicious side dish for burgers,
grilled meats, or anything, really. Leftovers are great served with
eggs the next morning.

1 tablespoon kosher salt
1 teaspoon paprika
1 teaspoon dried thyme
1 teaspoon garlic powder
1 teaspoon onion powder
Freshly ground black pepper to taste
1½ pounds sweet potatoes, peeled and cut into ½-inch batons
½ cup olive oil

1. Preheat the oven to 400°F. Line a rimmed baking sheet with
parchment paper.

2. In a small bowl, combine the salt, paprika, thyme, garlic powder, onion powder, and black pepper.

3. In a large bowl, combine the potatoes and olive oil, tossing to
coat. Season generously with the spice mix.

4. Spread the potatoes on the prepared baking sheet and bake
until tender and lightly browned, 20 to 30 minutes, turning once.

MENU

Easy Shredded
Pork Tacos with
Two Salsas

Roasted Chipotle
Salsa

Homemade Corn
Tortillas

Taco night comes
together in a very
tasty way with this
slow-cooked pork
filling, chipotle salsa,
and homemade corn
tortillas. Make the
salsa up to 3 days
ahead of time. The
pork filling cooks in
the slow cooker, but
it can be made in ad-
vance and frozen if
you prefer. The corn
tortillas can be made
several hours in ad-
vance and reheated
before serving.

Easy Shredded Pork Tacos with Two Salsas

Serves 4

`DAIRY-FREE` `GLUTEN-FREE` `SLOW COOKER` `MAKE-AHEAD` `FREEZER-FRIENDLY`

This shredded pork filling is effortless to create and full of flavor.

1 (2-pound) boneless pork shoulder roast or country strips
½ cup salsa verde (I like Trader Joe's.)
½ cup chopped onion, plus extra for taco assembly
1 tablespoon Mexican Spice Blend (page 81)
Homemade Corn Tortillas (page 222)
Shredded cabbage or lettuce
Chopped fresh cilantro
Roasted Chipotle Salsa (recipe follows)

1. Place the pork in a 4-quart slow cooker. Add the salsa verde, ½ cup chopped onion, and Mexican spice blend. Cook on High for 4 hours or on Low for 6 to 8 hours.

2. Shred the meat using two forks and stir the meat back into the drippings.

3. Assemble the tacos with the tortillas, meat, shredded cabbage, reserved chopped onion, chopped cilantro, and chipotle salsa.

MAKE IT AHEAD: Combine the uncooked pork, salsa verde, onion, and season-ing in a zip-top plastic bag and freeze for up to 1 month. Thaw completely in the refrigerator overnight before cooking in the slow cooker. Alternatively, you can cool the cooked, shredded meat (and all the drippings) and store in an airtight container in the refrigerator for up to 2 days or in the freezer for up to 1 month. Thaw in the refrigerator before reheating in the microwave or on the stovetop.

71

Have a conversation with your butcher. It's possible that there are discounts to be had just for the asking. Discuss with the butcher when he marks things for quick sale, if he offers bulk discounts, or what other options he has for folks shopping on a budget.

Roasted Chipotle Salsa

Makes 2 cups

`MEATLESS` `DAIRY-FREE` `GLUTEN-FREE` `MAKE-AHEAD`

Homemade salsa comes together quickly in a blender or food processor. The chipotle chile gives it a smoky flavor. Wrap leftover chipotles from the can individually in plastic wrap and store in the freezer.

1 (14.5-ounce) can fire-roasted diced tomatoes with green chiles, drained
½ cup fresh cilantro leaves
1 teaspoon minced garlic
1 canned chipotle chile in adobo sauce
Juice of 1 lime
Kosher salt and freshly ground black pepper

In a food processor fitted with a metal blade, combine the tomatoes, cilantro, garlic, chipotle, and lime juice. Pulse until well combined but still chunky. Season to taste with salt and pepper.

MAKE IT AHEAD: Store in an airtight container in the refrigerator for up to 4 days.

Homemade Corn Tortillas

Makes 16 to 20 tortillas

`MEATLESS` `DAIRY-FREE` `GLUTEN-FREE`

One day while we were dating, Bryan decided he would teach himself how to make tortillas. Persevering through trial and error, he has become a master at making great tortillas. I can make them, too, but he is by far the better tortilla maker. Our girls, aged 5 and 7, join him each time as part of the Tortilla Team. It may seem like overkill to make your own tortillas, but trust me: These are wonderful, and once you get the hang of it, you'll be pleasantly surprised at how easy it is to do. You may even be inspired to purchase an inexpensive tortilla press!

2 cups instant corn masa flour (I use Maseca.)
¼ teaspoon fine sea salt
2 cups warm water, or as needed

1. In a large bowl, combine the corn masa flour and salt. Stir in up to 2 cups of warm water until a soft dough forms. (The instructions on the bag of corn masa flour call for less water, but we prefer the texture when more water is added, so experiment to see what you like best.)

2. Roll the dough into golf ball–size balls and place on a baking sheet. Once all the dough is rolled into balls, cover the sheet with a damp paper towel. If you have enough helpers, you can press the tortillas while someone else rolls the balls, in assembly-line fashion.

3. Heat a griddle over medium heat and start pressing your tortillas in a tortilla press or between two plates. The tortillas should be 4 to 5 inches in diameter. We use a cut zip-top plastic bag to line the tortilla press since the dough has a tendency to stick to the press something fierce. You can also use waxed paper or parchment paper if you prefer.

4. As you press each ball into a tortilla, lay it on the hot griddle. Cook for 50 seconds on one side and then flip. Cook for another 50 seconds. The tortilla will puff up and then collapse during baking time and be lightly browned in spots. Remove from the griddle and cover them with a cloth towel to keep warm. These are best enjoyed the day they are made.

MENU

No-Egg Spinach
Meatballs

Herbed Onion
Gravy

Garlic Mashed
Potatoes

Meatballs and
gravy over garlicky
mashed potatoes just
might be my kids'
favorite things to
eat. There are never
any leftovers. All
components of this
meal can be made
in advance, cooled,
wrapped, and frozen
to enjoy later, mak-
ing it a great stand-
by meal.

No-Egg Spinach Meatballs

Makes 24 meatballs

`DAIRY-FREE` `MAKE-AHEAD` `FREEZER-FRIENDLY`

We've struggled with food allergies over the years, prompting me to experiment with a number of different combinations of ingredients. These meatballs are egg-free and absolutely delicious. They go beautifully with the onion gravy, but they're just as tasty with marinara sauce or barbecue sauce.

1 pound ground beef
1 cup fresh bread crumbs
1 cup finely chopped fresh spinach
¼ cup milk
¾ teaspoon kosher salt
½ teaspoon dried oregano
½ teaspoon dried thyme
½ teaspoon sweet paprika
⅛ teaspoon cayenne pepper
⅛ teaspoon freshly ground black pepper

1. Preheat the oven to 350°F. Line two rimmed baking sheets with heavy-duty aluminum foil. Spray the foil lightly with nonstick cooking spray.

2. In a large bowl, mix all of the ingredients just until everything is evenly distributed. Don't overmix, as that will make your meatballs tough.

3. Form the mixture into golf ball–size balls and place the meatballs on the prepared baking sheets. Bake the meatballs until they are cooked through, about 15 minutes.

MAKE IT AHEAD: Store the cooked and cooled meatballs in an airtight container in the refrigerator for up to 2 days or in the freezer for up to 1 month. If frozen, thaw the meatballs in the refrigerator, then reheat them in your choice of sauce on the stovetop.

Herbed Onion Gravy

Makes 2 cups

`MEATLESS` `MAKE-AHEAD` `FREEZER-FRIENDLY`

Besides the meatballs, this fragrant sauce is great over grilled or roasted meats, atop mashed potatoes or rice, or added to the filling for a potpie.

4 tablespoons (½ stick) butter
1 cup finely chopped onion
1 teaspoon minced garlic
¼ cup unbleached all-purpose flour
1¾ cups beef broth
¼ cup dry sherry
1 tablespoon chopped fresh parsley
1 teaspoon dried thyme
½ teaspoon dried tarragon
Freshly ground black pepper to taste

1. Melt the butter in a medium-size saucepan over medium heat. Add the onion and garlic. Cook until the onion has turned translucent, about 5 minutes. Add the flour and cook for 2 more minutes, stirring.

2. Slowly add the beef broth and sherry, stirring constantly. Add the parsley, thyme, tarragon, and pepper. Simmer until thickened.

MAKE IT AHEAD: Store the cooled gravy in an airtight container in the refrigerator for up to 3 days or in the freezer for up to 1 month.

72

CASH IT IN

If you set a grocery budget each month or week, pull that amount from the bank in cash and keep it in an envelope designated for grocery spending. Take a calculator shopping with you, if need be, but keep your spending to only what you can pay for with what's in the envelope. As you see the green stuff start to disappear, your brain will realize you're hitting your limit. Adjust your spending accordingly. Debit and credit cards deceive us into thinking we're not spending as much as we are. Cash never lies.

Garlic Mashed Potatoes

Serves 4

`MEATLESS` `GLUTEN-FREE` `MAKE-AHEAD`

Roasted garlic is a cheap and easy way to add tremendous flavor to any number of dishes. Here potatoes get an extra lift from the golden, caramelized garlic nuggets.

3 pounds medium russet potatoes, peeled and quartered
6 cloves roasted garlic (page 26)
4 tablespoons (½ stick) butter
1 cup hot milk
1 teaspoon kosher salt
Freshly ground black pepper to taste

1. Bring a large pot of salted water to a boil over high heat. Cook the potatoes until very tender when pierced with a fork, about 25 minutes. Drain the potatoes and transfer them to a large bowl.

2. Add the garlic cloves and mash the two together until the potatoes are smooth and the garlic is broken up a bit.

3. Add the butter and stir to combine. Stir in the milk, salt, and pepper. Mix well. Adjust the seasonings as desired and serve hot.

MAKE IT AHEAD: Cool the finished potatoes and transfer to a baking dish with a lid. Refrigerate for up to 3 days. When ready to serve, preheat the oven to 375°F. Bake the mashed potatoes, covered, until hot, about 30 minutes. Stir the potatoes before serving. Alternatively, reheat the potatoes in a saucepan with a bit of added milk to moisten and prevent sticking.

MENU

Grilled
Vinaigrette
Chicken Fillets

Summer
Vegetable
Kabobs

Orzo with
Tomatoes and
Basil

This is a perfect meal for summer. The chicken cooks quickly on the grill alongside the vegetable kabobs, while the pilaf cooks on the stove. Everything can be made in advance and served warm, at room temperature, or chilled.

Grilled Vinaigrette Chicken Fillets

Serves 4

DAIRY-FREE **GLUTEN-FREE** **MAKE-AHEAD** **FREEZER-FRIENDLY**

Marinated chicken is one of my favorite freezer meals. It's so simple to assemble trimmed chicken breasts and marinade in zip-top plastic bags and stash them in the freezer. The chicken marinates as it thaws on the day of serving.

½ cup white wine vinegar
1 teaspoon minced garlic
1 teaspoon dried thyme
½ teaspoon fine sea salt
¼ teaspoon freshly ground black pepper
¼ teaspoon paprika
⅓ cup olive oil
1 pound boneless, skinless chicken breast fillets

1. In a small jar or bowl, combine the vinegar, garlic, thyme, salt, pepper, and paprika. Place the lid on the jar and shake well or whisk until smooth. Add the oil and shake or whisk to emulsify.

2. Place the chicken pieces in a zip-top plastic bag or a glass dish with a lid. Pour the marinade over the chicken and turn to coat. Marinate in the refrigerator for 2 to 24 hours.

3. Prepare a hot fire in a charcoal or gas grill, or preheat the oven to 350°F. Grill the chicken pieces, turning once, until cooked through, about 20 minutes, or bake in a 9 x 13-inch baking dish for 30 to 40 minutes. The chicken is done when it reaches an internal temperature of 165°F.

MAKE IT AHEAD: Store the bag containing the chicken and marinade in the freezer for up to 2 months. Thaw the chicken completely in the refrigerator before grilling; it will marinate as it thaws. Alternatively, the cooled cooked chicken can be wrapped and stored in the refrigerator for up to 3 days or in the freezer for up to 1 month. If frozen, thaw in the refrigerator; reheat the chicken in the microwave if desired.

Summer Vegetable Kabobs

Serves 4

MEATLESS **DAIRY-FREE** **GLUTEN-FREE** **MAKE-AHEAD**

Even if my kids don't love all the vegetables involved, they still get excited about vegetables served on a stick. Mix and match the vegetables as you like. These make a festive addition to any grilled supper.

8 small button or cremini mushrooms
8 grape or cherry tomatoes
2 baby zucchini, cut into 1-inch chunks
1 medium bell pepper (any color), cut into squares
1 small red onion, cut into chunks
1 tablespoon olive oil
1 tablespoon white wine vinegar
1 teaspoon Dijon mustard
Kosher salt and freshly ground black pepper

1. Prepare a hot fire in a charcoal or gas grill.

2. Thread the vegetables on metal or soaked bamboo skewers, alternating and mixing up the order.

3. In a small bowl, combine the oil, vinegar, mustard, and salt and pepper to taste. Brush the vegetables with this mixture.

4. Grill the skewers until tender, 7 to 10 minutes, turning once.

MAKE IT AHEAD: Refrigerate the cooked skewers for up to 2 days. Let come to room temperature before serving.

73

SURF'S UP

Online grocery shopping can save you money. Large websites like Amazon ship groceries, often free of tax or shipping costs. Watch for deals and have the groceries brought to your door. If you agree to a regular delivery (every 1 to 6 months), you can get even lower pricing. (The same goes for household items. I have a regular shipment of toilet paper delivered so that I never worry about running out.)

Orzo with Tomatoes and Basil

Serves 4

MEATLESS DAIRY-FREE MAKE-AHEAD

Orzo is a type of pasta that resembles rice. It's often cooked into pilafs or turned into salads. Serve this dish hot, at room temperature, or chilled—it's good all ways.

1 cup orzo
2 tablespoons olive oil
2 garlic cloves, minced
2 teaspoons Greek Spice Blend (page 81)
Kosher salt and freshly ground black pepper
1 cup diced tomato
¼ cup chopped fresh basil

1. Bring a large pot of salted water to a boil over high heat. Cook the orzo according to the package directions. Drain well.

2. Place the hot pasta in a serving bowl and toss with the olive oil and garlic. Season with the Greek spice blend, and then with salt and pepper to taste. Gently fold in the tomatoes and basil.

MAKE IT AHEAD: Store the prepared orzo in an airtight container in the refrigerator for up to 2 days.

MENU

Pasta with
Roasted
Vegetable
Marinara Sauce

Buttery Italian
Bread Sticks

Herb-and-Spice
Green Beans

Pasta with red sauce, green beans, and warm bread has been a staple meal in our family forever. Kids of all ages love it. It's easy to pull together and affordable, making it a go-to meal any time of year.

Pasta with Roasted Vegetable Marinara Sauce

Serves 4 (makes 6 cups sauce)

MEATLESS   DAIRY-FREE   MAKE-AHEAD   FREEZER-FRIENDLY

As a college student and a young newlywed, I thought all pasta sauce came from a jar. It was surprising—and freeing!—to find out this wasn't true. Once I started making my own pasta sauce, there was no looking back. The money we saved by making a bulk batch was matched by the enjoyment we received from a flavorful, home-cooked sauce that wasn't overly sweet or salty.

This recipe makes a fairly large batch of sauce, making it a perfect candidate for freezing. Even if you're serving pasta for four people, you will use only half of the sauce. So put aside 3 cups so that you can make the Meaty Lasagna with Asiago Béchamel (page 158) another time.

ROASTED VEGETABLE MARINARA SAUCE
2 pattypan squash, trimmed and halved lengthwise
1 large zucchini, trimmed and halved lengthwise
1 medium eggplant, trimmed and halved lengthwise
4 garlic cloves, unpeeled
2 tablespoons olive oil
Kosher salt and freshly ground black pepper
1 (28-ounce) can crushed tomatoes
1 cup water
1 teaspoon dried basil
1 teaspoon dried oregano
1 teaspoon dried thyme
1 teaspoon dried parsley
⅛ teaspoon red pepper flakes
1 bay leaf

1 pound pasta of your choice

1. Preheat the oven to 400°F. On a large rimmed baking sheet, lay out the pattypan squash, zucchini, eggplant, and garlic. Brush with the olive oil and season generously with salt and pepper. Roast for 45 minutes.

2. Place the roasted squashes in a large stockpot. Scoop out the flesh of the eggplant and add that to the pot. Squeeze the garlic from its skins and add that to the pot, as well as the tomatoes, water, basil, oregano, thyme, parsley, red pepper, and bay leaf. Simmer for 20 minutes, covered but with the lid slightly ajar.

#74

CHILL OUT

Take up freezer cooking. By preparing several batches of an item, like pasta sauce, you benefit from bulk buying and bulk use of energy sources (both yours and the gas/electric company). A #10 can (108 ounces) of crushed tomatoes costs less than three bucks. Add some spices and you've got 10 dinners' worth of pasta sauce for about 50 cents a night. Plus, your homemade sauce tastes better than the jarred varieties.

3. Meanwhile, bring a large pot of salted water to a boil over high heat for the pasta.

4. Remove the bay leaf from the sauce and blend the mixture with an immersion blender until smooth. Alternatively, you can blend the mixture in batches in a food processor fitted with a metal blade or a blender. Be sure to vent the lid according to the manufacturer's directions.

5. Cook the pasta in the boiling water according to the package directions and serve with the sauce ladled over the top.

MAKE IT AHEAD: Cool the sauce and divide into portions as desired. Store in the refrigerator for up to 3 days or in the freezer for up to 2 months.

SAVE A BUNDLE THROUGH BULK BUYING

My local health food store has massive bins and dispensers of bulk foods, including nuts, flours, and grains. Typically I get the very best prices on oats and rice from these bins, as low as 69 cents per pound, which is a whopping savings compared with their name-brand packaged counterparts. Be sure to compare unit pricing to ensure that the bulk product is really the better deal. Store your bulk purchases appropriately in airtight containers so that you don't lose your investment to spoilage or insects.

Buttery Italian Bread Sticks

Makes 8 bread sticks

MEATLESS **MAKE-AHEAD** **FREEZER-FRIENDLY**

My kids used to love going to a family-style Italian restaurant near our home, where diners were offered unlimited bread sticks coated in butter and garlic. The restaurant has since gone out of business, but that doesn't mean we can't enjoy that same buttery goodness at home.

¾ cup water
4 tablespoons (½ stick) butter
2 cups unbleached all-purpose flour
1 tablespoon sugar
1½ teaspoons fine sea salt
1 teaspoon garlic powder
½ teaspoon dried Italian herb blend
1½ teaspoons active dry yeast
½ teaspoon minced garlic

1. Combine the water, 2 tablespoons of the butter, flour, sugar, salt, garlic powder, dried herbs, and yeast in the pan of your bread machine according to the manufacturer's directions. Set on the dough cycle and start the machine. (If making the dough by hand: Combine the water and 2 tablespoons butter in a small saucepan and warm slightly over medium heat. Transfer the mixture to a large bowl and add the sugar and yeast. Stir and allow the yeast to proof for 5 minutes. Add the flour, salt, garlic powder, and herbs. Stir to combine well. Turn the mixture out onto a lightly floured surface and knead for 5 minutes to create a smooth, elastic dough, adding more flour as necessary. Transfer to a greased bowl and turn the dough ball to coat. Allow to rise until doubled in bulk, about 1 hour.)

2. Meanwhile, preheat the oven to 400°F. Line a baking sheet with parchment paper or a silicone baking mat.

3. When the machine beeps or the dough has doubled in bulk, remove the dough from the pan or bowl and divide it into 8 equal pieces. Roll each piece into a 6-inch-long log and place a couple of inches apart on the prepared baking sheet.

4. Bake until golden brown, about 12 minutes.

5. Melt the remaining 2 tablespoons butter and stir in the minced garlic. While the bread sticks are still warm, brush the sticks with the garlic-butter mixture.

MAKE IT AHEAD: Bake the bread sticks and cool on a wire rack. Wrap and store at room temperature for up to 2 days or in the freezer for up to 1 month. When ready to serve, warm the bread sticks in a 350°F oven for about 5 minutes, and then brush on the garlic-butter mixture.

Surplus of fresh
herbs on hand? It's
a good problem to
have. Blend the herbs
with softened butter
and garlic to make
a compound butter
to serve on tonight's
steamed vegetables
or cooked meats, or
spread it on fresh
bread to broil in the
oven. Freeze the but-
ter to use later in the
month if you don't
have a use for it right
away.

Herb-and-Spice Green Beans

Serves 4 to 6

MEATLESS **DAIRY-FREE** **GLUTEN-FREE**

Each summer we get loads of green beans in our weekly produce
box. Often, I trim and blanch these for freezing so that we can enjoy
them throughout the year. You can use either fresh or frozen green
beans for this recipe.

4 cups green beans, trimmed
1 tablespoon olive oil
1 tablespoon minced garlic
1 tablespoon chopped fresh parsley
⅛ teaspoon dried dill
⅛ teaspoon dried thyme
⅛ teaspoon paprika
Kosher salt and freshly ground black pepper

1. In a large saucepan or skillet with a lid, steam the green beans
in 1 inch of water over medium-high heat until tender, about 10 minutes. Drain the beans and return them to the pan.

2. Place the pan over low heat. Add the oil, garlic, and parsley to
the pan and toss to combine. Add the dill, thyme, and paprika and
toss well. Season the beans to taste with salt and pepper.

TIPS FOR FREEZING

Preparing foods in bulk and freezing them in meal-size portions to enjoy later is a great way to save on food costs. You reap the benefits of bulk buying and getting a lower unit price on certain ingredients as well as bulk cooking, since you turn on the stove only once instead of several times. Not only that, but you also ensure that you've got a back-up plan for dinner that doesn't include a visit to the drive-thru.

Learning a few basics about freezing food will help you maximize your enjoyment on the other side of thawing.

- Never put hot food in the freezer. It will take too long to cool and will raise the overall temperature of your freezer, compromising other frozen items and allowing bacteria to grow at a rapid rate. Let the hot food stand on the counter until steam stops rising from it, then transfer it to the refrigerator to chill before freezing.

- Chill the food completely before freezing. You want your food items to freeze quickly, which reduces their chances of forming large ice crystals or developing freezer burn. Place it in the refrigerator for a few hours or overnight so that it has a chance to get cold all the way through before transferring it to the freezer.

- Label well. It's amazing how things change appearance when frozen. You don't want to confuse chocolate ice cream with beef gravy. Be sure to label each package with the date prepared, the name of the recipe, and the final preparation instructions so that you don't need to scramble for the recipe on the day of serving.

- Use it or lose it. While frozen food will keep indefinitely under a temperature of 0°F, very few home freezers maintain such a steady temperature. Keep a freezer inventory of what you have and use it up, ideally within 2 to 3 months for best taste and texture.

- Learn more about being freezer-friendly. My book *Not Your Mother's Make-Ahead and Freeze Cookbook* gives the complete 411 on how to cook and freeze foods to enjoy later, as well as more than 200 recipes.

Breakfast for Supper

Find yourself without a meal plan for supper? Or things didn't go the way you planned? No worries. Breakfast, particularly one that's home-cooked, makes a fabulous, quick dinner that is especially comforting after a hard day.

Breakfast foods are a fabulous option for good cheap eats. They generally feature eggs and an inexpensive protein, as well as a variety of baked goods and fruits and sometimes vegetables. My family breaks out in song and dance whenever we have breakfast for supper.

Mexican Oven Omelet 236
Easy Skillet Home Fries 238
Maple-Drizzled Fruit Salad 239

Spiced Vanilla Granola 240
Mango-Pineapple Breakfast Salsa 241

Poblano Chile Scramble 243
Chocolate-Pear Scones 244

Skillet Poached Eggs with Spinach 246
Oaty Maple Breakfast Cake 248
Monkey Salad 249

Yogurt-Cornmeal Pancakes 250
Turkey-Apple Sausage Patties 251
Spiced Vanilla Syrup 252

Chile and Corn Tortilla Egg Bake 253
Oven Hash Browns 254
Fun Fruit Kabobs 255

Coconut-Ginger Granola 256
Spiced Piña Colada Smoothies 257

Almond French Toast 258
Brown Sugar–Pear Compote 259
Malted Hot Cocoa Mix 260

Frittata with Sausage and Vegetables 261
Cucumber Salad with Scallion-Lime Dressing 262

MENU

Mexican Oven
Omelet

Easy Skillet
Home Fries

Maple-Drizzled
Fruit Salad

Our first date was breakfast at a little diner in Santa Barbara called Pavlakos. Bryan still waxes eloquent over their Mexican omelet, which I re-created in the form of an oven omelet. It's very much a make-ahead dish, which frees you to whip up home fries and a fancy fruit salad.

Mexican Oven Omelet

Serves 4

GLUTEN-FREE **MAKE-AHEAD**

Slide this flavor-packed omelet into the oven while you sip your first cup of morning java. To make the prep work even easier, make this the morning after taco night and use 1 cup of leftover taco meat.

2 cups chopped fresh spinach
4 ounces ground beef
½ cup chopped onion
¼ cup chopped red pepper
2 tablespoons chopped seeded jalapeños
6 large eggs
¼ teaspoon ground cumin
¼ teaspoon fine sea salt
⅛ teaspoon freshly ground black pepper
1 cup shredded cheddar cheese
¼ cup sliced black olives

1. Preheat the oven to 400°F. Grease a 9-inch pie plate with non-stick cooking spray.

2. Spray a large skillet with nonstick cooking spray. Sauté the spinach over medium heat until wilted, about 3 minutes. Transfer to the prepared pie plate.

3. Add the beef, onion, peppers, and jalapeños to the skillet and cook until the meat is browned and the onion has turned translucent, 10 to 15 minutes. Drain off the fat, and sprinkle this mixture over the spinach in the pan.

4. In a large bowl, beat the eggs; add the cumin, salt, and pepper. Pour into the pie plate. Top with the cheese, and sprinkle the olives evenly over the top.

5. Bake until puffy and golden, 15 to 20 minutes.

MAKE IT AHEAD: Prepare the dish through step 3. Cover and refrigerate overnight. In the morning, preheat the oven and proceed with step 4.

Easy Skillet Home Fries

Serves 4

MEATLESS **DAIRY-FREE** **GLUTEN-FREE**

Home fries are delicious and filling, giving you energy to take on the day. These are a tasty side dish for any meal just begging for potatoes.

¼ cup vegetable oil
1 cup chopped onion
2 pounds russet potatoes, peeled and cubed
1 garlic clove, minced
1 tablespoon chopped fresh parsley or 1 teaspoon dried parsley
1 teaspoon kosher salt
½ teaspoon sweet paprika
¼ teaspoon freshly ground black pepper
¼ teaspoon dried thyme
Pinch of cayenne pepper

1. In a large nonstick skillet with a lid, heat the oil over medium heat until shimmering. Add the onion and cook for 5 minutes.

2. Add the potatoes and garlic and increase the heat to high. Toss to coat. Add the parsley, salt, paprika, black pepper, thyme, and cayenne and toss again. Cover the pan and lower the heat to medium-low. Cook for 30 minutes, stirring once.

3. Uncover the pan and cook for 5 minutes more to crisp up the potatoes.

A special trip to the store for one item for supper often results in a bagful of unnecessary groceries and some overspending. Don't be afraid to make substitutions for ingredients you might not have on hand or to simply skip it.

Maple-Drizzled Fruit Salad

Serves 4

MEATLESS **DAIRY-FREE** **GLUTEN-FREE**

I was first served a similar salad at the Bed and Breakfast at Peace Hill, near Williamsburg, Virginia. How lovely to be served a plated fruit salad at breakfast! The FishKids are fans of any fruit salad; this one is a definite hit with them.

4 bananas, peeled and sliced
2 oranges, peel and pith removed, sliced into 6 rounds each
1 cup red grapes, halved
1 cup raspberries
4 teaspoons pure maple syrup
4 tablespoons sliced almonds, toasted

On each serving plate, arrange an equal portion of banana slices, orange rounds, grape halves, and raspberries. Drizzle 1 teaspoon maple syrup over each plate. Sprinkle 1 tablespoon almonds over each plate. Serve immediately.

Spiced Vanilla
Granola

Mango-Pineapple
Breakfast Salsa

This menu is quite versatile in terms of how the components can be combined. Serve the granola with milk and a side of the fruit salsa, layer the yogurt and fruit in a parfait, or assemble it banana-split style (see page 242). No matter how you serve it, it's a delicious and nutritious way to start the day.

Spiced Vanilla Granola

Makes 6 cups

`MEATLESS` `DAIRY-FREE` `GLUTEN-FREE` `MAKE-AHEAD`

This is one of our favorite recipes for granola. I can never keep enough on hand—it seems that my family practically inhales it.

6 cups rolled oats
½ teaspoon fine sea salt
1 cup honey
½ cup vegetable oil
1 teaspoon pure vanilla extract
1 teaspoon ground cinnamon
½ teaspoon ground ginger
½ teaspoon ground nutmeg
¼ teaspoon ground cloves

1. Preheat the oven to 300°F. Line a rimmed baking sheet with parchment paper or a silicone baking mat.

2. In a large bowl, combine the oats and salt.

3. In a small saucepan, combine the honey, oil, vanilla, cinnamon, ginger, nutmeg, and cloves. Heat over medium-low heat until warm, stirring.

4. Pour the liquid over the oats and stir to coat. Transfer the mixture to the prepared baking sheet and spread evenly, pressing the mixture down firmly.

5. Bake until golden brown, 40 to 45 minutes. Break into small clusters and bake for an additional 15 minutes. Let the baking sheet cool on a wire rack.

MAKE IT AHEAD: Store the cooled granola in an airtight container at room temperature for up to 1 week.

81

LOCATION IS EVERYTHING

Where you shop matters. Some grocery chains offer different pricing based on the zip code. I've seen big box stores within the same chain only five miles from each other offer significantly different pricing. With a cart full of foodstuffs, this can make a big difference at the checkout stand. If you live near a state line, it may even be worth your while to cross the border for grocery shopping.

Monkey Salad

Serves 4

MEATLESS **DAIRY-FREE** **GLUTEN-FREE**

This salad is addicting. I love it for its simplicity and its ease of preparation, not to mention the great combination of flavors.

4 bananas, peeled and sliced
1 cup unsalted roasted cashews
½ cup unsweetened coconut chips

Divide the banana slices among four serving bowls. Top each with ¼ cup cashews. Sprinkle 2 tablespoons coconut chips into each bowl. Do not stir. Enjoy immediately.

MENU

Yogurt-Cornmeal
Pancakes

Turkey-Apple
Sausage Patties

Spiced Vanilla
Syrup

Pancakes, sausage, and homemade spiced syrup? This is the makings of a fabulous weekend brunch or a surprise pancake supper to please the masses. The FishKids break out in applause when we have pancakes for supper, and I feel as if I'd won the Mother of the Year award. This meal is just the ticket to the red carpet.

Yogurt-Cornmeal Pancakes

Makes 22 (5-inch) pancakes

MAKE-AHEAD **FREEZER-FRIENDLY**

These thick, fluffy flapjacks have become my kids' favorite. Make up several bags of the dry mix so that you're always ready for pancakes. Using Greek yogurt will boost the protein content.

3 cups unbleached all-purpose flour
½ cup cornmeal
¼ cup sugar
1 tablespoon baking powder
1 teaspoon baking soda
1 teaspoon fine sea salt
2¾ cups milk
1 cup plain yogurt
⅓ cup vegetable oil
2 large eggs

1. In a large bowl, whisk together the flour, cornmeal, sugar, baking powder, baking soda, and salt.

2. In another large bowl, combine the milk, yogurt, oil, and eggs. Whisk until smooth.

3. Add the dry ingredients to the wet ingredients and fold to combine. It's okay if there are a few lumps.

4. Heat a griddle over medium heat. Pour the batter in ¼-cup portions onto the griddle and cook until the edges appear cooked and bubbles start to pop on the surface, 2 to 3 minutes. Flip and cook the other side for 2 to 3 minutes more.

MAKE IT AHEAD: Assemble the dry ingredients from step 1 in a zip-top plastic bag. Label with the recipe name and the list of wet ingredients to be added later. Store in the freezer until ready to use. Cooked pancakes can be cooled, wrapped, and frozen as well. They can be rewarmed in the microwave (for softer pancakes) or the toaster (for crisper pancakes).

82

BE SURE TO STRETCH

Proteins are usually the priciest of grocery items. Stretch meat and chicken purchases by making sautés, casseroles, skillet meals, and soups. Bulk up the dish with legumes, grains, or vegetables. Pack in the flavor and you won't mind skimping on the meat.

Turkey-Apple Sausage Patties

Makes 8 patties

`DAIRY-FREE` `GLUTEN-FREE` `MAKE-AHEAD` `FREEZER-FRIENDLY`

A while back, I realized that most commercial sausages have sugar added to them in addition to the excess salt and preservatives. *Sugar?* Making my own sausage patties is more economical, tastier, and better for my family, too.

1 pound ground turkey
1 small apple, peeled and grated (about ½ cup)
1 teaspoon garlic powder
1 teaspoon dried parsley
½ teaspoon kosher salt
¼ teaspoon dried thyme
¼ teaspoon freshly ground black pepper
¼ teaspoon paprika
¼ teaspoon rubbed sage
⅛ teaspoon cayenne pepper

1. In a medium-size bowl, mix all of the ingredients until thoroughly combined. Divide the mixture into 8 equal portions. Form each portion into a round patty.

2. In a large nonstick skillet over medium-high heat, cook the patties until cooked through, about 5 minutes on each side.

MAKE IT AHEAD: The patties can be formed 1 day ahead, covered, and refrigerated until ready to cook. Cooked patties can be stored in an airtight container in the refrigerator for up to 3 days or in the freezer for up to 1 month.

Spiced Vanilla Syrup

Makes 2 cups

`MEATLESS` `DAIRY-FREE` `GLUTEN-FREE` `MAKE-AHEAD`

Many commercial "pancake syrups" are just corn syrup with artificial flavoring. They're inexpensive, but *blech*. Real maple syrup, on the other hand, is real food, but it can be expensive. We've found that homemade sugar syrups can fill the gap from time to time. This one is flavored with vanilla extract and baking spices. Serve it on pancakes, over ice cream, or in coffee drinks.

1 cup dark brown sugar
1 cup water
1 teaspoon pure vanilla extract
½ teaspoon ground cinnamon
¼ teaspoon ground nutmeg
¼ teaspoon ground ginger
⅛ teaspoon ground cloves

In a medium-size saucepan, whisk together the brown sugar and water. Bring to a boil and boil for 3 minutes, stirring constantly. Stir in the vanilla extract, cinnamon, nutmeg, ginger, and cloves and remove from the heat. Serve warm, or cool to room temperature and store in the refrigerator.

MAKE IT AHEAD: Refrigerate the syrup in a covered jar or bottle for up to 2 weeks.

MENU

Chile and Corn
Tortilla Egg Bake

Oven Hash
Browns

Fun Fruit Kabobs

This hearty meal
comes together in no
time. The casserole
and the hash browns
can go into the oven
together. The fruit
kabobs are quick and
easy to assemble,
perfect to delegate to
children (or spouses).

Chile and Corn Tortilla Egg Bake

Serves 4

MEATLESS **GLUTEN-FREE** **MAKE-AHEAD**

Unlike the traditional egg bake that gets body from day-old bread, this casserole makes good use of tortilla chips. If you've got half a bag of broken pieces, this is the perfect vehicle for giving them new life. If you buy unsalted or low-salt chips, you may want to season the casserole with a bit of salt.

2 cups broken tortilla chips
6 large eggs, beaten
1 cup milk
1½ cups frozen corn kernels, thawed
1 cup shredded Monterey Jack or cheddar cheese
1 (4-ounce) can diced green chiles, drained, or ¼ cup chopped
    roasted chiles (see page 245)
1 teaspoon ground cumin
¼ cup chopped fresh cilantro
1 medium tomato, diced

1. Grease a 9-inch pie plate with nonstick cooking spray. Place the broken chips in the prepared pan.

2. In a medium-size bowl, combine the eggs, milk, corn, cheese, chiles, and cumin. Pour this mixture over the chips in the pan. Cover and refrigerate for 2 to 24 hours.

3. Preheat the oven to 400°F.

4. Sprinkle the cilantro and tomato over the top of the casserole. Bake until set, about 20 minutes.

MAKE IT AHEAD: Cover and refrigerate the unbaked casserole for up to 1 day.

Oven Hash Browns

Serves 4

MEATLESS DAIRY-FREE **GLUTEN-FREE**

I love to keep frozen shredded hash browns on hand for an easy, stopgap meal. While it doesn't take much work to peel and shred fresh potatoes, sometimes fatigue can get between you and a good dinner. This recipe helps, making quick work of oven-frying hash browns.

2 pounds frozen shredded potatoes
½ cup olive oil
1 teaspoon dried parsley
1 teaspoon garlic powder
1 teaspoon kosher salt
Freshly ground black pepper to taste

1. Preheat the oven to 400°F.

2. In a large bowl, combine the potatoes, olive oil, parsley, garlic powder, salt, and pepper. Bake for 20 minutes.

3. Flip the hash browns over in sections and continue baking until crispy, about 10 minutes more.

83

Don't leave a kitchen
full of food behind
when you go on vaca-
tion. Waste is a huge
cost to the grocery
budget. Use it up,
juice fresh produce,
freeze excess, or
pack it for the trip.
You'll save money
and come home to a
cleaner kitchen, too.

Fun Fruit Kabobs

Serves 4

MEATLESS **DAIRY-FREE** **GLUTEN-FREE**

I remember being at a Girl Scout campout once where a troop of
girls got to pick their breakfast from the trees. Their parents and
leaders had tied string around fruits, juices, and small cereal boxes
and hung them from the trees. It was such a simple thing, yet so
much fun. These fruit kabobs are like that—they're simple, but their
novelty turns them into something special.

  4 small bananas, peeled and thickly sliced
  8 ounces fresh strawberries
  8 ounces red grapes
  4 kiwis, peeled and thickly sliced

Thread the fruit onto eight skewers, alternating patterns and col-
ors. Serve immediately so that the bananas do not brown.

I know many a mom
who has served her
family popcorn and
smoothies for sup-
per. It's quite liberat-
ing, actually—and
not as crazy as it
sounds. You can do
one better by serv-
ing up rich, flavorful
Coconut-Ginger
Granola and frosty
Spiced Piña Colada
Smoothies.

Coconut-Ginger Granola

Makes 8 cups

`MEATLESS` `DAIRY-FREE` `GLUTEN-FREE` `MAKE-AHEAD`

Coconut chips are thick slivers of coconut, typically sold unsweetened. They caramelize in such a lovely way in this recipe; I confess,
I'd be apt to pick out all the coconut chips for myself if my kids
didn't catch me.

6 cups rolled oats
1 cup oat bran
1 cup unsweetened coconut chips or shredded coconut
½ teaspoon kosher salt
1 cup light brown sugar
½ cup coconut or vegetable oil
¼ cup water
1 teaspoon ground ginger

1. Preheat the oven to 300°F. Line a rimmed baking sheet with
parchment paper or a silicone baking mat.

2. In a large bowl, combine the oats, oat bran, coconut chips, and
salt. Set aside.

3. In a small saucepan, combine the brown sugar, oil, water, and
ginger. Stir over medium heat until the sugar dissolves.

4. Pour the liquid over the dry mixture and stir to coat. Transfer
the mixture to the prepared baking sheet and spread evenly, pressing the mixture down firmly.

5. Bake until golden brown, 40 to 45 minutes. Break into small
clusters and bake for an additional 15 minutes. Let the baking
sheet cool on a wire rack.

MAKE IT AHEAD: Store the cooled granola in an airtight container at room temperature for up to 1 week.

84

Smoothie bars charge a pretty penny for the blended drinks they sell. Make your own to save precious coin. Whip up a bulk batch and freeze it in individual freezer-safe jars. Pack frozen smoothies in everyone's lunch box for work or school for a refreshing treat at a fraction of the cost.

Spiced Piña Colada Smoothies

Serves 4

`MEATLESS` `DAIRY-FREE` `GLUTEN-FREE` `MAKE-AHEAD` `FREEZER-FRIENDLY`

The local smoothie bar makes a pretty mean piña colada–flavored smoothie. Virgin, of course. But I've found that it's cheaper and tastier to make it at home myself.

1 banana, peeled
1 cup light coconut milk
1 cup crushed ice
1 cup canned pineapple chunks, drained, juice reserved
½ cup pineapple juice reserved from can
1 teaspoon minced fresh ginger
¼ teaspoon ground cinnamon
¼ teaspoon ground nutmeg

Combine all of the ingredients in a blender. Blend until very smooth. Serve immediately.

MAKE IT AHEAD: Pour the blended smoothie mixture into four 1-cup freezer-safe containers with lids and freeze for up to 1 month. To thaw until drinkable, set out on the counter for 30 to 45 minutes. Stir before serving.

MENU

Almond French
Toast

Brown Sugar–
Pear Compote

Malted Hot
Cocoa Mix

This menu is the ultimate cold-weather comfort meal. While you sip hot cocoa and cook the French toast, the pear compote bakes in the oven. Jack Frost will successfully be held at bay.

Almond French Toast

Serves 4

`MEATLESS`

I've cooked this on an electric griddle as well as in a panini press. Both methods have their advantages. You can cook more at one time on an electric griddle, but with the panini press, the cooking is pretty much hands-free. You can also fry them up in a skillet or griddle on the stovetop. Choose the method that works best for you.

Instead of purchasing pre-ground almond meal, you can simply pulse whole raw almonds in a food processor until fine (be careful not to overprocess or they will turn into almond butter).

6 large eggs, beaten
1½ cups milk
2 tablespoons almond meal
2 tablespoons pure maple syrup
1 teaspoon pure vanilla extract
Melted butter, as needed
1 (12-inch) Italian loaf, thickly sliced, or 4 sub rolls, split horizontally

1. In a shallow dish, combine the eggs, milk, almond meal, maple syrup, and vanilla.

2. Heat a panini press or griddle. If using a griddle, grease it with melted butter.

3. Dip the bread pieces in the egg mixture, flipping to coat.

4. Cook the bread until toasted and browned, 5 to 10 minutes. If using a griddle, flip the bread once the first side is toasted.

Scan the manager's
specials during your
supermarket trip for
last-minute deals. Be
ready to change your
meal plan to suit
the markdowns you
discover. Just make
sure to read expira-
tion dates to ensure
you'll be able to use
the item before it
expires.

Brown Sugar–Pear Compote

Serves 4

`MEATLESS` `GLUTEN-FREE` `MAKE-AHEAD`

Pears bathe in sugar and spice, resulting in a dessert-like fruit
mixture that is great on French toast, pancakes, or even ice cream.
If you don't have cardamom, you can substitute cinnamon.

4 pears, peeled, cored, and chopped (about 3 cups)
½ cup dark brown sugar
½ cup water
1 teaspoon grated lemon zest
½ teaspoon ground cardamom
1 tablespoon butter, cut into pieces

1. Preheat the oven to 350°F.

2. Combine the pears, brown sugar, water, zest, and cardamom in
an 8-inch square baking dish. Toss to combine. Dot the surface with
the butter pieces. Bake until the pears are tender and the sauce
bubbles and thickens, about 45 minutes. Serve hot, warm, or cold.

MAKE IT AHEAD: Transfer the cooled compote to an airtight container and store
in the refrigerator for up to 3 days.

It's amazing the errors I've found at the grocery check-out stand. A $2.99 purchase once registered as $29.99. In a large order I might have missed that except for the fact that I checked my receipt before leaving the store. Don't be afraid to question even a few dollars or cents. It's your money.

Malted Hot Cocoa Mix

Makes about 5 cups mix

MAKE-AHEAD

This cocoa mix is adapted from one of Alton Brown's. I've added the flavor of malt as well as some additional spices for a tummy-warming treat that my kids love. You need 2 to 3 tablespoons of the mix for a cup of cocoa, so this makes for a lot of warm tummies.

2 cups confectioners' sugar
2 cups powdered milk
1 cup unsweetened cocoa powder
½ cup malted milk powder
2 teaspoons cornstarch
1 teaspoon fine sea salt
½ teaspoon ground cinnamon
¼ teaspoon ground nutmeg
Pinch of cayenne pepper

In a large bowl, sift together all of the ingredients. For each serving, measure out 2 to 3 tablespoons of the cocoa mix into a 6-ounce mug. Add boiling water. Stir to combine. Serve hot.

MAKE IT AHEAD: The mix will keep indefinitely in an airtight container at room temperature.

MENU

Frittata with
Sausage and
Vegetables

Cucumber Salad
with Scallion-
Lime Dressing

One evening while I
was prepping vege-
tables for pizza night
(see page 86), I real-
ized that I had all the
makings for a deli-
cious Italian egg dish
and a side salad. I
chopped extra ingre-
dients, and *voilà!*—or
whatever they would
say in Italy—the next
day we had a scrump-
tious sausage and
vegetable frittata
that came together
with very little work.

Frittata with Sausage and Vegetables

Serves 4

MAKE-AHEAD **FREEZER-FRIENDLY**

Loaded with sausage and veggies, this egg dish can be served for
breakfast, brunch, lunch, or supper.

8 ounces Italian sausage links
½ cup chopped green bell pepper
¼ cup chopped yellow or red onion
¼ cup sliced black olives
1 cup shredded cheddar cheese tossed with 1 tablespoon
    unbleached all-purpose flour
6 large eggs, beaten

1. Preheat the oven to 400°F. Grease a 9-inch pie plate with nonstick cooking spray.

2. In a large skillet over medium heat, cook the sausages until
cooked through. When cool enough to slice, slice the sausages thinly.

3. Layer the sausage, pepper, onion, olives, and cheese in the
bottom of the prepared pan. Pour the eggs over the top.

4. Bake until the eggs are set, 25 to 30 minutes.

MAKE IT AHEAD: Place the assembled, unbaked frittata in the freezer until firm,
about 2 hours. Wrap tightly and store in the freezer for up to 1 month. Completely thaw the frittata in the refrigerator before baking, adding 5 to 10 minutes
of baking time since the pan will be cold.

87

Track your expenses.
Keep a running log
each week or month
to see how much
money you're spend-
ing on food costs.
This is crucial as a
way to audit spend-
ing, especially in
homes where more
than one person
might be shopping.

Cucumber Salad with Scallion-Lime Dressing

Serves 4

`MEATLESS` `DAIRY-FREE` `GLUTEN-FREE` `MAKE-AHEAD`

This salad is crisp and refreshing and can be made ahead. It's a
nice change from fruit as part of a breakfast-for-dinner meal. It's
also great for topping sandwiches.

1 large cucumber, thinly sliced
1 red bell pepper, seeded and thinly sliced
3 tablespoons Scallion-Lime Dressing (page 89)

In a small bowl, toss the cucumbers and pepper with the dressing. Chill until ready to serve.

MAKE IT AHEAD: Refrigerate in an airtight container for up to 2 days. The vegetables will soften as they marinate in the dressing.

WEREWOLF MEALS

These "buy one get one" (BOGO) meals allow you to cook once but eat twice. The two meals build on similar ingredients and may even share some cooking preparation and methods. The bulk of the cooking can be done on night one; on night two, you add a few things, change a few things, and *voilà*—dinner is on the table. (The men in my family say that I should call these Werewolf Meals, because they turn into something else the next evening.)

This is a great way to stretch your ingredients, maximize your time investment, and, of course, save money. Check out these meal pairings to practice the method. Pretty soon, you'll be able to give new life to any leftovers you have in the fridge.

• Once you've enjoyed a Classic Roast Chicken dinner (page 94), be sure to make up a batch of Homemade Chicken Stock (page 97). Use that along with leftover mashed potatoes to prepare Potato-Leek Soup (page 50). Serve Honey Whole-Wheat Bread (page 52) on the side.

• Prep for pizza night typically involves a round of slicing and dicing vegetables and cheeses. Do double slicing-and-dicing duty when you make Supreme Sausage Pizza (page 86) and Spinach-Apple Salad with Scallion-Lime Dressing (page 89). Use the leftover vegetables to make Frittata with Sausage and Vegetables (page 261) and Cucumber Salad with Scallion-Lime Dressing (page 262).

• We love Asian flavors at our house, and many Asian meals share common ingredients. While you're chopping vegetables and marinating chicken for the Asian Chicken Salad with Rice Noodles (page 189), double your efforts so that you can make the Chicken Summer Rolls (page 266) in a jiffy later in the week.

• A potpie is a wonderful way to follow up a roast dinner, whether it's chicken, pork, or beef that you've roasted. Make Beef Potpie with Flaky Cheddar Crust (page 206) a day or two after you've enjoyed the Pot Roast with Herbed Red Wine Sauce (page 196) and Parsleyed New Potatoes (page 197). While you're making the pie crust for the Deep-Dish Apple-Cranberry Pie (page 198), also make the dough for the potpie. You'll have to wash the food processor just once, but you'll enjoy double the rewards.

Meals On the Run

A meal on the run is one that can easily be packed in a cooler and thermos. It's not too inelegant to eat at your desk or too awkward to hold in your lap at the ball field or the park. It's a little bit of comfort when you're forgoing a restaurant meal in order to save money. It's a brief respite to grab some nourishment when you can't eat at home.

Though, truth be told, all of these meals are just as satisfying eaten at the kitchen table as they are in the bleachers or at the office.

Chicken Summer Rolls 266
Sunny Dipping Sauce 267

Tortellini-Chickpea Pasta Salad 268
Baby Cakes 271

Loaded Italian Subs 272
Mom's Macaroni Salad 274
Lemon-Pecan Biscotti 275

Cajun Grilled Chicken Salad with Creamy Scallion Dressing 276
Lemon-Blueberry Corn Muffins 279

Chicken Salad Wraps with Apples, Almonds, and Grapes 280
Pineapple *Agua Fresca* 282
No-Bake Cereal Bars 283

Vegetable, Beef, and Barley Soup 284
Garlic-Herb Soft Pretzels 286

Chipotle Turkey Sandwiches 290
Quinoa Salad with Black Beans and Feta Cheese 291
Spiced Carrot Quick Bread 292

Poor Man's Chicken Caesar Salad 294
MinTea 297
Orange–Chocolate Chip Cookies 299

Thanksgiving Chef Salad 300
Brownie Cheesecake Bars 301

MENU

Chicken Summer
Rolls

Sunny Dipping
Sauce

Asian takeout is one
of the most tempt-
ing of "faster foods."
Loaded with crunchy
vegetables and
fragrant sauces, it
pleases the senses in
wonderful ways. I've
found that making
our own is a happy
solution that suits the
budget as well as the
taste buds. Try your
hand at these sur-
prisingly quick and
easy summer rolls
wrapped in rice paper
with a homemade
nut-free dipping
sauce. Serve with
Homemade Lemon-
ade (page 66).

Chicken Summer Rolls

Serves 4

`DAIRY-FREE` `GLUTEN-FREE` `MAKE-AHEAD`

After spending a small fortune at our favorite Asian restaurant, I
finally learned how to make summer rolls, or salad rolls, at home for
a light supper. It feels so exotic to soften the rice paper rounds and
create tight packages bursting with flavor. They are fun to pack in
lunches as well.

½ cup reduced-sodium soy sauce
1 tablespoon toasted sesame oil
1 teaspoon minced garlic
¼ teaspoon red pepper flakes
1 pound boneless, skinless chicken breasts or thighs, cut into
    ¼-inch strips
14 rice paper rounds
½ head napa cabbage, thinly sliced
1 red bell pepper, seeded and cut into matchsticks
1 cup daikon radish matchsticks
1 cup carrot matchsticks
½ cup chopped fresh cilantro
Sunny Dipping Sauce (recipe follows) or other dipping sauce of
    your choice, for serving

1. In a small bowl, whisk together the soy sauce, sesame oil,
garlic, and red pepper flakes.

2. Place the chicken in a zip-top plastic bag or glass dish with a
lid. Add the marinade and toss to coat. Allow the chicken to marinate in the refrigerator for 2 to 24 hours.

3. Remove the chicken from the marinade and discard the marinade. Cook the chicken in a large skillet over medium-high heat until
cooked through, 10 to 15 minutes, stirring often. Transfer to a plate
to cool, then chill in the refrigerator until ready to roll, about 1 hour.

4. Soften the rice paper rounds in water one at a time according
to the package directions. Place a small amount of cabbage, red
pepper, radish, carrot, cilantro, and chicken on each one and roll it
up. After you roll each one, keep them covered with a damp paper
towel to prevent them from drying out. Package the rolls in an airtight container, leaving a little space in between them if you can so
that they don't stick together. You can tuck a damp paper towel in
between if you like. Enjoy immediately or chill the rolls until ready to
serve. Serve the rolls with the dipping sauce.

MAKE IT AHEAD: Prepare the rolls up to 1 day in advance; store in an airtight
container in the refrigerator.

#88

EXPLORE THE WORLD

Ethnic grocery stores not only offer a great variety of international ingredients, but they also sell basic produce and meat at very economical prices. They are great sites to buy exotic spices at a discount as well.

Sunny Dipping Sauce

Makes about ½ cup

`MEATLESS` `DAIRY-FREE` `GLUTEN-FREE` `MAKE-AHEAD`

This is my take on the nutty dipping sauce at my favorite Asian restaurant. It's so much cheaper to prepare and enjoy it at home! Due to nut allergies in my family, I make this sauce with sunflower butter, but feel free to use your favorite nut butter instead. It also makes a great dipping sauce for fresh vegetable sticks and pot stickers.

3 tablespoons sunflower seed butter
2 tablespoons rice vinegar
2 tablespoons reduced-sodium soy sauce
1 tablespoon toasted sesame oil
¼ teaspoon red pepper flakes

In a small jar or a bowl, combine all of the ingredients. Shake or whisk well to combine. Serve immediately or chill until ready to serve.

MAKE IT AHEAD: Store the sauce in an airtight container in the refrigerator for up to 3 days.

Pack a filling one-dish-meal pasta salad, loaded with veggies and chickpeas, for a meatless Monday lunch. Finish it off with some little home-baked "cakes," which are actually cookies—a great portable dessert no matter what you are serving beforehand!

Tortellini-Chickpea Pasta Salad

Serves 4

MEATLESS   MAKE-AHEAD

Pasta salad has always been one of my go-to meals. If I add hearty ingredients like beans or cheese, the men in my midst are appeased. If I add veggies, I'm a happy camper. So, naturally, this salad has both.

1 (12-ounce) package cheese tortellini (fresh, dried, or frozen)
⅓ cup red wine vinegar
Juice of ½ lemon
½ teaspoon minced garlic
½ teaspoon dried oregano
Kosher salt and freshly ground black pepper
⅓ cup extra-virgin olive oil
2 cups cooked or canned chickpeas (rinsed and drained if canned)
2 cups chopped fresh spinach
1 (10-ounce) package grape tomatoes
¼ cup chopped peeled carrots

1. Bring a large pot of salted water to a boil over high heat and cook the tortellini according to the package directions. Drain and let cool slightly.

2. In a small jar or bowl, combine the vinegar, lemon juice, garlic, oregano, and salt and pepper to taste. Place the lid on the jar and shake well or whisk until smooth. Add the olive oil and shake or whisk again to emulsify.

3. In a large bowl, combine the tortellini, chickpeas, spinach, tomatoes, and carrots. Pour the dressing over the salad and toss gently to combine. Adjust the seasonings as desired. Pack in individual serving containers and serve chilled or at room temperature.

MAKE IT AHEAD: Store the finished salad in the refrigerator for up to 4 days.

GET YOUR KITCHEN READY FOR VACATION

You're getting ready to leave town; you've got your bags packed; you're looking forward to some rest and relaxation. Before you go, consider spending a few hours in the kitchen. Say what?

Yes, really. An hour or two in your kitchen before you leave town can save you lots of money and heartache during and after your trip. If you don't, you could be wasting a ton of food and, in turn, a ton of money. It's in your best interests to get the kitchen ready for vacation, too. Here's what you can do to not waste good food while you're away.

1. EAT IT UP.
Serve leftovers in the last few days before a trip so that you can use up what you have and not let it go to waste.

2. JUICE IT.
Homemade juices and smoothies are a great way to use up produce while it's still fresh.

If the vegetable drawers are full, make juice. If you don't have a juicer, you can make smoothies with many of the fruits and vegetables that you might have on hand. (If you're interested in learning more about juicing, check out my book *Best 100 Juices for Kids*. It includes juice recipes that folks of every age will enjoy.)

3. FREEZE IT.
If you have the time, prep freezer meals with the food you have left in the fridge. If not, then take a few minutes to make those items freezer-friendly. Wrap, label, and freeze any leftovers that are still worth saving.

4. TAKE IT WITH YOU.
When we know we will have access to a kitchen on vacation, we pack meals for the road and for our stay. Packing food from home can save you money during your trip and help you avoid wasting money when food goes bad before you can eat it up. Plus, if you've got food allergies to account for, bringing food from home means you can have an easier time enjoying meals that suit everyone.

5. STORE IT PROPERLY.
If you're going to be gone for only a short time, make sure that you store in the refrigerator the fruits and vegetables that might ripen too quickly on the counter.

6. SHARE IT.
Friends and neighbors may be more than happy to take that gallon of milk or that basket of peaches off your hands. Bless them.

7. DITCH IT.
Throw out what is bad or very close to it. It's not going to make you love your kitchen more to come home to things that might be stinky, slimy, or rotten.

Bon voyage!

#89

DESSERT ON A DIME

Buy chocolate candy on clearance after holidays like Valentine's Day, Easter, Halloween, and Christmas. Chop and use it as a substitute for chocolate chips in baking. You won't believe how low the prices will go, and chocolate keeps well for months.

Baby Cakes

Makes 3 dozen cookies

`MAKE-AHEAD` `FREEZER-FRIENDLY`

When I was little, my dad always called my sisters and me "Baby Cakes" as a term of endearment. He also always seemed to have candy in his coat pockets or in his car. Always. These cake-like cookies filled with candy are named in his honor.

Use your favorite candy or whatever is on clearance in your store's holiday section.

1 cup sugar
¾ cup (1½ sticks) butter
2 large eggs
1 teaspoon pure vanilla extract
2⅓ cups unbleached all-purpose flour
1½ teaspoons baking powder
¼ teaspoon fine sea salt
½ cup small candy pieces, such as candy-coated chocolates,
   chopped candy bars, or crushed toffee

1. Preheat the oven to 350°F. Line two baking sheets with parchment paper or silicone baking mats.

2. In a large bowl, cream together the sugar and butter. Add the eggs and vanilla and beat until well combined.

3. Stir in the flour, baking powder, and salt. Fold in the candy.

4. Scoop the dough into rounded tablespoons and place 2 inches apart on the prepared baking sheets.

5. Bake until firm and beginning to brown, 8 to 10 minutes. Cool on a rack before wrapping in plastic wrap or storing in individual zip-top plastic bags.

MAKE IT AHEAD: Layer the cookies in an airtight container and store at room temperature for up to 1 week or in the freezer for up to 1 month.

MENU

Loaded
Italian Subs

Mom's Macaroni
Salad

Lemon-Pecan
Biscotti

A good sub sandwich plus a small cup of deli salad plus a cookie for dessert equal the makings of a fabulous boxed lunch. This is worth skipping the gossip around the water cooler for.

Loaded Italian Subs

Serves 4

`MAKE-AHEAD`

Once upon a time, I worked for the University Dining Services at UC Santa Barbara. I woke up every morning at five o'clock to go make sandwiches like this one for hundreds of professors and college students. My family is thrilled when I find cold cuts at a good price, because they know we'll enjoy these subs soon after. We like ours with homemade mayonnaise jazzed up with garlic and herbs, but feel free to drizzle on a little vinaigrette if you prefer.

4 Italian sub rolls
½ cup mayonnaise, preferably homemade (recipe follows)
1 garlic clove, minced
1½ teaspoons dried basil
1 teaspoon dried oregano
Kosher salt and freshly ground black pepper
8 slices ham (about 8 ounces)
20 slices salami (about 5 ounces)
8 slices provolone cheese (about 5 ounces)
2 medium tomatoes, sliced
½ small red onion, sliced
1½ cups shredded lettuce
8 pepperoncini peppers

1. Cut the sub rolls in half lengthwise, but do not cut all the way through on one side; leave a hinge.

2. In a small bowl, combine the mayonnaise, garlic, basil, oregano, and salt and pepper to taste. Spread 1 to 2 tablespoons of the herbed mayo on the inside surfaces of each roll.

3. Layer 2 slices ham, 5 slices salami, and 2 slices cheese on each roll.

4. Divide the tomato, onion, and shredded lettuce among the sandwiches. Close each sandwich tightly and wrap securely in plastic wrap. Serve immediately or chill until ready to serve. Serve with pepperoncini on the side (or, if you like, tuck the pepperoncini into the sandwiches).

MAKE IT AHEAD: These subs can be prepared up to 1 day in advance, if you leave the bread dry (no mayo or vinaigrette). Pack the spread separately for the freshest flavor.

HOMEMADE MAYONNAISE

Makes 1 cup

I never in a million years thought that I would make my own mayonnaise. It sounded difficult. And a little scary. I got lots of coaching from my food blogger friends Mandi Ehman and Shaina Olmanson and found that it wasn't so hard after all.

I experimented with different recipes (whole eggs and/or different types of oils) and two different methods (immersion blender and food processor), landing on an adaptation of Shaina's Sriracha Mayo recipe. The food processor turned out to be my go-to gadget. I use pasteurized eggs for this, stocking up when they are on sale. This makes me feel "on the safe side," but you can use regular eggs, too; just make sure they are very fresh and come from a reliable source. I also found that using a blend of light olive oil and sunflower oil gives it a milder taste than straight olive oil.

We use this basic mayonnaise on sandwiches, in potato and macaroni salads, in chicken salad, and in dressings. Go ahead, give it a try!

1 pasteurized egg yolk
2 teaspoons freshly squeezed lemon juice
2 teaspoons white wine vinegar
¼ teaspoon fine sea salt
½ cup light olive oil
¼ cup sunflower oil

1. In a food processor fitted with a metal blade, blend the egg yolk, lemon juice, white wine vinegar, and sea salt until smooth.

2. Combine the oils in a glass measuring cup. While the food processor is running, add the oils in a very thin stream until an emulsion is formed and the mixture thickens. Scrape down the sides of the bowl as needed to make a smooth emulsion.

3. Spoon the mayonnaise into a glass jar. Store, covered, in the refrigerator for up to 5 days.

School lunches can be pricey, especially if you buy those prepackaged snack boxes. You can easily and more economically slice cheeses and meats and package them along with some crackers in bento-style boxes or brown bags for your kids' lunches. Include a fun home-baked goodie and pack some home-made applesauce in a small cup with a lid. Easy-peasy—and half the price.

Mom's Macaroni Salad

Serves 4

`MEATLESS` `MAKE-AHEAD`

This is the macaroni salad that my mom made for us when I was growing up. It's still one of my favorites. Mom used jarred mayo, but if you make my homemade version, it will turn this into something extra-special.

8 ounces small macaroni, such as shells, elbows, or mini penne
½ cup mayonnaise, preferably homemade (page 273)
1 cup chopped celery
½ cup chopped red onion
½ cup finely cubed cheddar cheese
1 tablespoon chopped fresh dill or 1 teaspoon dried dill
Kosher salt and freshly ground black pepper

1. Bring a large pot of salted water to a boil over high heat. Cook the macaroni according to the package directions. Drain, rinse, and let cool.

2. In a large bowl, combine the pasta, mayonnaise, celery, onion, cheese, dill, and salt and pepper to taste. Stir gently to combine. Pack in individual serving containers and chill until ready to serve, about 1 hour.

MAKE IT AHEAD: Store the finished salad in the refrigerator for up to 4 days.

Take along food and drink when you go on road trips. Convenience stores, fast-food restaurants, and gas stations provide expensive and unhealthful fare. Pack a cooler full of good cheap eats for lunch and snacks.

Lemon-Pecan Biscotti

Makes 2 to 3 dozen cookies

MAKE-AHEAD   **FREEZER-FRIENDLY**

I like to end a meal with a little bit of sweet, but not too much sweet. These twice-baked cookies are crisp and crunchy, with pecan and lemon flavors to punctuate the end of the meal.

3 large eggs
1 teaspoon pure vanilla extract
½ teaspoon pure lemon extract
1 teaspoon grated lemon zest
1 cup granulated sugar
2⅓ cups unbleached all-purpose flour
1 teaspoon baking soda
¼ teaspoon fine sea salt
1 cup pecan pieces

GLAZE (OPTIONAL)
1 cup confectioners' sugar
2 teaspoons grated lemon zest
1 tablespoon freshly squeezed lemon juice

1. Preheat the oven to 300°F. Line a baking sheet with parchment paper or a silicone baking mat.

2. In a large bowl, beat the eggs, vanilla, lemon extract, and lemon zest with a handheld mixer. Beat in the granulated sugar until frothy.

3. Stir in the flour, baking soda, and salt. Fold in the pecans.

4. Form the dough into a 10-inch-long loaf down the center of the parchment paper. Bake for 50 minutes.

5. Remove the baking sheet from the oven. Leave the oven on. Wait for 5 to 10 minutes, then slice the large cookie log on the bias into ½-inch-thick slices.

6. Place the slices back on the baking sheet, cut sides down, and bake for 25 minutes. Turn the cookie slices over and bake for another 25 minutes. Cool on a rack.

7. If using the glaze, combine the confectioners' sugar, lemon zest, and lemon juice in a small bowl. Drizzle this over the cooled cookies and let set completely before storing in individual zip-top plastic bags.

MAKE IT AHEAD: Store the cooled biscotti in an airtight container at room temperature for up to 1 week or in the freezer for up to 1 month. (If freezing, do not glaze the cookies until you are ready to serve.)

Cajun Grilled
Chicken Salad
with Creamy
Scallion Dressing

Lemon-Blueberry
Corn Muffins

Salad and bread has
been one of my fa-
vorite meal pairings
for years. This par-
ticular combination
evokes flavors of the
South: Cajun-spiced
chicken, buttermilk
dressing, and corn
muffins. Y'all are
gonna love it.

Cajun Grilled Chicken Salad with Creamy Scallion Dressing

Serves 4

`GLUTEN-FREE` `MAKE-AHEAD`

Entrée salads are my go-to meals for making sure I'm getting enough fruits and vegetables in my diet. I love to pack them for picnics and meals on the run. If I make them more than a few hours ahead of time, I just make sure to package the dressing separately so nothing gets soggy.

1 pound boneless, skinless chicken tenders
2 tablespoons Cajun Spice Blend (page 80)
6 cups torn salad greens
1 cup grape tomatoes
1 cup small broccoli florets
1 medium carrot, peeled and shredded
¼ cup sunflower seeds
Creamy Scallion Dressing (recipe follows)

1. Prepare a hot fire in a charcoal or gas grill.
2. Season the chicken tenders generously with the spice blend on both sides.
3. Grill the chicken, turning once, until the chicken has reached an internal temperature of 165°F, about 10 minutes. Set aside to cool.
4. In four bowls or packable containers with lids, divide the salad greens, tomatoes, broccoli, carrot, and sunflower seeds. Add the cooled chicken pieces. Drizzle with dressing or pack it separately.

MAKE IT AHEAD: Store the grilled chicken and prepped veggies in airtight containers in the refrigerator for up to 2 days before assembling the salads.

#92

FORGET CAESAR: ALL HAIL SALES!

In the old days, I planned meals based on what I wanted to eat. That meant I paid $5 a pound for chicken breast. Too much! Now, I plan on having chicken only when it's on sale. Or, better yet, I buy extra on sale to freeze and then have chicken when I want it.

creamy scallion dressing

Makes about 1½ cups

`MEATLESS` `GLUTEN-FREE` `MAKE-AHEAD`

1 cup buttermilk
¼ cup mayonnaise, preferably homemade (page 273)
¼ cup chopped fresh parsley
¼ cup chopped scallions
1 teaspoon minced garlic
¼ teaspoon freshly ground black pepper
⅛ teaspoon sweet paprika

In a medium-size bowl, whisk together the buttermilk and mayonnaise until smooth. Stir in the parsley, scallions, garlic, pepper, and paprika. Enjoy immediately or chill until ready to serve.

MAKE IT AHEAD: Store the dressing in an airtight container in the refrigerator for up to 3 days.

93

A DOLLOP'LL DO YA

Freeze dollops of yogurt on a plastic-lined baking sheet and then store the frozen blobs in a freezer bag in the freezer to use later in smoothies or sauces. This is a great way to save small portions or uneaten containers before they go bad.

Lemon-Blueberry Corn Muffins

Makes 12 muffins

MAKE-AHEAD **FREEZER-FRIENDLY**

Lemons and blueberries make great partners in these tasty corn muffins. Bake a batch or two, and then cool, wrap, and freeze so that you have a ready snack, breakfast, or side dish in the weeks to come.

1½ cups unbleached all-purpose flour
¾ cup sugar
½ cup cornmeal
1 tablespoon baking powder
1 teaspoon baking soda
1 teaspoon fine sea salt
1 cup plain yogurt, Greek yogurt, or sour cream
½ cup milk
2 large eggs
⅓ cup vegetable oil
1 teaspoon grated lemon zest
1 cup blueberries

1. Preheat the oven to 400°F. Line a 12-cup muffin pan with paper liners.

2. In a large bowl, whisk together the flour, sugar, cornmeal, baking powder, baking soda, and salt.

3. In another bowl, whisk together the yogurt, milk, eggs, oil, and zest. Add the wet ingredients to the dry ingredients and fold just until combined. Fold in the berries.

4. Divide the batter among the 12 muffin cups. The cups will be fairly full. Bake until the muffins are lightly browned and a tester inserted comes out with only a few crumbs attached, about 20 minutes. Cool on a rack.

MAKE IT AHEAD: Cooled muffins can be stored in an airtight container at room temperature for up to 2 days or in the freezer for up to 1 month.

MENU

Chicken Salad
Wraps with
Apples, Almonds,
and Grapes

Pineapple *Agua
Fresca*

No-Bake Cereal
Bars

These clever wraps
taste just as good
at home as they do
when we're out and
about. Bursting with
protein and fresh
produce, they're a
tasty and nutritious
alternative to PB &
J. Pack a thermos
of pineapple *agua
fresca* and finish off
the meal with choco-
late rice cereal treats.

Chicken Salad Wraps with Apples, Almonds, and Grapes

Serves 4

DAIRY-FREE GLUTEN-FREE MAKE-AHEAD

Bread often gets soggy if you make sandwiches ahead, but when you make lettuce wraps, there's no chance of that. There *is* a high chance of intense flavor satisfaction, though. I like those odds. Choose a sturdy lettuce or a soft cabbage so it will hold your filling without breaking.

2 cups cubed cooked chicken
½ cup red grapes, halved
1 cup diced apple
2 scallions, chopped
½ cup mayonnaise, preferably homemade (page 273)
2 teaspoons apple cider vinegar
¼ teaspoon dried thyme
⅛ teaspoon freshly ground black pepper
4 to 8 large lettuce or napa cabbage leaves
2 tablespoons sliced almonds

1. In a large bowl, combine the chicken, grapes, apple, and scallions.

2. In a small bowl, whisk together the mayonnaise, vinegar, thyme, and black pepper. Pour the dressing over the chicken mixture and toss to coat. Serve immediately or cover the bowl and refrigerate until ready to serve.

3. Divide the chicken salad mixture among four plastic contain-ers with lids, packing the lettuce or cabbage leaves separately. Top each salad portion with a sprinkling of sliced almonds. Before eat-ing, diners can portion out the salad onto the lettuce leaves and roll up, burrito-style.

MAKE IT AHEAD: The chicken salad can be stored in an airtight container in the refrigerator for up to 3 days.

94

WATER, WATER EVERYWHERE

Drink water instead of cheap sodas and sugar-laden "sports drinks." You'll feel better and save money. Add citrus slices or fresh herbs to your ice water for a little pizzazz.

Pineapple Agua Fresca

Serves 4

`DAIRY-FREE` `GLUTEN-FREE` `MAKE-AHEAD`

An *agua fresca* (Spanish for "fresh water") is a refreshing drink typically made with fruit and a bit of sugar. You can use many different fruits, so feel free to experiment with berries or melons in place of the pineapple.

1 (20-ounce) can crushed pineapple
Juice of 1 lime
¼ cup sugar
2 cups cold water

1. Combine the pineapple, lime juice, sugar, and a little of the water in a blender. Blend to a smooth consistency.
2. Stir in the remaining cold water and liquefy. If your blender doesn't have a liquefy setting, strain the mixture, pressing on the solids to remove as much juice as possible.
3. Chill in a thermos or in individual to-go cups until ready to serve.

MAKE IT AHEAD: You can store the *agua fresca* in the refrigerator for up to 1 day.

No-Bake Cereal Bars

Makes 12 to 16 bars

`GLUTEN-FREE` `MAKE-AHEAD`

These bars are my adaptation of Rice Krispies treats. I like to use salted butter in this recipe, but use either salted or unsalted according to your preference and what you have on hand. Check your oats to make sure they are gluten-free, if that is a concern. Serve the bars chilled for the best texture.

8 tablespoons (1 stick) butter
½ cup light brown sugar
½ cup honey
1 teaspoon pure vanilla extract
4 cups crisp rice cereal
1 cup chocolate-flavored rice cereal
1 cup rolled oats
½ cup sunflower seeds, chopped nuts of your choice, dried
    cranberries, or raisins
2 tablespoons mini chocolate chips

1. Line a 9 x 13-inch baking pan with aluminum foil or parchment paper with the edges hanging over the sides.

2. In a large stockpot over medium heat, melt the butter. Add the sugar and honey and bring to a boil, stirring. Add the vanilla and remove from the heat.

3. Stir in the cereals, oats, and seeds until well incorporated.

4. Spoon the mixture into the prepared pan, sprinkle with the chocolate chips, and press firmly so the chips adhere. Cover and chill until firm, about 1 hour.

5. Grasp the edges of the foil and remove from the pan. Peel off the foil and cut the cereal mixture into 12 to 16 bars. Wrap each bar individually in plastic wrap and store in the refrigerator.

MAKE IT AHEAD: Store the wrapped bars in the refrigerator for up to 4 days.

MENU

Vegetable, Beef,
and Barley Soup

Garlic-Herb Soft
Pretzels

Soup and bread make
for a great, filling
meal wherever you
find yourself. Pack a
thermos of hot soup
and some garlicky
herb pretzels for your
next tailgating party,
Little League game,
or school board
meeting.

Vegetable, Beef, and Barley Soup

Makes 8 to 10 cups

`DAIRY-FREE` `MAKE-AHEAD` `FREEZER-FRIENDLY`

This soup beats the canned variety by a long shot. Full of vegetables and barley, it's hearty and delicious. Freeze individual portions in freezer-to-microwave containers to pack for lunches, quick snacks, or dinners.

1 tablespoon olive oil
1 pound chuck steak, cubed
1 cup chopped onion
1 cup chopped peeled carrot
½ cup chopped celery
½ cup pearl barley
4 cups vegetable broth
1 (15-ounce) can tomato sauce
2 cups cooked or canned chickpeas (rinsed and drained if canned)
½ cup chopped green bell pepper
½ cup frozen petite peas, thawed
1 teaspoon herbes de Provence
1 teaspoon kosher salt
¼ teaspoon freshly ground black pepper

1. In a large stockpot over medium heat, heat the oil until shimmering. Brown the steak cubes on all sides for 5 minutes.

2. Add the onion, carrot, celery, and barley to the pot. Cook until the onions turn translucent, 5 to 7 minutes.

3. Stir in the broth, tomato sauce, chickpeas, bell pepper, peas, herbes de Provence, salt, and pepper. Simmer until the barley and vegetables are tender, 20 to 30 minutes.

MAKE IT AHEAD: Store in an airtight container in the refrigerator for up to 4 days or in the freezer for up to 1 month.

95

A number of gro-
cery stores offer free
delivery service for
orders placed online.
The sale prices still
apply, meaning you
can have someone
else do the shopping
and driving, saving
you fuel costs as
well as the price of
those impulse buys
you just might have
thrown into the cart
while you were there.

Garlic-Herb Soft Pretzels

Makes 12 pretzels

MEATLESS **MAKE-AHEAD** **FREEZER-FRIENDLY**

Soft pretzels are a tasty yet expensive treat at the mall or amusement park. In desperation, we once paid $7—for one pretzel!
These pretzels, however, are healthier, tastier, and far more economical than the commercially prepared versions. The only bad
part is that you'll be hard-pressed to keep them on hand. They will
disappear in a flash.

1 cup milk
½ cup water
1 tablespoon honey
3 cups unbleached all-purpose flour
1 cup white whole-wheat flour
1¼ teaspoons fine sea salt
½ teaspoon garlic powder
¼ teaspoon dried oregano
¼ teaspoon dried basil
¼ teaspoon dried parsley
1 tablespoon active dry yeast
¼ cup baking soda
Kosher salt, poppy seeds, and/or sesame seeds, for sprinkling

1. Combine the milk, water, honey, flours, salt, garlic powder,
oregano, basil, parsley, and yeast in the pan of your bread machine
according to the manufacturer's directions. Set to the dough cycle
and start the machine. (If making the dough by hand: Combine
the milk, water, and honey in a medium-size saucepan and warm
slightly over medium heat. Transfer the mixture to a large bowl and
add the yeast. Stir and allow the yeast to proof for 5 minutes. Add
the flours, salt, garlic powder, oregano, basil, and parsley. Stir to
combine well. Turn the mixture out onto a lightly floured surface
and knead for 5 minutes to create a smooth, elastic dough, adding
more all-purpose flour as necessary. Transfer to a greased bowl
and turn the dough ball to coat. Allow to rise until doubled in bulk,
about 1 hour.)

2. Line 2 baking sheets with parchment paper or silicone baking
mats. When the machine beeps or the dough has doubled in bulk,
remove the dough from the pan or bowl and divide it into 12 equal
parts. Roll each dough portion into an 18-inch-long rope. Shape
the rope into a horseshoe. Twist the sides of the horseshoe, about
halfway up, around each other twice. Flip the ends over onto the U
of the horseshoe. Press to seal. Continue until all of the pretzels
are shaped.

3. Preheat the oven to 450°F. Bring a large stockpot of water to a boil over high heat.

4. Add the baking soda to the pot of water, stir, and return to a boil. Drop the formed pretzels, one at a time, into the soda bath. Boil for about 30 seconds and then use a slotted spoon to transfer to the prepared baking sheets. Sprinkle the pretzels with coarse salt and/or seeds, if desired.

5. Once all the pretzels have been "bathed," bake them until golden, 9 to 10 minutes. Let cool on a rack.

MAKE IT AHEAD: The baked and cooled pretzels can be wrapped individually in plastic wrap and stored in a zip-top plastic bag at room temperature for up to 3 days or in the freezer for up to 1 month. Thaw them on the counter before serving. Pretzels can be reheated in a 350°F oven for 5 minutes, if desired.

BROWN-BAGGING IT ON A BUDGET

P acking a lunch, whether for work or school, can be a great way to save on food costs. Consider these costs-cutting strategies when you're thinking about meals on the run.

1. MAKE YOUR OWN CONVENIENCE ITEMS.

The aisles of the grocery store are filled with all kinds of packaged goods in individual-size servings that make packing a lunch pretty easy. But the convenience is yours at a price. You can easily repackage bulk purchases into smaller containers or portions and make your own lunch box items. Consider this strategy for crackers, cheese cubes or slices, sliced meats, trail mix, yogurt, and applesauce. Take a larger, less expensive package or a homemade batch of something and divide it into individual reusable containers. At the start of the week, you can prepare many packets "assembly line" style and thus make lunch packing easier for the coming days.

2. BAKE SOMEONE HAPPY.

Browsing the baked goods aisle, I've noticed that boxed crackers, granola bars, and cookies cost a minimum of $3. Surely you can find these items for a lower price if you watch for coupons and good sales. However, if you're working around a food allergy as we are, or you are looking toward reducing your use of processed foods, or you just don't have time to troll the sales, it's just as easy—and often cheaper—to make your own. It certainly tastes better.

3. VEG OUT.

Buy in-season produce when it's on sale and use it to fill out your brown bag. Carrot and celery sticks, cucumber slices, broccoli florets, and red bell pepper spears all go well with the Creamy Scallion Dressing on page 277 or the Easy Homemade Hummus on page 126. Salads are easy to pack, especially if the dressing is on the side.

Rather than buying small packages of fruit salads or apple slices, prepare your own fruit items and spend less. Berries, homemade applesauce, sliced apples, grapefruit sections, pineapple spears, and grape clusters are all easy enough to prep at home. Make things as appealing and as easy to eat as possible: Remove the berry stems, treat the apple slices with lemon juice to prevent browning, section the grapefruit, and cut the grapes into small clusters.

4. KEEP IT CHILL.

Make sure that you're practicing proper food storage techniques to prevent spoilage. Keep your cool when it comes to brown-bagging it. Sometimes refrigeration is available at school or work, and sometimes you're on your own. An insulated cooler or lunch bag is a great alternative, as are reusable ice packs that you can refreeze at night. We keep a few extras on hand in case we forget to return them to the freezer. Freeze juices and yogurts to keep them cool. They should thaw by lunchtime.

5. USE REUSABLE PACKAGING.

Reusable packaging can be a great way to save money. Not only are you keeping more plastic and paper from entering a landfill, but you are also saving money by not buying the same things over and over again. My kids love the sectioned plastic boxes with lids that you can buy in the wraps aisle of the grocery store. They are reusable but can eventually be recycled when they've done their time in the lunch box. There are all kinds of reusable packaging that you can buy or make yourself.

Lunchtime can very easily be affordable, nutritious, and fun. Just think outside the box a little bit.

MENU

Chipotle Turkey
Sandwiches

Quinoa Salad
with Black Beans
and Feta Cheese

Spiced Carrot
Quick Bread

Hitting the road
sometime soon?
Whenever we head
out for the day, we
like to pack food
for the ride—that
way we eat better
and spend less. This
menu makes for
great road trip food.

Chipotle Turkey Sandwiches

Serves 4

DAIRY-FREE **MAKE-AHEAD**

This, one of my favorite sandwiches ever, is a mix of cultures: French baguette, all-American turkey breast, and Southwestern chipotle mayonnaise. Then I throw in some tomato and sweet onion for good measure. You'll be pleasantly surprised at the combo of great flavors. If you can't get your hands on a good baguette, use your favorite sandwich roll.

½ cup mayonnaise, preferably homemade (page 273)
1 canned chipotle chile in adobo sauce, chopped
2 French baguettes, halved crosswise and split open
8 ounces sliced deli turkey
2 medium tomatoes, sliced
½ sweet onion, such as Vidalia, sliced
4 large lettuce leaves

1. In a small bowl, combine the mayonnaise and chipotle chile. Spread the chipotle mayonnaise on the top of each baguette half.

2. On the bottom of each baguette half, layer the turkey, tomato, onions, and lettuce. Place the top of the baguette on each sandwich.

MAKE IT AHEAD: Wrap and refrigerate the sandwiches up to 1 day ahead, but for the freshest flavor, package the mayonnaise separately from the sandwiches and spread it on right before serving.

96

While shopping, check displays and the backs of product packaging for coupons. Often you can save a couple of bucks just by redeeming the "peelies" (coupons that peel off the package) or the coupon tear pads in the aisle. No scissors required.

Quinoa Salad with Black Beans and Feta Cheese

Serves 4

GLUTEN-FREE   **MAKE-AHEAD**

Quinoa is a seed that looks like a grain and acts like a cereal. Confusing? That's okay; all you really need to know is that it tastes great as a hot side dish or cold in a salad and that it is high in protein, making it a fun and easy way to go meatless.

1 cup quinoa, rinsed and drained
1 cup cooked or canned black beans (rinsed and drained if canned)
1 cup chopped tomato
⅔ cup frozen corn kernels, thawed
⅓ cup crumbled feta cheese
¼ cup chopped fresh cilantro
⅓ cup white wine vinegar
1 teaspoon Dijon mustard
Kosher salt and freshly ground black pepper
⅓ cup olive oil

1. Cook the quinoa according to the package directions. Transfer to a bowl to cool slightly, then cover and chill thoroughly, 1 to 2 hours.

2. In a large bowl, combine the quinoa, black beans, tomato, corn, feta, and cilantro. Stir gently to combine.

3. In a small jar or bowl, combine the vinegar, mustard, and salt and pepper to taste. Place the lid on the jar and shake or whisk until smooth. Add the olive oil and shake or whisk again to emulsify. Toss the salad with enough of the dressing to coat.

MAKE IT AHEAD: The dressed salad can be stored in an airtight container in the refrigerator for up to 1 day. Alternatively, you can refrigerate the salad and dressing separately for up to 4 days.

A recent-model chest freezer costs only about $38 a year to run. If you've got the space, it's worth the investment. You can save big on grocery costs by buying foods in bulk, like meat or fish, and storing them in the freezer.

Spiced Carrot Quick Bread

Makes 2 (8½-inch) loaves

`MEATLESS` `MAKE-AHEAD` `FREEZER-FRIENDLY`

You hear all about zucchini bread and banana bread, but rarely about carrot bread. Seeing as they are so amazingly cheap to buy, it seems a shame not to use carrots in baked goods. So, I tried it— with fantastic results. This recipe makes two loaves, so you can eat one right away and freeze the other for future good cheap eats. You can use the optional glaze or do like my friend JessieLeigh does and serve it with a cream cheese spread.

1 cup vegetable oil
4 large eggs
½ cup buttermilk
1½ teaspoons pure vanilla extract
2½ cups granulated sugar
2 cups shredded peeled carrots
4 cups unbleached all-purpose flour
1½ teaspoons baking powder
1½ teaspoons fine sea salt
1½ teaspoons ground cinnamon
1 teaspoon grated lemon zest
½ teaspoon baking soda
½ teaspoon ground nutmeg
½ teaspoon ground ginger
¼ teaspoon ground cloves

GLAZE (OPTIONAL)
½ cup confectioners' sugar
1 tablespoon milk

1. Preheat the oven to 350°F. Spray two 4½ x 8½-inch loaf pans with nonstick cooking spray.

2. In a large bowl, beat together the oil, eggs, buttermilk, and vanilla. Stir in the sugar until well incorporated. Stir in the carrots.

3. In another large bowl, combine the flour, baking powder, salt, cinnamon, lemon zest, baking soda, nutmeg, ginger, and cloves. Whisk to blend. Add the dry ingredients to the wet ingredients and fold to combine.

4. Divide the batter between the prepared pans and bake until a tester comes out with just a few crumbs attached, about 1 hour. Cool the loaves on a wire rack.

5. If making the glaze, whisk the confectioners' sugar with the milk in a small bowl. Drizzle the glaze over the cooled loaves.

MAKE IT AHEAD: The glazed loaves can be stored in an airtight container at room temperature for up to 3 days. Unglazed loaves can be wrapped in plastic wrap and stored in zip-top plastic bags in the freezer for up to 1 month. Thaw at room temperature and glaze before serving, if desired.

MENU

Poor Man's
Chicken Caesar
Salad

MinTea

Orange–
Chocolate Chip
Cookies

I was a child of the 1980s, which means that I became an adult in the '90s. And that means that I love Caesar salad. One just follows the other. Caesar salad was all the rage in the '90s, and at my house it still is. It's perfect to pack in a lunch box or to eat at home. Serve with minty iced tea and a few cookies for dessert.

Poor Man's Chicken Caesar Salad

Serves 4

`MAKE-AHEAD`

In the old days, this salad was not a frugal affair, especially when you bought prepared croutons and dressing. I've cut the costs in several ways for my version. Marked-down bread from the grocery store (or leftover bread that you've got on the counter) becomes homemade croutons. The less expensive but just as flavorful Romano cheese stands in for pricey Parmigiano-Reggiano. Leftover grilled chicken adds protein to the salad and makes it a meal. I make my own dressing, and I buy the romaine lettuce on sale whenever possible. It's very little effort—and very little expense—for such huge rewards.

1 tablespoon mayonnaise, preferably homemade (page 273)
Juice of ½ lemon
1 teaspoon minced garlic
Kosher salt and freshly ground black pepper
¼ cup olive oil
1 large head romaine lettuce, torn into bite-size pieces
2 cups chopped cooked chicken
1 cup Homemade Croutons (page 296)
¾ cup shredded Romano cheese

1. In a small jar or bowl, stir together the mayonnaise, lemon juice, garlic, and salt and pepper to taste. Add the olive oil, stirring to combine well.

2. In four bowls or packable containers with lids, layer the lettuce, chicken, croutons, and cheese.

3. When ready to serve, toss the salad with the dressing. Season with additional pepper, if desired.

MAKE IT AHEAD: The salad (minus the croutons) and the dressing can be made and refrigerated separately for up to 3 days. Add the dressing and croutons to the salad right before serving.

#98

BRED BONANZA

Day-old bread is a blessing in disguise. Usually stores start reducing their bread prices several days before the sell-by date. Snatch it up at low prices and turn it into all kinds of yummy goodness: croutons, French toast, bread crumbs, egg bakes, crostini, panzanella, and bread pudding.

homemade croutons

Makes 2 cups

`MEATLESS` `DAIRY-FREE` `MAKE-AHEAD` `FREEZER-FRIENDLY`

I can make a gallon of croutons for about 75 cents when I buy day-old bread. It's worth the 15 minutes of effort for great-tasting salad toppings.

2 cups bread cubes
2 tablespoons olive oil
¼ teaspoon dried Italian herb blend
¼ teaspoon garlic powder

1. Preheat the oven to 375°F. Line a baking sheet with parchment paper or a silicone baking mat.

2. In a large bowl, combine the bread cubes and olive oil. Toss to coat. Season with the Italian herbs and garlic powder.

3. Bake, stirring a couple of times to promote even browning and prevent burning, until crisp and golden brown, 10 to 15 minutes. Cool before adding to salads.

MAKE IT AHEAD: Cooled croutons can be stored in an airtight container at room temperature for up to 4 days or in the freezer for up to 1 month.

#99

JUST BREW IT

Homemade iced tea is an affordable and delicious alternative to expensive bottled beverages. Boxed teas go on sale or clearance often throughout the year, cutting your costs even more. Keep a pitcherful of iced tea on hand for an easy and refreshing beverage. Tote a bottle to work and on road trips to avoid pricey bottled versions.

MinTea

Serves 4

MEATLESS   DAIRY-FREE   GLUTEN-FREE   MAKE-AHEAD

Bottled sweet teas are expensive—and full of sugar! Save money by brewing tea at home and sweetening it yourself.

4 black tea bags
¼ cup chopped fresh mint
2 cups boiling water
2 tablespoons honey
4 cups ice cubes

1. Place the tea bags and mint leaves in a heatproof glass pitcher or bowl. Pour the boiling water over and steep for 5 minutes. Remove the tea bags and strain out the mint leaves. Stir in the honey until dissolved.

2. Put the ice in a large thermos. Pour the hot tea over the ice. Serve chilled.

MAKE IT AHEAD: Store the iced tea in the refrigerator for up to 4 days.

#100

HONEY, I SHRUNK THE CHOCOLATE

Use mini chocolate chips instead of regular-size chips to get a bigger distribution of chocolaty goodness without using more product. You will find that you can get away with using less in many of your favorite baking recipes.

Orange–Chocolate Chip Cookies

Makes about 3 dozen cookies

MAKE-AHEAD   FREEZER-FRIENDLY

These cookies are favorites at our house. They are full of flavor thanks to the chocolate, cinnamon, and orange zest. Feel free to try other combinations, such as ginger and lemon zest or dried cherries and lime zest (with or without the chocolate chips).

1 cup (2 sticks) butter
1 cup dark brown sugar
½ cup granulated sugar
2 large eggs
1 teaspoon pure vanilla extract
1½ cups rolled oats
1½ cups unbleached all-purpose flour
1 teaspoon baking soda
1 teaspoon fine sea salt
½ teaspoon ground cinnamon
Grated zest of 1 orange
1 cup mini chocolate chips

1. Preheat the oven to 375°F. Line two baking sheets with parchment paper or silicone baking mats.

2. In a large bowl, cream together the butter and sugars. Add the eggs and vanilla and beat until well combined.

3. Grind the oats in a blender or food processor until powdered. Add to the butter-sugar mixture along with the flour, baking soda, salt, cinnamon, and orange zest, stirring to combine. Fold in the chocolate chips.

4. Place the dough by rounded tablespoons about 2 inches apart on the prepared baking sheets.

5. Bake until set, 8 to 10 minutes. Cool on a rack.

MAKE IT AHEAD: Store the cooled cookies in an airtight container at room temperature for up to 5 days or in the freezer for up to 1 month.

This meal is perfect for holiday travel time, when you've got some leftover roast turkey and maybe a bag of nuts to dip into. The brownies mix up quickly and chill in the refrigerator or cooler until you're ready for dessert.

Thanksgiving Chef Salad

Serves 4

GLUTEN-FREE **MAKE-AHEAD**

This is a great salad for using up leftover roast turkey, and the cranberries, Gorgonzola, and nuts add to the autumn theme. These are also ingredients that typically go on sale around Turkey Day. My friend Jen refers to this kind of salad as a "party in your mouth," since all the flavors play so nicely together.

¼ cup balsamic vinegar
¼ teaspoon dried basil
¼ teaspoon fine sea salt
⅛ teaspoon freshly ground black pepper
⅓ cup olive oil
5 ounces baby spinach or mixed baby greens
2 cups cubed leftover roast turkey (or turkey deli meat)
1 cup dry-roasted almonds
1 cup crumbled Gorgonzola cheese
1 cup dried cranberries

1. In a small jar or bowl, combine the vinegar, basil, salt, and pepper. Place the lid on the jar and shake well or whisk until smooth. Add the olive oil and shake or whisk again to emulsify.

2. Divide the greens among four bowls or plastic containers with lids. Divide the turkey, almonds, Gorgonzola, and cranberries among the salads. When ready to serve, toss the salads with enough dressing to coat.

MAKE IT AHEAD: The salad and dressing can be refrigerated separately for up to 4 days.

#101

Cake and brownie mixes are highly overrated, especially when the from-scratch counterpart tastes so much better, costs much less, and can be customized to your tastes. To save time, prepare your own baking mixes. Bag up the dry ingredients in advance, being sure to mark what ingredients still need to be added, as well as baking times.

Brownie Cheesecake Bars

Makes 16 squares

MAKE-AHEAD   FREEZER-FRIENDLY

A full cheesecake can be an elaborate and expensive affair. But you can get all the cheesecake flavor you crave, plus portability, with this rich brownie-based crust in just a matter of minutes. The holidays are the perfect time to grab cream cheese at a premium price.

BROWNIE CRUST
½ cup sugar
⅓ cup unbleached all-purpose flour
⅓ cup unsweetened cocoa powder
¼ teaspoon baking powder
¼ teaspoon fine sea salt
¼ cup vegetable oil
1 large egg
½ teaspoon pure vanilla extract

CHEESECAKE
1 (8-ounce) package cream cheese, softened
½ cup sugar
1 large egg
½ teaspoon pure vanilla extract
⅛ teaspoon fine sea salt

1. Preheat the oven to 350°F. Line an 8-inch square baking pan with parchment paper, allowing the paper to hang over the edges.

2. To make the brownie crust, in a large bowl, whisk together the sugar, flour, cocoa powder, baking powder, and salt. Add the oil, egg, and vanilla and blend until just combined. Spoon the thick batter into the prepared pan and spread it evenly.

3. To make the cheesecake, in another bowl, beat the cream cheese until light and fluffy. Add the sugar, egg, vanilla, and salt. Pour this mixture over the chocolate mixture in the pan. Bake until set, 25 to 30 minutes.

4. Cool to room temperature, then grasp the edges of the parchment to remove from the pan. Cut into 2-inch squares and, if desired, wrap individually in waxed paper. Chill until ready to serve.

MAKE IT AHEAD: Store the wrapped bars in the refrigerator for up to 4 days or in a zip-top plastic bag in the freezer for up to 1 month.

Acknowledgments

Twenty years ago I dreamed of writing a cookbook. This is my third. How did I get here?

Crafting a great book takes many hands, mouths, and eyeballs. Great thanks are in order.

Thank you to the team at The Harvard Common Press: to Bruce Shaw, Adam Salomone, and Dan Rosenberg for giving ear to my ideas as well as the space to run with them. To Valerie Cimino, Karen Wise, and Kelly Messier for the most excellent feedback, editing, and correcting. To Pat Jalbert-Levine for her extraordinary attention to detail. To Virginia Downes and Elizabeth Van Itallie for adding style and beauty to the finished product.

Big thanks to my agent, Alison Picard, for sharing her expertise and for always guiding me in the right direction.

Thank you to my blog readers at Life as Mom and Good Cheap Eats. Your enthusiasm for and support of my recipes and writing make all the hard work worth it. Thanks to friends and family who offered input and served as taste testers, including but not limited to: Allie, Anne, Carrie, Cristina, Danielle, Debbie, Janel, JessieLeigh, Jessika, Lynn, Michelle, Rosalie, Shari, Sharon, and Sheila.

Thank you Mom, Dad, Jamie, Janel, John, and Jace; I imagine you're used to my crazy ways by now. Thanks for putting up with me.

Special thanks to my six precious children, who understand what it means when I answer the question, "What's for dinner?" with the reply, "An experiment." You are my best and favorite guinea pigs. Thank you for sharing your good-natured feedback with me. You make me a very rich woman.

Deep gratitude goes to my sweet husband, Bryan, who has encouraged me to follow my dreams even when it meant more work for him. This kid-raising, homeschooling, recipe-testing, cookbook-writing, blog-posting life wasn't exactly what we planned for twenty years ago, but I can't imagine a better life, thanks to having you to share it with.

My ultimate thanks to Jesus, who has given me all good things.

Measurement Equivalents

LIQUID CONVERSIONS

U.S.	METRIC
1 tsp	5 ml
1 tbs	15 ml
2 tbs	30 ml
3 tbs	45 ml
¼ cup	60 ml
⅓ cup	75 ml
⅓ cup + 1 tbs	90 ml
⅓ cup + 2 tbs	100 ml
½ cup	120 ml
⅔ cup	150 ml
¾ cup	180 ml
¾ cup + 2 tbs	200 ml
1 cup	240 ml
1 cup + 2 tbs	275 ml
1¼ cups	300 ml
1⅓ cups	325 ml
1½ cups	350 ml
1⅔ cups	375 ml
1¾ cups	400 ml
1¾ cups + 2 tbs	450 ml
2 cups (1 pint)	475 ml
2½ cups	600 ml
3 cups	720 ml
4 cups (1 quart)	945 ml
(1,000 ml is 1 liter)	

WEIGHT CONVERSIONS

U.S./U.K.	METRIC
½ oz	14 g
1 oz	28 g
1½ oz	43 g
2 oz	57 g
2½ oz	71 g
3 oz	85 g
3½ oz	100 g
4 oz	113 g
5 oz	142 g
6 oz	170 g
7 oz	200 g
8 oz	227 g
9 oz	255 g
10 oz	284 g
11 oz	312 g
12 oz	340 g
13 oz	368 g
14 oz	400 g
15 oz	425 g
1 lb	454 g

OVEN TEMP. CONVERSIONS

°F	GAS MARK	°C
250	½	120
275	1	140
300	2	150
325	3	165
350	4	180
375	5	190
400	6	200
425	7	220
450	8	230
475	9	240
500	10	260
550	Broil	290

Note: All conversions are approximate.

Cilantro
  -Onion Dressing, 136
  and Shrimp Pasta, 60, 61
Cinnamon-Chocolate Meringues, *144*, 145
Coconut
  -Ginger Granola, 256
  Monkey Salad, 249
  Spiced Piña Colada Smoothies, 257
Coffee
  Salted Caramel *Affogato*, 46, *47*
Cookies
  Almond, Lui's Kitchen, 171
  Baby Cakes, *270*, 271
  Chocolate-Cinnamon Meringues, *144*, 145
  Double-Chocolate Oatmeal, 212
  Ginger-Orange Crisps, 191
  Lemon-Pecan Biscotti, 275
  Orange–Chocolate Chip, 299
Corn
  and Chile Tortilla Egg Bake, 253
  Grilled, with Basil Butter, 152
  Pepper, and Red Onion Salad, 188
  -Potato Chowder, 28
  Quinoa Salad with Black Beans and Feta
    Cheese, 291
  Salsa, Smoky, 185
  Sautéed, with Thyme, 122
Cornbread, Herbed Garlic, *203*, 204
Cornmeal
  Cheesy Jalapeño Cornbread, 63
  Cheesy Polenta, 32
  Herbed Garlic Cornbread, *203*, 204
  Lemon-Blueberry Corn Muffins, *278*, 279
  Rich and Creamy Polenta, 139
  -Yogurt Pancakes, 250
Corn Tortillas, Homemade, 222
Couscous
  Colorful Herbed, 163
  Curried, *127*, 129
Cranberry(ies)
  -Apple Pie, Deep-Dish, 198
  No-Bake Cereal Bars, 283

and Pecans, Broccoli Slaw with, 27
-Pesto Pasta Salad, 134
Spinach-Apple Salad with Scallion-Lime
    Dressing, 89
Thanksgiving Chef Salad, 300
Winter Greens and Citrus Salad, 207
Cream, Honey-Ginger, 36
Croutons, Homemade, 296
Cucumber(s)
  Greek Spinach Salad, *127*, 130
  Salad with Scallion-Lime Dressing, 262
Cumin
  Chicken Legs, Grilled, 121
  -Scented Cabbage Salad, 76
Curly Endive and Romaine Salad with Meyer Lemon
    Dressing, 159
Curried Couscous, *127*, 129
Curried Roasted Potatoes, 100
Cutting boards, 12

D

Dairy-free recipes, designation for, 14
Desserts
  Baby Cakes, *270*, 271
  Baked Apple Porcupines, 30
  Brownie Cheesecake Bars, 301
  Chocolate-Cinnamon Meringues, *144*, 145
  Cream Cheese and Nectarine Tart, 153
  Deep-Dish Apple-Cranberry Pie, 198
  Double-Chocolate Oatmeal Cookies, 212
  Fruit and Cream Tart, 148
  Ginger-Orange Crisps, 191
  Lemon-Blueberry Crumble, 58
  Lemon-Pecan Biscotti, 275
  Lemon Pie with Honey-Ginger Cream, 36
  Lui's Kitchen Almond Cookies, 171
  Maple Fried Apples, 120
  Mixed Berry Pie with Cinnamon and Lemon,
    194–95, *195*
  No-Bake Cereal Bars, 283
  Orange–Chocolate Chip Cookies, 299
  Salted Caramel *Affogato*, 46, *47*

Dill Carrots, Buttery, 78
Dilly Dip for Vegetables and Chips, 214
Dips and spreads. *See also* Salsa
    Chunky Guacamole, 184
    Dilly Dip for Vegetables and Chips, 214
    Easy Homemade Hummus, 126, *127*
    Homemade Mayonnaise, 273
    Hot Cheese Dip with Sun-Dried Tomatoes, 48
    Jalapeño Cheese Dip with Homemade
      Tortilla Chips, 72, *73*
    Spready Cheese, 213
    Sunny Dipping Sauce, 267
Dressings. *See also specific salad recipes*
    Cilantro-Onion, 136
    Herbed Feta, 59
    homemade, money saved with, 137
    Honey-Ginger, 190
    Lemon-Basil Vinaigrette, 44
    Meyer Lemon, 159
    reusing jars for, 41
    Scallion, Creamy, 277
    Scallion-Lime, 89
Drinks
    Homemade Lemonade, 66, *66*
    Malted Hot Cocoa Mix, 260
    MinTea, 297
    Pineapple *Agua Fresca*, 282
    Salted Caramel *Affogato*, 46, *47*
    Spiced Piña Colada Smoothies, 257

E

Eggplant
    Roasted Vegetable Marinara Sauce, 229–30
Egg(s)
    Bake, Chile and Corn Tortilla, 253
    dishes, safe cooking temperatures, 117
    Frittata with Sausage and Vegetables, 261
    Mexican Oven Omelet, 236, *237*
    Poblano Chile Scramble, 243
    serving ideas, 244
    Skillet Poached, with Spinach, 246, *247*
    yolks, uses for, 145

Enchiladas, Poblano Chile, 18, *19*
Equipment, 12–13, 122

F

Fish
    safe cooking temperatures, 117
    Spiced, with Garlic-Lemon Butter, 138
Food processors, 12
Food scales, 12
Fransconi Potatoes, 119
Freezing foods, tips for, 230, 233, 292
French Toast, Almond, 258
Frittata with Sausage and Vegetables, 261
Fruit. *See also specific fruits*
    and Cream Tart, 148
    Kabobs, Fun, 255, *255*
    Salad, Maple-Drizzled, 239, *239*
    seasonal, buying, 148

G

Garlic
    butter, leftover, uses for, 140
    Buttery Italian Bread Sticks, 231
    Cornbread, Herbed, *203*, 204
    Garlicky Grilled Cheese Sandwiches, 25
    Garlicky Quinoa Pilaf, 181
    -Herb Soft Pretzels, 286–87, *287*
    Mashed Potatoes, 225
    -Parmesan Texas Toast, 211
    Roasted, 26
    Roasted Broccoli with, 33
    Roasted Tomato Sauce, 43
    Rolls, Cloverleaf, 29
Ginger
    -Coconut Granola, 256
    -Honey Cream, 36
    -Honey Dressing, 190
    -Orange Carrots, 180
    -Orange Crisps, 191
Gluten-free recipes, designation for, 14
Grains. *See also* Cornmeal; Oats; Rice
    Garlicky Quinoa Pilaf, 181

Quinoa Salad with Black Beans and Feta
Cheese, 291
Vegetable, Beef, and Barley Soup, 284, *285*
Granola
Breakfast Banana Splits, 242, *242*
Coconut-Ginger, 256
Spiced Vanilla, 240
Grapes
Apples, and Almonds, Chicken Salad Wraps
with, 280, *281*
Fun Fruit Kabobs, 255, *255*
Maple-Drizzled Fruit Salad, 239, *239*
Gravy
Chicken, Spicy Creamy, 98
Onion, Herbed, 224
Greek Spice Blend, 81
Greek Spinach Salad, *127*, 130
Green Beans
Grilled, 147, *147*
Herb-and-Spice, 232
Roasted, 115
Greens. *See also* Lettuce; Spinach
Baby, with Lemon-Basil Vinaigrette, 44
Cajun Grilled Chicken Salad with Creamy Scallion
Dressing, 276
Creamy Kale with Sun-Dried Tomatoes, 103
Curly Endive and Romaine Salad with Meyer
Lemon Dressing, 159
Thanksgiving Chef Salad, 300
Guacamole, Chunky, 184

H

Ham
buying on sale, 176
Honey-Mustard Baked, 174, *175*
Loaded Italian Subs, 272
and Mac and Cheese Casserole, 56
safe cooking temperatures, 117
Hamburger Buns, Homemade Sourdough, *217*,
218
Hamburgers, Spiced, with Lemon–Blue Cheese
Butter, 216–17, *217*

Handheld mixers, 12
Hash Browns, Oven, 254
Herbed Feta Dressing, 59
Herbed Garlic Cornbread, *203*, 204
Herbed Onion Gravy, 224
Herb(s). *See also specific herbs*
-and-Spice Green Beans, 232
dried, buying and storing, 45
fresh, growing, 45
fresh, storing, 45, 60, 184, 232
fresh, using up, 184, 232
-Garlic Soft Pretzels, 286–87, *287*
growing your own, 211
Holiday dinners, on a budget, 160
Home Fries, Easy Skillet, 238
Hominy
Chili Bean Soup, 91
and Pumpkin, Beef Stew with, 210
Honey
-Ginger Cream, 36
-Ginger Dressing, 190
-Mustard Baked Ham, 174, *175*
Whole-Wheat Bread, 52
Whole-Wheat Pizza Dough, 88
Hot Cocoa Mix, Malted, 260
Hot Dog and Sausage Buffet, 164–65, *165*
Hummus, Easy Homemade, 126, *127*

I

Ice cream
Salted Caramel *Affogato*, 46, *47*
Immersion blenders, 12

K

Kale, Creamy, with Sun-Dried Tomatoes,
103
Knives, 12

L

Lamb, safe cooking temperatures, 117
Lasagna
Meaty, with Asiago Béchamel, 158

Lasagna (continued)
  Turkey and Spinach, with Feta Cheese, 202–3, *203*
Leek(s)
  -Potato Soup, 50, *51*
  Skillet Poached Eggs with Spinach, 246, *247*
Leftovers
  adding to rice bowls, 21
  freezing, 85
  safe cooking temperatures, 117
  using up, 199, 219, 263
Lemon(s)
  -Basil Vinaigrette, 44
  -Blueberry Corn Muffins, *278*, 279
  -Blueberry Crumble, 58
  –Blue Cheese Butter, 216
  freezing juice and zest, 36
  Homemade Lemonade, 66, *66*
  Lemony Linguini with Broccoli and Mushrooms, 49
  Meyer, Dressing, Curly Endive and Romaine Salad with, 159
  -Pecan Biscotti, 275
  Pie with Honey-Ginger Cream, 36
Lettuce
  ChiChi's Italian Salad, 83
  Chicken Salad Wraps with Apples, Almonds, and Grapes, 280, *281*
  Chopped Vegetable Salad, 132, *133*
  Curly Endive and Romaine Salad with Meyer Lemon Dressing, 159
  Make-Your-Own Burrito Bar, 182
  Mexican Tossed Salad, 85
  Michèle's *Salade*, 41
  Poor Man's Chicken Caesar Salad, 294, *295*
  Red and Green Salad with Cilantro-Onion Dressing, 136
  Tossed Salad with Mediterranean-Spiced Dressing, *203*, 205
  Winter Greens and Citrus Salad, 207

Lime-Scallion Dressing, 89
Lunches, on a budget, 274, 275, 288–89

M

Mac (and Ham) and Cheese Casserole, 56
Malted Hot Cocoa Mix, 260
Mango-Pineapple Breakfast Salsa, 241
Maple Breakfast Cake, Oaty, 248
Maple-Drizzled Fruit Salad, 239, *239*
Maple Fried Apples, 120
Mayonnaise, Homemade, 273
Meal planning tips, 49, 53, 76, 248, 259, 277
Meat. *See also* Beef; Pork
  adding grains and vegetables to, 251
  bone-in, buying, 105
  -free meals, money saved with, 20
  grinding your own, 109
  marked down, buying, 132
  safe cooking temperatures, 116–17
Meatballs, No-Egg Spinach, 223
Meatless recipes, designation for, 14
Meatloaf, Cajun Turkey, 101
Meat thermometers, 12
Meringues, Chocolate-Cinnamon, *144*, 145
Mexican Oven Omelet, 236, *237*
Mexican Spice Blend, 81
Mexican Tossed Salad, 85
Milk, freezing, 63
Mint
  MinTea, 297
  -Yogurt Sauce, *127*, 128
Monkey Salad, 249
Muffins
  Banana-Walnut, Mini, 79
  Corn, Lemon-Blueberry, *278*, 279
Mushroom(s)
  Asian Vegetable Skewers, *169*, 170
  and Broccoli, Lemony Linguini with, 49
  Gravy, Salisbury Steak with, 114
  Marinara, Fire-Roasted, 31
  and Root Vegetables, Pot Roast with, 110, *111*

Spiced Hamburgers with Lemon–Blue Cheese
   Butter, 216–17, *217*
and Spinach Pizza with Roasted Tomato
   Sauce, 42
Summer Vegetable Kabobs, 227, *227*
Supreme Sausage Pizza, 86, *87*

N

Nectarine and Cream Cheese Tart, 153
Noodle(s)
   Beef Stroganoff Soup, 91
   Mac (and Ham) and Cheese Casserole, 56
   Rice, Asian Chicken Salad with, 189
   Soup, Chicken, 91
Nuts. *See also* Almond(s); Pecan(s); Walnut(s)
   Asian Chicken Salad with Rice Noodles, 189
   Lemon-Pecan Biscotti, 275
   Monkey Salad, 249
   No-Bake Cereal Bars, 283

O

Oats
   Coconut-Ginger Granola, 256
   Double-Chocolate Oatmeal Cookies, 212
   Lemon-Blueberry Crumble, 58
   No-Bake Cereal Bars, 283
   Oaty Maple Breakfast Cake, 248
   Orange–Chocolate Chip Cookies, 299
   Spiced Vanilla Granola, 240
Olives
   Chopped Vegetable Salad, 132, *133*
   Frittata with Sausage and Vegetables, 261
   Mexican Oven Omelet, 236, *237*
   Supreme Sausage Pizza, 86, *87*
   Tossed Salad with Mediterranean-Spiced
      Dressing, *203*, 205
Omelet, Oven, Mexican, 236, *237*
Onion(s)
   and Broccoli, Bryan's, 162
   -Cilantro Dressing, 136
   Gravy, Herbed, 224
   and Peppers, Classic Sautéed, *165*, 166

and Squashes, Balsamic Grilled, 140, *141*
Orange(s)
   Asian Chicken Salad with Rice Noodles, 189
   –Chocolate Chip Cookies, 299
   -Ginger Carrots, 180
   -Ginger Crisps, 191
   Maple-Drizzled Fruit Salad, 239, *239*
   Winter Greens and Citrus Salad, 207

P

Pancakes, Yogurt-Cornmeal, 250
Pantry challenges, 43, 71
Parsleyed New Potatoes, 197
Pasta. *See also* Noodle(s)
   Buttery Orzo Pasta, 105, *105*
   Colorful Herbed Couscous, 163
   Curried Couscous, *127*, 129
   Lemony Linguini with Broccoli and Mushrooms,
      49
   Meaty Lasagna with Asiago Béchamel, 158
   Mom's Macaroni Salad, 274
   Orzo with Tomatoes and Basil, 228
   Peanut Butter Chicken and, 64
   with Roasted Vegetable Marinara Sauce,
      229–30
   Salad, Cranberry-Pesto, 134
   Salad, Tortellini-Chickpea, 268
   Shrimp and Cilantro, 60, *61*
   Turkey and Spinach Lasagna with Feta Cheese,
      202–3, *203*
Peanut Butter
   Chicken and Pasta, 64
Pear
   –Brown Sugar Compote, 259
   -Chocolate Scones, 244
   and Spinach Salad with Raspberry Vinaigrette,
      112
Pecan(s)
   and Cranberries, Broccoli Slaw with, 27
   -Lemon Biscotti, 275
Pepper(s). *See also* Chile(s)
   Asian Vegetable Skewers, *169*, 170

Peppers (contined)
  Chicken Summer Rolls, 266
  Corn, and Red Onion Salad, 188
  Cucumber Salad with Scallion-Lime Dressing, 262
  Frittata with Sausage and Vegetables, 261
  Gussied-Up Sausage and Vegetables, 99
  Mexican Tossed Salad, 85
  and Onions, Classic Sautéed, *165*, 166
  Summer Vegetable Kabobs, 227, *227*
  Supreme Sausage Pizza, 86, *87*
Pesto
  -Cranberry Pasta Salad, 134
  freezing, 134
  Spinach, 143
  -Spinach Pizza, Grilled, 142, *143*
Pie Crust, Versatile Buttery, 37
Pie(s)
  Apple-Cranberry, Deep-Dish, 198
  Lemon, with Honey-Ginger Cream, 36
  Mixed Berry, with Cinnamon and Lemon, 194–95, *195*
Pilaf
  Brown Rice, 102
  Buttery Orzo, 105, *105*
  Quinoa, Garlicky, 181
Piña Colada Smoothies, Spiced, 257
Pineapple
  Agua Fresca, 282
  Asian Vegetable Skewers, *169*, 170
  Barbecue Sauce, Tangy, 150
  Chicken, Grilled, 168, *169*
  -Mango Breakfast Salsa, 241
  Sauce, 169
  Spiced Piña Colada Smoothies, 257
Pizza
  individual-size, 88
  Spinach and Mushroom, with Roasted Tomato Sauce, 42
  Spinach-Pesto, Grilled, 142, *143*
  Supreme Sausage, 86, *87*
Pizza Dough, Honey Whole-Wheat, 88

Polenta
  Cheesy, 32
  Rich and Creamy, 139
Popovers, Easy-Peasy, 193
Pork. *See also* Ham; Sausage(s)
  Chops, Blackened, 135
  Roast, Ale-Braised, 118
  safe cooking temperatures, 117
  Shredded, Tacos, Easy, with Two Salsas, 220
  Slow Cooker Pulled, Sandwiches, 186
Potato(es). *See also* Sweet Potato(es)
  Beef Stew with Pumpkin and Hominy, 210
  -Corn Chowder, 28
  Curried Roasted, 100
  Easy Skillet Home Fries, 238
  Fransconi, 119
  Garlic Mashed, 225
  -Leek Soup, 50, *51*
  leftover, serving ideas, 100
  New, Parsleyed, 197
  Oven Hash Browns, 254
  Poblano Chile Scramble, 243
  Pot Roast with Mushrooms and Root Vegetables, 110, *111*
  Salad, Favorite, 137
  Scalloped, Tastiest-Ever, *175*, 177
  Smashed, 95
  Vegetable Chowder, 91
Potpie, Beef, with Flaky Cheddar Crust, 206
Pots and pans, 12
Poultry. *See also* Chicken; Turkey
  safe cooking temperatures, 117
Pretzels, Soft, Garlic-Herb, 286–87, *287*
Pumpkin
  and Hominy, Beef Stew with, 210
  -Onion-Poppy Rolls, 57
Pumpkin seeds
  Winter Greens and Citrus Salad, 207

Q

Quinoa
  Pilaf, Garlicky, 181

Salad with Black Beans and Feta Cheese, 291

R

Radishes
 Asian Chicken Salad with Rice Noodles, 189
 Chicken Summer Rolls, 266
 Cumin-Scented Cabbage Salad, 76
 Greek Spinach Salad, *127*, 130
Raspberries
 Maple-Drizzled Fruit Salad, 239, *239*
Recipes
 accompaniments, 13–14
 costs and yields, 13–14
 dairy-free, 14
 freezer-friendly, 14
 gluten-free, 14
 make-ahead, 14
 meatless, 14
 slow cooker, 14
Rice
 Arroz con Pollo, 75
 and Bean Bowls, *22*, 23
 and Bean Soup, 91
 bowls, for easy meals, 21
 Brown, Pilaf, 102
 Cajun Shrimp and Sausage, 77
 Chicken, and Black Bean Soup, 67
 Confetti, 123
 Make-Your-Own Burrito Bar, 182
 White, Stovetop, 172, *172*
 Zesty Mexican, 21
Rolls
 Cloverleaf Garlic, 29
 Pumpkin-Onion-Poppy, 57
 Sourdough, 68
 Sweet, Mom's, 178

S

Salad(s)
 Baby Greens with Lemon-Basil Vinaigrette, 44
 Broccoli Slaw with Pecans and Cranberries, 27
 Cabbage, Cumin-Scented, 76
 ChiChi's Italian, 83
 Chicken, Asian, with Rice Noodles, 189
 Chopped Vegetable, 132, *133*
 Coleslaw with a Kick, 187
 Corn, Pepper, and Red Onion, 188
 Cranberry-Pesto Pasta, 134
 Cucumber, with Scallion-Lime Dressing, 262
 Curly Endive and Romaine, with Meyer Lemon Dressing, 159
 Fruit, Maple-Drizzled, 239, *239*
 Grilled Chicken, Cajun, with Creamy Scallion Dressing, 276
 Macaroni, Mom's, 274
 Michèle's *Salade*, 41
 Monkey, 249
 Pear and Spinach, with Raspberry Vinaigrette, 112
 Potato, Favorite, 137
 Quinoa, with Black Beans and Feta Cheese, 291
 Red and Green, with Cilantro-Onion Dressing, 136
 Roasted Beet, with Herbed Feta Dressing, 59
 South of the Border Slaw, 20
 Spinach, Greek, *127*, 130
 Spinach-Apple, with Scallion-Lime Dressing, 89
 Thanksgiving Chef, 300
 Tortellini-Chickpea Pasta, 268
 Tossed, Mexican, 85
 Tossed, with Mediterranean-Spiced Dressing, *203*, 205
 Winter Greens and Citrus, 207
Salisbury Steak with Mushroom Gravy, 114
Salsa
 Breakfast, Mango-Pineapple, 241
 Corn, Smoky, 185
 Roasted Chipotle, 221
 Tomato, Chunky, 35

Salted Caramel *Affogato*, 46, *47*
Sandwiches
  Chicken Salad Wraps with Apples, Almonds,
    and Grapes, 280, *281*
  Chipotle Turkey, 290, *290*
  Garlicky Grilled Cheese, 25
  Loaded Italian Subs, 272
  Sloppy Fo's, 82
  Slow Cooker Pulled Pork, 186
Sauce(s). *See also* Salsa
  Dipping, Sunny, 267
  Fire-Roasted Mushroom Marinara, 31
  Herbed Onion Gravy, 224
  Lemon–Blue Cheese Butter, 216
  Mint-Yogurt, *127*, 128
  Pineapple, 169
  Pineapple Barbecue, Tangy, 150
  Roasted Tomato, 43
  Roasted Vegetable Marinara, 229–30
  Spicy Creamy Chicken Gravy, 98
Sausage Patties, Turkey-Apple, 251
Sausage(s)
  and Hot Dog Buffet, 164–65, *165*
  Loaded Italian Subs, 272
  Pizza, Supreme, 86, *87*
  and Shrimp Rice, Cajun, 77
  Sloppy Fo's, 82
  and Vegetables, Frittata with, 261
  and Vegetables, Gussied-Up, 99
Scallion
  Dressing, Creamy, 277
  -Lime Dressing, 89
Scones, Chocolate-Pear, 244
Seafood
  buying on sale, 162
  Cajun Shrimp and Sausage Rice, 77
  safe cooking temperatures, 117
  Shrimp and Cilantro Pasta, 60, *61*
  Spiced Fish with Garlic-Lemon Butter,
    138
  Zesty Baked Shrimp with Panko, 161
Sesame Broccoli, 65

Shellfish
  Cajun Shrimp and Sausage Rice, 77
  safe cooking temperatures, 117
  Shrimp and Cilantro Pasta, 60, *61*
  Zesty Baked Shrimp with Panko, 161
Sherried Black Bean Tomato Soup, 192
Shrimp
  and Cilantro Pasta, 60, *61*
  and Sausage Rice, Cajun, 77
  Zesty Baked, with Panko, 161
Slaw(s)
  Broccoli, with Pecans and Cranberries, 27
  Coleslaw with a Kick, 187
  South of the Border, 20
Sloppy Fo's, 82
Smoothies, Spiced Piña Colada, 257
Soft Pretzels, Garlic-Herb, 286–87, *287*
Soup(s). *See also* Stew(s)
  Bean and Rice, 91
  Beef Stroganoff, 91
  Black Bean Tomato, Sherried, 192
  Butternut Squash and Carrot, Simplest, 39
  Chicken, Black Bean, and Rice, 67
  Chicken Noodle, 91
  Chili Bean, 91
  Chili Bean, Fired-Up, 62
  made with leftover vegetables, 106
  Potato-Corn Chowder, 28
  Potato-Leek, 50, *51*
  Stone, 90–91
  Tomato, Creamy Herbed, 24
  Vegetable, Beef, and Barley, 284, *285*
  Vegetable Chowder, 91
Sourdough Hamburger Buns, Homemade, *217*,
  218
Sourdough Rolls, 68
Sourdough Starter, 69
Spice Blends
  Cajun, 80
  Greek, 81
  Mexican, 81
  storing, 98

Spinach
  -Apple Salad with Scallion-Lime Dressing, 89
  Asian Chicken Salad with Rice Noodles, 189
  Meatballs, No-Egg, 223
  Mexican Oven Omelet, 236, *237*
  Mexican Tossed Salad, 85
  and Mushroom Pizza with Roasted Tomato
    Sauce, 42
  and Pear Salad with Raspberry Vinaigrette,
    112
  Pesto, 143
  -Pesto Pizza, Grilled, 142, *143*
  Salad, Greek, *127*, 130
  Skillet Poached Eggs with, 246, *247*
  Thanksgiving Chef Salad, 300
  Tortellini-Chickpea Pasta Salad, 268
  and Turkey Lasagna with Feta Cheese, 202–3,
    203
Squash. *See also* Zucchini
  Beef Stew with Pumpkin and Hominy, 210
  Butternut, and Carrot Soup, Simplest, 39
  and Onions, Balsamic Grilled, 140, *141*
  Pumpkin-Onion-Poppy Rolls, 57
  Roasted Vegetable Marinara Sauce, 229–30
Stew(s)
  Armchair Quarterback Chili, 215
  Beef, with Pumpkin and Hominy, 210
  Spicy No-Bean Chili, 167
Stock
  homemade, saving money with, 102
  Homemade Chicken, 96, 97
Stone Soup, 90–91
Strawberries
  Fun Fruit Kabobs, 255, *255*
Summer Rolls, Chicken, 266
Sunflower seeds
  Cajun Grilled Chicken Salad with Creamy Scallion
    Dressing, 276
  Cranberry-Pesto Pasta Salad, 134
  No-Bake Cereal Bars, 283
Sweet Potato(es)
  Oven Fries, Seasoned, 219

Pot Roast with Mushrooms and Root
    Vegetables, 110, *111*
Syrup, Spiced Vanilla, 252

T

Tacos
  Easy Shredded Pork, with Two Salsas, 220
  Paso Mom, *108*, 109
Takeout, avoiding, 208–9
Tarts
  Cream Cheese and Nectarine, 153
  Fruit and Cream, 148
  Vegetable, Versatile, 40
Tea
  buying on sale, 297
  MinTea, 297
Thermometers, 12
Thyme, Sautéed Corn with, 122
Tomato(es)
  Avocado and Black Bean Salsa, 107
  and Basil, Orzo with, 228
  Black Bean Soup, Sherried, 192
  Broiled Bruschetta, 156, *157*
  Chopped Vegetable Salad, 132, *133*
  Fired-Up Chili Bean Soup, 62
  Fire-Roasted Mushroom Marinara, 31
  Roasted, Sauce, 43
  Roasted Chipotle Salsa, 221
  Roasted Vegetable Marinara Sauce, 229–30
  Salsa, Chunky, 35
  Soup, Creamy Herbed, 24
  Summer Vegetable Kabobs, 227, *227*
  Sun-Dried, Creamy Kale with, 103
  Sun-Dried, Hot Cheese Dip with, 48
  Tortellini-Chickpea Pasta Salad, 268
  Tossed Salad with Mediterranean-Spiced
    Dressing, *203*, 205
Tortellini-Chickpea Pasta Salad, 268
Tortilla Chips
  Cheesy Beefy Chili Bake, 84
  Chile and Corn Tortilla Egg Bake, 253
  Homemade, *73*, 74

Tortilla Chips (continued)
  Mexican Tossed Salad, 85
Tortillas
  Corn, Homemade, 222
  Make-Your-Own Burrito Bar, 182
  Paso Mom Tacos, *108*, 109
  Poblano Chile Enchiladas, 18, *19*
  Simple Bean Tostadas, 34, *35*
Tostadas, Simple Bean, 34, *35*
Turkey
  -Apple Sausage Patties, 251
  buying on sale, 176
  Meatloaf, Cajun, 101
  safe cooking temperatures, 117
  Salisbury Steak with Mushroom Gravy,
    114
  Sandwiches, Chipotle, 290, *290*
  Spicy No-Bean Chili, 167
  and Spinach Lasagna with Feta Cheese,
    202–3, *203*
  Thanksgiving Chef Salad, 300

V

Vanilla Syrup, Spiced, 252
Veal, safe cooking temperatures, 117
Vegetable(s). *See also specific vegetables*
  Beef, and Barley Soup, 284, *285*
  and Chips, Dilly Dip for, 214
  Chopped, Salad, 132, *133*
  Chowder, 91
  growing your own, 130
  leftover, making soup with, 106
  Mixed-Up, Stir-Fry, *105*, 106
  seasonal, buying, 148
  Skewers, Asian, *169*, 170

  Summer, Kabobs, 227, *227*
  Tart, Versatile, 40
  Vinaigrette, Lemon-Basil, 44

W

Walnut(s)
  -Banana Mini Muffins, 79
  Pear and Spinach Salad with Raspberry
    Vinaigrette, 112
Water, adding citrus or herbs to, 282
Whipped cream
  Honey-Ginger Cream, 36
Whole-Wheat Honey Bread, 52
Whole-Wheat Honey Pizza Dough, 88
Wine, leftover, storing, 197
Wraps, Chicken Salad, with Apples, Almonds,
  and Grapes, 280, *281*

Y

Yogurt
  Breakfast Banana Splits, 242, *242*
  -Cornmeal Pancakes, 250
  freezing, 279
  -Mint Sauce, *127*, 128

Z

Zucchini
  Asian Vegetable Skewers, *169*, 170
  Balsamic Grilled Onions and Squashes, 140,
    141
  Chicken, Black Bean, and Rice Soup, 67
  Chopped Vegetable Salad, 132, *133*
  Gussied-Up Sausage and Vegetables, 99
  Roasted Vegetable Marinara Sauce, 229–30
  Summer Vegetable Kabobs, 227, *227*

About the Author

Sharon Leppellere

Jessica Fisher's two very popular blogs, Life as Mom and Good Cheap Eats, have established her as a go-to authority on cooking for a family cheaply, creatively, and nutritiously.

Good Cheap Eats is Jessica's third cookbook. Her bestselling first book, *Not Your Mother's Make-Ahead and Freeze Cookbook*, offered a wealth of clever ideas for feeding a family inexpensively and well. Her second book, *Best 100 Juices for Kids*, brought the juicing revolution home for the entire family, children included. A widely cited figure in the world of food blogs and "mom blogs," she has also written online for The Kitchn, Life Your Way, Money Saving Mom, $5 Dinners, and The Art of Simple and in print for more than 85 regional parenting publications. Jessica's readers recognize that she walks the talk: She is the mom to, and primary cook for, four young sons and two young daughters. She lives with her husband and children in the San Diego area.